FORE Wₗ

Tales of a Woman at War
...with the Military System

Or

Cockups, Conspiracies & Misogyny in the British Army (1983 – 2020)

(Thinking of joining up and not middle class, white and male? You should read this first....)

Diane Allen OBE

CRANTHORPE
MILLNER

First published (2020)

ISBN 978-1-912964-37-6 (Paperback)

www.cranthorpemillner.com

Cranthorpe Millner Publishers

ACKNOWLEDGEMENTS

In writing this book, I spent a lot of time with military colleagues as well as my own memories. I have done my best to present a true and accurate picture of events as I recall them. Inevitably, memory fades with time and opinions differ slightly of any event. With the more recent events, some names, ranks and organisations have been changed.

I hope, in reading this book, the reader will gain true insight into the way the British Army works – the good, humorous moments, but also the bad and the plain ugly. In its current state, I would not recommend it as a career to any family member or friend, but I do remain optimistic that with effort and more importantly the will to change, it can become the great career choice I felt it was when I first signed up.

My time in the military stirs mostly good memories and it was only the final few years where a different narrative evolved – that of a military over-tasked, under-resourced and, at times, under-appreciated by the citizens it serves, the government that funds it and sadly, also by some of its own leadership. The military still attracts great people who want to serve – I hope and wish it finds ways to retain the best in the future and stops allowing its top talent to walk away.

I wish to acknowledge all those brave military comrades that I have served alongside – for their humour, professionalism and willingness to put themselves in harm's way to protect others. Especially, and with such warmth, to every member of WRAC 4 who shared the incredible experience of being the first women at Sandhurst. Most of my military family are still alive; a few sadly are not. We will remember them.

And finally, some individual thanks to a few.

To Barbara (not her real name) who took on the onerous task of reading the terrible first draft of this book – you have shared so many key moments of my military career. To Smiley (also not his real name) who shared many a gin & tonic with me as we figured out ways to overcome the dreaded military bureaucracy. Your wit and intellect were a pleasure to share – don't forget to write your own story soon. And to all the headquarter staff and colleagues at the specialist intelligence unit who stood by me during that dreadful eighteen months of investigations into my conduct – you kept me sane.

To the cohort of female friends in my home village, who offered a shoulder to cry on when I went through the appalling military complaints process – Juliet, Jane and Hillary – you are all amazing.

To Caro, who came along at just the right time and polished up the final draft professionally – I don't believe I would have reached an audience without you - you believed in my story and brought it to life. And to Kirsty at Cranthorpe Millner Publishers, for all the hard work in getting to the final product. I simply could not have done it without your skill.

And finally, finally, my thanks to Newall, my soul mate, who watched me suffer in those final military years and felt helpless at times to protect me from the obstructive military processes that caused such pain. With all my love. You were there when I needed you.

Introduction

For thirty years, give or take the odd, interesting detour, the British Army was my life.

I joined up as a teenager, keen on sport and not sure what career to choose, and by the end I was a senior officer with an OBE and a proud service record. I served in both the regular army and the reserves and because of who I am, I gave both my all.

Becoming part of the military is a tough journey, but the Army suited me. I have a warrior spirit and I have always been drawn to what used to be traditionally male roles: *defender of the people, leader, intelligencer, explorer.* I am quite comfortable in these roles, as are many other women.

In many ways I was lucky to join when I did; it was an exciting time because my generation of women in the military were at the forefront of a great deal of change. Not the immediate change of a world war or severe economic depression, but structural and societal change that was turning so many old ways of doing things upside down. I was 'at war' in the sense of being at the forefront of the changing role of women in the Army.

I thought I could make a real difference. Believed that a woman could do it all. But what I learned was that to make a difference I needed power and that was not readily on offer within the military – power was controlled by upper middle-class white males. I did find some wonderful comrades, but I also came across deep pockets of hostility, particularly in the later years and I don't mean from the Enemy, but from those who should have been on my side. And what I learned was that, despite all the protestations to the contrary, equality on paper is not equality in reality.

This is not to say that women have not come a long, long way, and I feel proud to have played my part. I was one of the first intake of women at Sandhurst. We were a small group and we broke through many barriers. Those 'firsts' we achieved are now accepted by the Army as routine. I like to think we helped to pave the way. When I look at what women are achieving now: the Army's 2018 all-women Ice Maidens' team who walked solo across Antarctica, a female general, women in combat roles and commanding units, women paragliding off Everest, sailing singlehandedly round the world and training anti-poaching squads in Africa, it reminds me how far we have come.

But it has been a journey and a fight – we still have a way to go, both in being accepted and in making the rules, rather than having to live by the rules others have made. I have seen the change and acceptance of women in junior roles, but there is less willingness to open access to senior roles. Why are women such a threat that we must fail to promote through subterfuge rather than competition? Why am I now witnessing a re-glazing of the 'glass ceiling' that reinforces male public school dominance and keeps women from the boardroom as well as the corridors of military power?

Throughout my time in the Army I fought my own battles and forged new paths, but in the end, I hit a line I could not cross and I bounced hard off that ceiling. I had been side-lined and refused promotion after an unfounded malicious complaint against me by a disgruntled soldier. He knew what he was doing when he warned me that he could destroy my career if I challenged his poor behaviours. And he was right, for even though I was completely vindicated, that, it seemed, didn't make a difference. It had given those who wanted to hold me back the excuse they needed. I remember the moment when I finally accepted that I could do no more. I walked into the office of my long-term mentor and sat down. I had crossed the Rubicon, had my sudden and irrevocable realisation and I said, 'Old friend, I am going to have to leave'. Realising that I could not stay was incredibly sad. I felt I had more to give, so much more to do.

I didn't set out to be a role model for women. Nor did I set out to leave the Army – twice. But those things happened and so this is my story of walking through the corridors of male privilege; of observing the Establishment, the privilege afforded to the Household

Cavalry, the Guards and Rifles (and others) and the long-reaching influence of Eton and masonic handshakes.

It is also my explanation of why the Army is struggling to recruit and retain today. Why it will continue to struggle to recruit women, ethnic minorities and to hold on to its talent. And a look at why Reserves, now an increasingly vital part of a pared back army are still being treated as second-class by too many full-time soldiers, even before they meet them as individuals – a strange bigotry the Army seems reluctant to address. How the deliberate lack of a just and independent system to resolve internal conflicts, such as discrimination, bullying and bias is holding the Army back in preparing to win external conflicts.

Because that is what you and I pay the Army to do. To provide lethal force in defence of the UK and its allies, if called to do so. In my view, we don't currently have an army that we can be proud to serve in or that can deliver that defence. We did when I joined, so what has changed? More importantly, how do we get that back?

Last year (2019) is 100 years since the Women's Royal Army Corps (the WRAC) association formed and one year since all roles in the military opened to women. A good time to take stock of progress, to capture the journey taken – good, bad and just plain comical. Mine is that insider's story – of how we got there, from first women at Sandhurst Officer training in the 1980s, with expectations of leaving on marriage, to the current day. I want to share how the Army got here – and what various pockets within the military think about it.

It is way too late to fix my career now – the patriarchy has found a way to stop my progress, but I can still use my voice to help the next generation of women – that becomes my next mission. I want us to have the Army we need, a meritocracy, not the Army we currently have, a defensive, blundering and bureaucratic dinosaur, unwilling to face up to change and haemorrhaging out its most talented as they realise that who you know still matters more than what you know.

The Army and I are now in the process of a messy divorce, but the alternative was to keep quiet about my experiences.

This is my journey through change – loss, grieving, fighting, winning and losing. The story of picking my battles and learning to stand up for my own rights as well as those of others. I was witness to many inequalities in my years of service, but I didn't always speak up.

I'm speaking up now. Through this book and to the Defence Select Committee. I have joined up with others who have lost their military careers - by speaking truth to power, standing up for their values and upholding their 'leadership vows', of serving our soldiers above ourselves.

In July 2019, the Amy finally admitted it does still have a problem, with 'new measures announced to stamp out inappropriate behaviour in the armed forces,' and acknowledgement it is running a deliberately obstructive complaints system. Of course, it didn't do this voluntarily-it was pushed into this, by voices such as mine who were willing to speak up.

The Head of the Army has declared he will 'shift cultures' and set up a Defence Authority to see that it does. I have seen these declarations before. Change requires a will to change. And in a top-down organisation like the Army, that means our senior leaders need to want it to change. I will be watching and monitoring.

In the meantime, I want to speak on behalf of the generation of women who experienced the rampant misogyny of the 80s as well as those who are living through the more covert biases and bigotry of today. It wasn't all bad - as pioneering military women, we had a lot of fun and brilliant experiences along the way. And we dated, even married, quite a few of those male officers as well, because many serving British women and men are exactly the sort of characters you would want to marry: reliable, resilient, faithful and kind. But there are still too many holding minorities back within the British Army – a small, but toxic cohort of senior, misogynistic white middle class males. These are the enemy of Good. Of a high-class British Army. They are not the ones you would want to marry.

So even though I am leaving I will continue to fight.

I will remain a Woman at War.

Chapter One
Military Guinea Pigs

Of course I am not worried about intimidating men. The type of man who will be intimidated by me is exactly the type of man I have no interest in.
Chimamanda Ngozi Adichie

It was early in the morning in mid-September and the first autumn winds were blowing so hard that we strained to hear the orders being hurled our way by a frustrated drill sergeant, as we shuffled awkwardly into a straggling attempt at a parade.

The new uniform wasn't helping. Uncomfortable trousers, hairy shirts and scratchy, round-necked jumpers. The whole ensemble, all of it in olive green, was topped off by a stiff new beret perched flat on the top of my head in a look referred to by those in the know as the 'helicopter landing pad'. Flattering it wasn't.

This was my first day at Sandhurst, the elite Royal Military Academy where all officers in the British Army receive their initial training. I was eighteen, but with my face scrubbed clean and my short, dark hair tucked out of sight behind my ears, I looked even younger.

It had already been a long morning. Up at six, we had to parade in our civvies (civilian clothes) and then stand in line to wait for our uniforms to be issued, get them on and stand in line again to be inspected – over and over again, or so it seemed. Today that first day is known as 'ironing board Sunday'. We carried kitbags of uniforms to our rooms and during the course of the day were shown how to keep our rooms tidy, how to iron uniforms, how to keep the ablution blocks clean, how to salute, how to recognise ranks and how to address people.

It was 1983 and I was the second youngest in the first group of women admitted to Sandhurst to train alongside the men. We weren't the first women in the Army – that had happened in 1917. Nor were we the first to be commissioned. But we were the first to complete the same course as the men in the same location. We all knew that we'd been handed a great opportunity. Equality was on the march and we were at the cutting edge.

My world had shifted almost overnight from a girls' school to, until now, all-male Sandhurst. And I was wildly excited. The only information I had about officer training came from watching *An Officer and a Gentleman*. I couldn't wait to be one of those glamorous officers. I knew I was a little fish leaping into a big pond, but I was a strong swimmer and I was determined to make it.

I had left a boyfriend behind and exchanged him for 38 women, ranging in age from 18 to about 28. We came from all sorts of backgrounds: daughters of senior military officers, ex-police officers, graduates and schoolgirls. It was rare for the Army to combine graduates with non-graduates, but we were too small an intake for them to do otherwise. We were designated Windsor Company and split into two platoons.

Our instructors were friendly but formal; we were addressed as 'Miss' plus our surnames. So, I was Miss Allen, which felt strange after a lifetime of Diane. But I soon learned that military instructors have finely honed the skill of making it clear just how low you are in the pecking order while addressing you with unimpeachable politeness.

We were guinea pigs in a whole new world, and we had no idea what to expect. Our arrival was greeted with a wide range of responses. There were those who ridiculed and laughed at us, those who thought we'd been provided as 'totty', and those who were simply hostile. Whatever happened, their faces said, the girls couldn't, and wouldn't, be allowed into the boys' world. Let alone have a chance to be better than the boys.

Thankfully we had our own directing staff who ran Windsor Company and who were nearly all women. They taught us basic drill and military law, oversaw our uniform and inspected our rooms. They also did their best to help us with the transition to military life and to buffer us from some of that hostility.

We were told we would be confined to camp for the first two weeks, so if we were missing anything on the kit list, we had to borrow or make do. There was only one public phone to contact the outside world so there was always a queue to phone home. We didn't mind, it was all just part of the newness and the fun. But while we were convinced we were ready for the Army, it was quickly apparent that it wasn't quite ready for us.

For a start there was our accommodation. Until then women who entered the Army officer training had trained separately at the WRAC College at Camberley, eight miles – and a whole world – away from the men's college, which stood within the vast area of heathland that was known as the Barossa military training area. Now, we women recruits stood next to the men as equals, training side by side. Or at least that was the theory. We were supposed to be accommodated at Sandhurst but ended up sleeping in college rooms in the old location in Camberley and being ferried the eight miles to Sandhurst every day in the back of an open four-ton lorry. We had to climb up a rope to get into it, all without scuffing our neatly polished shoes or creasing our clothes. The Army just said our accommodation wasn't ready – make do, so we did.

Then there were the boots. They hadn't bargained on anyone with small feet so when a couple of the women said they were size four the sergeant in charge looked perplexed and said the smallest they had was size seven. None of us had feet that big. Our boots would need to be specially made and that would take weeks, so his short-term solution was multiple pairs of socks. We felt like clowns, clumping about in our massive boots, our feet clammy inside three or four pairs of socks.

The rest of the uniform wasn't much better. It was designed for men, which meant everything was the wrong shape and there were no smaller sizes. The result was that we were almost all missing items of army kit and we looked like some kind of rag-tag militia, in a combination of ill-fitting army uniform and civvy clothes. I was tall and slim, so the trousers were too short (I had grown eight inches since being thrown out of ballet for being too tall and was now just under six foot) and the jumpers were man-shaped. Our hair had to be either short or long enough to put up in a bun, but if you had a bun, your helmet would be perched forward, covering your eyes. This was known at the time as the 'Private Benjamin' look after the Goldie Hawn film that had come out a couple of years earlier.

We all agreed that there had to be an award for the designer who managed to make army uniform look equally bad on every woman. As for the DMS (Directly Moulded Soles) boots, not only did we have to wear them several sizes too big, but even when we eventually got the right sizes, they cut into our ankles so badly that they were nicknamed Designed to Mutilate Soldiers. Second only to the dreaded boots on the horror scale were puttees: strips of cloth you had to wrap around the lower leg and ankle. They were intended to provide ankle support and prevent debris and water from entering the boots or pants, but they did neither and were a complete pain to wear.

Fortunately, puttees were abandoned by the Army a few years later.

In some areas of etiquette confusion reigned. We were told not to wear makeup in uniform (the men were more likely to take us seriously) but in the evenings, when we were tired after long hours training, we were admonished for not wearing makeup as we didn't look 'feminine' enough.

Our time was scripted almost to the hour, seven days a week. We would wake around 6 am, work until around 10 pm and rush from lesson to lesson, changing clothes, catching transport and doing extra duties. We were expected to be five minutes early for everything and we were permanently sleep-deprived, so when the opportunity arose it was easy to nod off. Both men and women fell asleep in darkened lecture theatres, on buses and even in trenches.

Most days started with physical training, which was my favourite part of the day. I was young and sporty, and I enjoyed the early morning runs and workouts. I was one of the few who wasn't injured during the course. Before arriving at Sandhurst, I had spent the summer at a karate camp where my sister and I were the top two women, winning most of our fights. Good preparation, as it turned out, for the battles ahead.

Morning training was followed by classroom study, military skills training, weapon-handling and more inspection parades. The pressure was always on, as we were told, many times a day, that as the first women at

Sandhurst we 'mustn't let the side down'. We were responsible, it seems, for providing a positive example for all the women who would follow us. And we felt it keenly. I had always been a bit of a rebel and before I left home a good friend had said, 'All that marching and shouting and taking orders, you won't make it through the first week'. He knew me pretty well, so I was worried. But I was determined to see it through, not only because I was competitive and would never have let myself quit, but because I was desperate not to go back home.

Not that my resolve wasn't sorely tested. The challenges came thick and fast. I spent most of my first couple of weeks feeling ravenous. I was a vegetarian, but at that time the Army didn't cater for vegetarians, so the only option was to leave the meat and eat the rest. I lost nearly a stone before I realised I had to start eating meat.

As one of the youngest, and a natural tomboy, I felt like the ugly duckling next to the older women. I had absolutely no idea how to dress for the social functions, how to wear jewellery or make-up or how to make polite small talk. In the evenings we were expected to wear our own clothes, but even then, as I quickly discovered, there were rules.

I had arrived with two small suitcases and my idea of 'casual and fashionable' was drain-pipe jeans (not allowed), a T-shirt with the Sex Pistols on it (inappropriate message), a pair of Han Solo-style black trousers with piped red seams, a Sheena Easton-style turquoise jump suit and Flashdance leg-warmers – all the rage at that time.

Wearing cotton sweatbands on your wrists was also trendy then but, I discovered, hardly potential officer wear. I turned up in a pair on my first day and was nicknamed Superbrat, after tennis tantrum king John McEnroe, for the rest of term.

Luckily some of the older recruits took me under their wing and taught me what to do and what to wear. Once we were allowed to leave the campus, they whisked me into Laura Ashley – the epitome of feminine at that time – and kitted me out with chintzy skirts, frilly blouses and demure frocks that were not me at all. I wore them all with good grace, determined to grow up quickly and join the swans.

Inevitably, as we ran the gauntlet of condescending looks, dubious jokes and outright sexism we began to feel a sense of 'them and us' and to bond within our own group. At the end of the first week we held a party in one of our dorms and, as we swigged bottles of cheap wine, a 'we can do this' spirit was born. Sandhurst didn't really want us, but we weren't going to let it break us. That bond helped us all through – each time one of our number flagged, the rest of us encouraged her on, and by the end we were so close that many of us would stay in touch throughout our time in the Army and beyond.

I struggled with the level of exactitude required. Our rooms always had to be kept tidy, in case of spot inspections. Naturally messy, I found it a challenge to keep my things neat and ordered.

Every day for the first couple of weeks I was picked out in line-ups for transgressions with my uniform. I had never noticed or cared about an untucked shirt, the angle of a beret or the exact length of my hem (we paraded in barrack dress of pleated skirts, tight-starched shirts with strange little green cravats, V-necked jumpers and forage caps), but by the end of the first couple of weeks I realised that it was easier to do it right the first time than to keep being ordered back on parade again for repeat inspections. The first time I managed a line-up without being picked out was a real moment of triumph.

At times, during those first few weeks we were there, you could smell the fear. And it came from every direction: men, women, staff, students. I have no idea what preparations were made in advance to get women into Sandhurst, certainly it was a big deal, and inevitably there was the usual range of reactions- what in business terms is known as the human traffic light response:

Green Lighters: Good to go, change no problem, enthusiastic enablers. The supportive few.

Amber Lighters: Willing to go along with it, a bit sceptical but let's see how it goes. The hesitant majority.

Red Lighters: Not up for it, will actively sabotage, block and fight it. The destructive few.

Those in charge at Sandhurst appeared to be green, touching on amber – they were trying to find out what women could do. In practice this meant that one week we would carry the same packs as the men, but if there were injuries, we might carry nothing for the next

15

few weeks. We did the same military field exercises and used the same weapons, but also trained on other weapons 'more appropriate for women'. The Sterling sub-machine gun and 9mm pistol were both considered acceptable. Women had only just been allowed to carry weapons at all and then only for self-defence. So initially we were only taught how to make safe the standard army weapon, the SLR 7.62 calibre self-loading rifle, but were not allowed to fire it.

We kept a mandatory diary. Mine says there were also worries about whether we could hold our own in inter-college quizzes and debates (we did), whether we could tab (march) at the same pace as the men with full kit (we couldn't, as a group, but we tried) and how we were going to be included in the full syllabus when our accommodation – with our many changes of clothing – was eight miles away. It was tough, but we managed it.

I learned that bias comes from unexpected angles; the Sandhurst academics were not so much anti-women as universal in their dislike of teaching a mixed course of graduates and non-graduates. They refused to take questions from those of us who didn't have degrees. We were easily spotted since we wore white bands and collar insignia while the graduates did not. So, it was a major point of pride when I won the overall academic prize at the end of the course.

The level of misogyny from the minority of Red Lighters did surprise me. We were denied attendance at firepower demonstrations at Warminster as 'it would be all about tanks and armour and women would probably be bored'. We were told to never talk about 'women's problems' and there were plenty of derogatory jokes about women. At times we were hidden from the view of the Commandant or given menial tasks the men weren't expected to do, like cleaning the classrooms after the men were allowed to leave. It was my first taste of being treated as second class simply because of my gender and the first time it dawned on me that to change the rules you need to become a rule-maker.

One of the other women recorded in her diary that the men at Sandhurst had been instructed (by a full-on Red Lighter) not to talk to the women, on the basis that if we were not made welcome then it might be possible to reverse the decision to have women admitted. An attitude that might well make our lives harder but would never turn the clock back.

Things weren't helped by the fact that we didn't have real equality or parity with the men. That would come much, much further down the line. We were members of the WRAC, the Women's Royal Army Corps, which came into existence in 1949 to replace the wartime ATS, the Auxiliary Territorial Service, of which the Queen was the most famous member. And while the civilian perception of these organisations was of girl-warriors, in reality women were given more sedentary trades such as clerks, posties, truckies and stewardesses.

Women of my generation were already seeking more variety and gradually abandoning the WRAC to join other regiments. The WRAC would be disbanded eight years later in 1992 – it was a necessary phase for integrating women, but it created separate standards and roles and separation created inequality, so that women were always going to be seen as 'second-class'.

At Sandhurst the military lessons on doctrine and tactics were delivered by male officers; the only female staff were at Camberley. And with no women on site at the academy, sexism was the order of the day. The standard presentation format was to use a slide deck and a projector. The instructors had worked out that the most effective way to keep young, sleep-deprived male students awake was to put in a photo of a naked woman about every tenth slide. There was panic when they realised they now had a mixed audience. To change the carousels meant a long-winded process of taking out each slide and moving the others up, so for a while it didn't happen. At first, we tolerated this – and some of the poses were something of an education for me as an 18-year-old. But some instructors took this to mean they could continue. They would tell us that the Army was 'a man's world, so we might as well get used to seeing these images'. It was only when we started to leave pictures of naked men around on the chairs and to sneak one or two slides of naked men into the carousels that the offending slides were removed.

Some of the sergeant-majors struggled to allow women on their parade squares, those hallowed squares of tarmac on every military base. Soldiers never just amble across them; we walk around or march smartly across.

Until we arrived only men had stood on them and the change was genuinely painful for some traditionalists.

Most of the male students were Amber Lighters, too busy getting through the course themselves to worry about us, but there were a few who didn't like having us there. During parade rehearsals some of them changed our marching tunes to the Stripper Theme. And when it came to the end of course revues, women were usually portrayed by the men in partial uniform with fishnet stockings.

That first term I made the mistake of mentioning that I was agnostic. Army culture encourages a strong relationship with faith and what my confession taught me was not to confess again. I was made a 'chapel member' for the first term, which meant rising early to set up the church for congregations, bringing in flowers and preparing services. I also met the padre once a week and arranged his diary. All this I found extremely tedious, so I asked to switch roles and in the second term was made the 'bar member'. This was no easier; at the end of every evening, I had to calculate how much we had drunk and re-order stock.

I grew up fast. I found I liked the discipline and the instructors; their cynical humour and professionalism gave me the parenting I was looking for. I found out quickly where I was good: sport, log-races, assault courses, adventure training and team tasks, as well as where I needed to apply myself: concentration, written tests and attention to detail. And I struggled with giving verbal briefings. I couldn't easily manage talking at the same time as placing acetates in the projector to illustrate my points, and speaking on tape, when we had to record a radio interview, was painful.

To my dismay, I wasn't great at military tactics either. The enemy force at Sandhurst was the Gurkhas, a wonderful group of professional infanteers. When I oversaw the tactics, we seemed to lose to these guys every time. I was better at playing the enemy myself and good with radios (no surprise that I would join the Signals and Intelligence after training). I was also learning that charging in was not always the best approach. I had new scars on my knees to show this, after diving through a window after a smoke-grenade was thrown, without checking first how far it was to the basement floor.

Being tall for a woman, I was required to short step when marching and I constantly tripped over my own feet. A lot of infantry troops are actually quite short and wiry – shorter legs and strong muscles is a good mix for moving fast across difficult ground.

For relaxation I joined the karate club – a welcome breather from being a potential officer – and played hockey for the men's team. There were two of us women who joined, the other was a former international player. The memo when we finally got permission to play for the men's team (the first women to play sport for Sandhurst), was 'when you turn up, wear a short skirt'. The skirt wasn't a problem, it was the college shirts which were open almost to the waist; we had to go and borrow safety pins.

We did a lot of adventure training too. We rode horses before classes and took part in a group outdoor adventure week in Wales, climbing Snowdon, kayaking and orienteering. I loved all of that. And as time went on we developed a good camaraderie with most of the men, whose apprehension about us diminished as they saw that we were as serious as they were about completing the course.

As autumn became winter, we felt the chill. The Army kit of that time was pretty basic (none of the thermals, down and specialist gloves included now) and most of it didn't fit us properly, so as the temperature dropped we piled on several layers of civvy clothes underneath our uniforms, giving us a decidedly odd look on parade. To add to our discomfort, we were still being driven from Sandhurst to our dorms eight miles away in the back of an open lorry. Enduring that in skirts and jumpers in midwinter left many of us blue with cold.

Despite everything I ended the first term feeling that I belonged and happy to be there. There wasn't anything else at that stage that I wanted to do with my life, and I felt I was among like-minded people. I loved the rhythm of army-life almost immediately and while I struggled with the constraints, youth and adaptability were on my side and I knew I would stick it out – at least until the end of training.

Chapter Two
Choosing the army

I hope the fathers and mothers of little girls will look at them and say, 'Yes, women can.'
Dilma Rousseff

I walked past the window of the Army recruitment office, glancing surreptitiously at it. A few yards up the street I turned and walked back past. My heart was thudding with excitement and nerves. After a couple more trips, up and down the street I finally gathered my courage and went in.

An overweight, middle-aged man in a uniform was sitting behind the desk.

'Hello, son.'

He looked up at me again and did a double take. 'Oh, sorry love. I'll get one of the women to talk to you.'

He disappeared and a woman, not in uniform, appeared in his place.

'Hello. Are you enquiring for yourself?'

I nodded. She took a pile of papers from a drawer and ran through a lot of questions. When we got to education, I said I had nine O Levels.

She looked up and smiled. 'Well, you will want to be an officer then?'

Officer sounded good. I said yes.

About a month later I received a letter asking me to go to Guildford for assessment and enclosing a rail warrant. It also said I should prepare a short talk to bring with me. I got busy pasting press clippings about Sally Ride, the first American woman in space, onto a large piece of cardboard.

With this under one arm and my overnight bag in the other, I set off. I nearly missed a connection and I left my precious Sony Walkman on the train, but I did hang onto my cardboard presentation.

The selection, which lasted a couple of days, involved solving team tasks, writing essays, planning challenges, debating, going over assault courses, and the talks, or 'lecturettes'. The selection team was all women and they seemed happy with me, although they did tell me to read up a little more on current affairs. My level of sophistication at that stage extended to science fiction, episodes of *The Professionals*, the exploits of Illya Kuryakin in *The Man from Uncle* and the kids from *Fame* so it was probably a fair criticism.

A couple of weeks later another letter arrived. I had been accepted for officer training. I was to report to Sandhurst on September 23.

I was jubilant. I had done it. I was seventeen and I was joining the Army.

Why the Army? Well, my path to that pivotal moment when I stepped into the recruitment office was in some ways a classic one. I was looking for a vocation, something that would absorb my passion and my energy. I didn't want to go to university, but I wanted to leave home. As a small girl I'd dreamed of being a ballerina, then an astronaut, neither remotely viable. When I shot up into a lanky colt a head taller than the others in the class my ballet teacher stopped casting me in main roles and gave me the role of 'tree, which the smaller ones can dance around'. A few years later, I auditioned for a role as one of the children in *The King and I* and was cast instead as an Amazon guard. Both these episodes were a shock to me, and I understood that doors were closing. After that I wanted to be an astronaut, but I got sick just rolling down a hill. I thought again. Adventurer? I applied for Operation Drake; a round-the-world ocean voyage aimed at young people. It was 1978 and I was 14. I received a very polite letter of rejection saying I was too young. I moved onto full contact karate and here I did find a successful niche as one of the best women in the region, although it wasn't going to give me a career.

At sixteen I was sent off for work experience helping in a primary school, but after a week with 5-year olds, I knew I was definitely not cut out to be a teacher. So, what next? I read a glossy brochure showing the Army as a vocation, an adventurous way of life, with exotic travel and physical challenge. It sounded good to me so I told my careers adviser I might like to join the Army. She signed me up to the Combined Cadet Force (CCF) at a local private school (the girls' grammar school I attended didn't have CCF). I was given a slip of paper with a date, an address and a sergeant's name and told to find my way there.

I immediately loved the cadets. We met once a week after school and I was soon promoted to corporal. We wore itchy over-sized army clothing, ate terrible food (including chocolate so old it had a white film across it) and fired what seemed like enormous rifles. All perfect preparation for the real thing.

I was the middle one of five children, with an older brother and sister and a younger brother and sister. I had learned independence, probably far too much of it, from an early age. We weren't well off, so I had been working since I was 11, first in a chip shop, later as a waitress, then delivering newspapers and after that getting up at five every morning before school to write up newspaper rounds and run the shop. Although I struggled with confidence, I was determined that not having money wasn't going to stop me doing things and nor was lack of access to a car. Dad wasn't one to offer lifts and Mum didn't drive, so I went everywhere on a battered boy's racing bike

When I was 16 Dad left us. He was 14 years younger than my mother and they hadn't been happy for a long time. I have a memory of him announcing that there were 'just too many of you' and walking out. My memory might be playing tricks but regardless, we were all devastated. After that I didn't have a lot of contact with him. My parents refused to see or speak to one another again and the atmosphere, whether at my mother's or my father's, was tense and unhappy. Not long afterwards Dad moved to Somerset and after that I barely ever saw him. He got on well with my two older siblings but had very little to do with me or the two younger ones.

In my late twenties I had some therapy to try to resolve the anger and hurt that I felt. It did help, and I understood that by going into the Army I was trying to prove myself as well as to escape, but the wound my father left will probably always be there.

My mother, at 55, was left with five teenagers and very little money. She learned to drive at the same time I did, and she managed to keep things going for us, for which she deserves credit. But she and I struggled to get on, so life at home was not easy. I wanted to make my own way in the world, and the Army seemed to give me the perfect route. It also gave me the structure I was craving, since structure had been largely absent at home. I knew instinctively that the comfortable predictability of institutional life would help to calm the chaos I felt inside. Carl Jung wrote of the attraction of institutions for young, confused souls. I didn't read his work until my late twenties, but when I did, I instantly recognised myself.

I had looked at the police and all the armed forces and, truth be told, the Army won simply because I got a reply before the RAF and the Royal Navy got back to me, and it beat the police because it offered accommodation and travel.

As I signed up, I wasn't looking to make a big statement. It wasn't warrior or princess. In fact, the character of Princess Leia in Star Wars had shown me that I could be both and that pleased me. I liked a lot of activities more commonly associated with boys, but I was happy being a girl. I never wished I could be a man.

I was part of the age group that would become known as Generation X. We came after the baby boomers and before the millennials. My generation was defined by shifting societal rules, as latchkey kids (as our mothers as well as fathers went out to work) and children of divorce. We were seen as cynical, disaffected, yet entrepreneurial. That sounded like me. Even as a teenager I never thought that class, gender and background would hold me back. I would be part of a meritocracy and the Army brochure, at least to my teenage eyes, seemed to reflect all those worthwhile principles.

I had no concept of the difference between soldier and officer. I was told by my career's advisor and by the woman in the recruitment office that I had enough qualifications to go for officer, so that was the route I took. But I'd have been just as happy joining the ranks.

There were, and have always been, those who questioned my choice of the Army.

Friends I asked said their image of the Army was being shouted at, obeying mindless orders and killing

27

people. But, as I discovered at the selection, what the Army was looking for was physical robustness, a sense of adventure, enthusiasm and a competitive spirit. It was, and still is, about being robust enough for the military way of life. Certainly in the early years.

As a teenager I saw myself, romantically, as choosing bravery above all else, like the character Tris in the book and film *Divergent*. Later I would reflect at length on what it was all about for me and what is worth fighting for. I believe that everyone will fight for something. A few years ago, I came across the Gloria Steinem quote, 'From pacifist to terrorist, each person condemns violence – and then adds one cherished case in which it may be justified'. So now when I get into discussions about why we need an army I ask:

Would you fight if your child was threatened? Your family?

Would you fight for your way of life – freedom of speech, education, what you wear?

Would you fight on behalf of others' freedoms? Neighbours, country, comrades?

The answer to all of these, for me, is yes.

General Norman Schwarzkopf said that all good soldiers are anti-war, yet still 'there are things worth fighting for'. I don't think the Army chooses those who want war, but rather those willing to fight for peace. But we accept that war will come looking for us one day or another and we will be there to fight. I was reminded of this while watching the London Bridge terrorist attack in

June 2017. People had to run for their lives. Some were just lucky, some combined luck with physical robustness as they escaped. I imagine all were grateful for those from our armed military and police, who swiftly ended that attack by driving among the terrorists and shooting them. This was not a situation that could be resolved peacefully. There was a young army officer nearby who had made sure the civilians he was with were safe and then ran towards the incident to help. When interviewed, he simply said it was what he was trained to do.

Like him, like so many in the Army, I had a warrior spirit. I have a sister who shares that spirit. Bruce Lee was our idol and we practised karate all the time. My younger brother tells a tale of how he tried karate years later, not knowing it was the same club we had been part of. In the pub afterwards, they were talking about two women who could really fight. He knew instantly who they meant.

In 1983 when I joined up it was just over a year since the Falklands War, Margaret Thatcher had won a landslide election victory and there was an ongoing, bitter counter-terrorism conflict in Northern Ireland. Russia was still in control of the Soviet Union and America was introducing its 'Star Wars' programme (its strategic defence initiative) and posting nuclear missiles in Europe. In Britain, that had resulted in the mass protests at the RAF base in Greenham Common.

The British Army was generally well-liked. It was over 320,000 strong, with a big footprint, including Germany, Cyprus, Northern Ireland, Hong Kong, Belize and Brunei. But what the Falklands campaign had made clear was that its doctrine was old and narrow, and it wasn't very fit. The main fighting experience since World War Two had been on the streets in Northern Ireland. Women in the Army were still, with rare exceptions, separated into their own branches and there were no clear plans for integration. The Army top brass had realised it was time to re-write its manuals and become more forward-thinking and enlightened and I joined just as the rule book was changing. The Army was updating clothing, equipment, fitness standards and doctrine. Lesson plans were altered at Sandhurst not just because there were women there, but because of the Falklands experience. The instructors were literally ripping up manuals in front of us. Everything from weapon drills to tactics and first aid was being re-written.

I didn't know any of this as I packed my two suitcases and boarded the train for Sandhurst, wondering how I would cope with being confined to camp for the first two weeks. In the event I barely noticed that we couldn't leave camp, because every moment of my day was filled during that first term. It was full-on through to a Christmas break and after a brief visit home I went back early and joined the Sandhurst ski trip. It was my first time on big snow, and I loved it. We all wore bright orange, army-issue cagoules, trained on hugely long skis and learned by pointing our skis downhill and seeing how far we could go before falling over.

It was on the ski trip that a Sandhurst instructor did his best to seduce me. He was at least ten years older and there were explicit rules against instructors fraternising with students, but none of this stopped him from trying his luck. When I refused to sleep with him, he took it cheerfully, winking and telling me, 'No hard feelings, I had to give it a try'. I took it cheerfully too, I had no idea that what he did was against the rules and didn't tell anyone but my friend, who said it had happened to her too. Looking back at the photograph of that time, I look like a child next to him. But it didn't upset me, and he accepted it when I said no.

Lots of us dated the male officer cadets. We were a novelty and we enjoyed it. I had poems written for me, I was serenaded with a guitar and several times I visited huge country estates with well-heeled male cadets. But our course was short – just six months, so there was little time for deep or meaningful distractions. The second term of training involved more time in the classroom and that was tough for me; I failed quite a few written tests and had to repeat them. It was before word processors, so essays were handwritten and if we made an error we had to start again. The expectations on all of us were higher in the second term; my ability to iron was found wanting and I was disciplined for cutting my hair too short rather than deal with hairnets and clips.

Being one of the tallest in the group, I was always on the end of the row when marching. Soldiers in squad are placed so that the shortest are in the middle; the tall ones are the 'markers' for the others to fix their position from. For me it felt like being back in that ballet class while the smaller ones danced around me. Right hand markers stand around a lot so I would often get called out for daydreaming. The punishment was usually to be hauled out of the squad and to briefly take the role of the sergeant-major, which I actually quite enjoyed.

On rare home visits I was no longer interested in rekindling the home-town romance I'd left behind or seeing old haunts. I knew that after Sandhurst I would probably be going abroad for several years. My friends laughed at the new language I spoke. I described biff-chits (sick-notes), back-squadding (being moved back a term), beastings (being physically pushed in training), brews (tea), things that were gopping (terrible), and Jacking it (quitting). I related how we washed our dhobi (laundry), ate scoff (food), slept in doss bags (sleeping bag), that I was a Rupert (officer), that I carried a gat (gun), used beer tokens (money), got things buckshee (free), could be chin-strapped (really tired), would bimble along (walk out of step), that things were bone (rubbish, poor), how we visited pad friends (married officers living out) and went on stag (guard-duty). I had become institutionalised remarkably quickly.

Our final exercise was called Pons Asinorum – Bridge of Asses. This term is used to mean a critical test, separating the bright sparks from the dunces. We women approached this exercise collaboratively, for us completing the final exercise was about getting all of us through. In our minds there were no dunces. We had become a band of sisters, and all of us knew, and have known ever since, that we would unfailingly help one another if called on.

The two-day exercise was held in February in freezing weather, so cold that they almost cancelled it. We set off wearing military uniform with weapons and backpacks, rations and military radios. We were given a series of grid references and had to take it in turns to navigate across the military training area. At each stopping point we were set a task to complete before moving on to the next. Some tasks were given by a staff member in person, some by radio and sometimes we met 'enemy' and had to react. We got to sleep for a few hours at a time, taking it in turns to be on guard duty to prevent hostile approaches at night. In the bitter cold we marched as quickly as we could between activities, but when we stopped to sleep, we had only our basha, a single, waterproof camouflage sheet, to cover us. One woman became so hypothermic her lips swelled and she started to speak utter nonsense, so she had to be casevacced – casualty evacuated, until she warmed up and could return.

We took it in turns to carry the heavier kit like radios and stoves, we shared our warm clothes when sleeping and took it in turns to have the warmer middle spot and the draughty outside positions (like penguins) under the basha. And we all made it through.

The final passing-out parade was, and still is, known as the Sovereign's parade. The cadets march in front of the Sovereign's representative and the adjutant rides a white charger up the steps of Old College. When we started the preparation for this parade, it became clear there was no plan for how to integrate us women into it. As they struggled to make it work the plan kept being changed, and each change meant more rehearsals and required bussing us back and forth for the extra sessions.

The problem was stride length. The pace of the women in skirts, versus the men in trousers didn't match. There was a suggestion that we shorten our skirts to march at the same pace as the men. Some of our male fellow students loved that one. But our sergeant-major had our backs. He started to jail any man he saw smirking. That meant a few hours in the on-barracks facility. Not that serious but still demeaning enough to wipe the leery looks off their faces.

Each time we practised, we would start at the front and gradually the men's squads behind would start catching up, even when they were ordered to short step. The whole episode was divine comedy; we could hear our drill sergeant shouting, 'Fast as you can ladies, the men are catching you', but our skirts would not allow a wider pace. If you try to push the pace in a tight skirt, you fall over. Trust me, I know.

Step-length wasn't the only problem. Women were also not allowed to carry weapons on the parade, 'in case it gave the wrong impression'. We tried carrying nothing, swinging both arms, but our tunics rode up and it looked messy. We needed to hold something. The suggested solutions were increasingly desperate; we tried a handbag, a short cane, even just keeping one arm by our side. Each looked more ridiculous than the last.

Eventually the decision was made that we would stand at the side of the parade and only march on, carrying nothing and with arms swinging smartly, for the final lap. The senior sergeant-major was aware of the smug looks of some of the men and the demoralised women as he addressed us before the event. He ignored the men as he said, 'Remember ladies, you will own that parade square that day. People will not remember the men who march this year, they will see the first women, you will be standing at the very front, your every step watched. You will do this proudly and you will make me proud.' We were all grateful, he got us through it. And he was right, the media attention was huge; all of us were photographed and interviewed and all the national papers carried the story of the first women graduates from Sandhurst.

Thirty of us graduated and were commissioned on April 6, 1984. As a non-graduate my first rank would be a second-lieutenant or 'one-pip wonder'. Soldiers called 'one-pippers' the baby officers, but I felt very grown-up.

Eight of our 38 had dropped out. It was a testament to our determination that there weren't more who didn't make it. At one stage, there were only nine of us still standing; four were in hospital, six were sick and others were excused physical activities and wearing boots. We had cases of hypothermia, concussion, broken bones, bruises and sprains. It wasn't that women couldn't hack the course, but that we needed uniform, equipment and training designed for us. Everything at Sandhurst at that time was designed for men. Not surprisingly it suited them better.

The sisterhood scored many firsts. I was selected to turn a page of the book in the main Sandhurst chapel, the first time a woman had done it. The sergeant-major who trained me for the role told me, 'Don't worry, you're on your own out there so you can't be out of step for a change'. Despite his sarcasm I glowed with pride.

We also attended the Sandhurst final ball in our own right. This was when we would appear looking wonderful in our beautifully made 'mess kit' (military evening dresses) – except that they weren't ready in time. All the men's were ready, but the company who held the contract to provide the female mess kit wasn't up to the task; they kept delaying the final fittings until a week before the ball and at that point none of the dresses fitted us- they were badly made and completely unwearable. All officers get a one-off allowance to pay for their first mess kit and ours had been paid direct to the company by the Army – we ended up in dispute with them for months. To be fair, the mess kit evening wear for women was awful, a hideous gold-braided, square-necked gown with a long green sash attached to it. When I did finally get mine, weeks later, I barely ever wore it. Not only was it horribly unflattering but the green sash was only attached by a press-stud so young male officers used to rip it off and run away with it.

Meanwhile – what to wear to the ball? I had no alternative evening gown. At the last minute I was given an address in Camberley for a small, designer dress shop. The sales assistant took pity on me and picked one out. It was expensive but perfect and lasted me for the next ten years. And the ball was memorable; the Army knew how to do big social events. We rode bucking broncos in those evening dresses, danced the whole night to a band and drank champagne at breakfast. It was a great way to celebrate the end of our course.

Towards the end of our time at Sandhurst each of us filled in a form, known as the 'dream sheet' to say where we wanted to be posted – and we had up to three choices. We could ask for exotic options like Brunei, Hong Kong and Cyprus but traditionally first tours were either on mainland Europe or in the UK. A few weeks later, each of us was called into the office to be given our posting orders. Mine was for my first choice – Krefeld in Germany. I was delighted, I had studied German at school, visited on exchange and loved the culture.

I left Sandhurst, aged 19, with hugs and promises to stay in touch with the other Sandhurst sisters. We were all off in different directions and some of us would not meet again for many years, but our promise to stay in touch held true.

My two suitcases had been replaced by two large wooden crates full of kit which would be shipped out to Germany for me. Postings are a huge part of army life and I couldn't wait to begin my first one.

Chapter Three
Germany

The supreme art of war is to subdue the enemy without fighting.
Sun Tzu, *The Art of War*.

I had phoned the woman already in the role I was to fill, and she agreed to pick me up from the airport. I booked a military flight from RAF Brize Norton in Oxfordshire and set off with just a rucksack to last me until the kit arrived. Arriving at Brize Norton alongside 'real' soldiers was my first sighting of the military world beyond Sandhurst. Until then I had only been on school exchanges to France and Germany, so it was a big step up for me and I felt suddenly part of a parallel world, alongside the civilian one.

As I arrived in Dusseldorf, I still had little idea of what, exactly, I was going to be expected to do. At Sandhurst I had been trained to manage soldiers. But I hadn't yet gone beyond the theory to the reality of hands-on leadership. And while the men at Sandhurst would move on to a second phase of training in their future specialist areas, we WRAC officers were administrators, phase two training was not considered necessary and that meant heading straight to a unit and getting on with the job.

I would be working in a Signals unit, responsible for army communications. I had applied for sponsorship by the Royal Signals but missed out on their quota so I wouldn't actually be a Signals officer, but I was to be attached to the unit.

The woman I was replacing grinned as she welcomed me to Krefeld. She handed me the keys to a land rover and said it would be my work vehicle for the whole tour (very different to today where each military journey requires a long administrative process to justify borrowing a vehicle from the pool). My licence to drive military vehicles, it seemed, was simply a question of practising over the next few weeks.

That first day the HQ was having a barbecue on the sports field and had taken the afternoon off. As I arrived, one of the senior officers passed me a beer. I muttered something about starting my duties and he grinned, 'Relax, you are out of training now'. I began to feel I was going to enjoy this posting.

As a single officer I was accommodated in the officers' mess. Officers had their own rooms along a series of corridors with communal living rooms and bars. Men and women were mixed in together, but we had separate male and female bathrooms. We all tended to keep our doors unlocked and open and wander casually into each other's rooms. For me it was a great way to live, I made plenty of friends and we had a lot of parties. We were expected to keep our rooms tidy but they were never inspected, which came as a big relief to me. The senior officers were housed on a separate corridor, a long way from the youthful exuberance and noise of the younger ones.

My mother had been worried about my choice of career, even more so when I was posted abroad. I flew out only weeks after the Libyan embassy siege in London and the murder of WPC Yvonne Fletcher so there was high tension with Libya and the IRA also had an ongoing European bombing campaign targeting the military. But none of this worried me in the least; I was young and free and excited that the world was opening up.

Britain, and the Army, was far less diverse then. White, Anglo-Saxon, male was dominant. Being gay was still a military offence, women were required to leave if they became pregnant (when this changed later some who had been forced out received compensation) and getting married was an acceptable reason for women to resign. Roles for women remained limited; we were still not authorised to participate in combat or carry weapons and we were allocated a lead WRAC officer responsible for the moral values and standards of 'the girls'.

The nicknames of the time said it all. The WRAC was 'warm, round and cuddly' and we women were 'lumpy-jumpers' or 'the Doris-brigade'. Women would spell out WRAC, but men would pronounce it as 'rack' and would define it as 'something you screwed up against a wall'. And service women were called by their first names, not by their rank, while men were addressed by their rank and last name.

The British culture of the time set the tone for army culture. Women were established in the workplace but were still expected to 'know their place', although a few were starting to speak up. Margaret Thatcher was in power and, like her or loathe her, she was showing that a woman could lead. Princess Diana was finding a voice and influence beyond the traditional Windsor 'wife of' role. Popular TV shows of the time like *The Sweeney*, *The Professionals* and *Juliet Bravo* were inherently sexist. It was a time of gender inequality, virtually no health and safety, low litigation fear, more controlled public communications and hardly any environmental concerns.

Life was also slower; we had to find a public phone to make calls when not at home and there was no concept of 24/7 life. We were enjoying our relationship with Europe, with trade and travel barriers coming down. And Britain was becoming more globally aware – Bob Geldof's Band Aid was a response to the famine in Ethiopia and we were all reading George Orwell's *1984* with its totalitarian 'big-brother' state level of intolerance of individuality.

In Germany the British Army of the Rhine (BAOR) was a throwback from World War ll. By the time I arrived it had reduced in size from its 1940s peak, but it was still about 50,000 strong. No longer an occupational force, it was more a deterrent against the threat of Soviet troops sweeping across the European plains. Germany's spiritual capital was still divided into East and West by the Berlin Wall. The British, the Americans and the French each held responsibility for defending a section of West Berlin, while the Soviet Union held East Berlin. The inner German border was about 100 miles from the 'island' of West Berlin and military personnel could only access West Berlin via controlled routes; the military train, flights or driving along a designated corridor through the East. This was the height of the Cold War and the border was effectively the front-line between Soviet ideology and that of the West. It spawned some great films and books, including John le Carré's *Smiley* series. Britain and its allies had stationed manpower, artillery and other heavy weaponry strategically to counter the threat, but by 1984 it was a time of relative peace and army activity was dominated by what was known as contingency training. This meant large-scale exercises, and I arrived at the start of the biggest one since the end of the war: Exercise Lionheart.

Although the common civilian perception is of soldiers as 'killing machines', in the 1980s, other than the short conflict with Argentina and insurgency in Northern Ireland, very few members of the armed forces were engaged in real fighting. Training tactics and doctrine were designed around winning without (or with minimal) fighting. This included precision strikes, avoiding casualties and careful target planning. Operations such as

Lionheart were intended to rehearse these responsible and careful tactics, but also to demonstrate the West's willingness to defend borders against a Soviet incursion.

During the exercise over 100,000 troops, regular and reserve, were on the move with tanks and armoured personnel carriers, conducting amphibious crossings of the vast German waterways. Inevitably, my first impression of the military in Germany was very dynamic. Everyone had a war-fighting role and mine, practised during Lionheart, involved taking a small team of soldiers in land rovers to tops of hills and setting up mobile re-broadcasting stations. I had a technical sergeant with me, and we drove around for weeks, moving in and out of military sites.

Most women by now were being trained on weapons, although still not officially carrying them for anything other than self-defence. I was lucky as the Royal Signals were pretty good at integrating women, even then, and they expected us to be trained and capable on all weapons and to do nearly all the tasks expected of the men. I was an excellent pistol shot, slightly less good with long barrelled weapons. During Lionheart my team and I spent a lot of time rehearsing scenarios and firing weapons and I seem to recall we shot a lot of sheep – or at least the German farmers claimed we did.

I enjoyed my role in Lionheart, but there were other women who felt frustrated. One told me later, 'My war role in the event of a Soviet invasion was to escort women and children to the Ports. I had far more training skills than that'. The Army had a long way to go to catch up with the potential of its women soldiers.

For me, those first few months in Germany were everything I had hoped for. I had money and few responsibilities, I played sport and travelled, and I made friends and partied. I was mentored by the seniors and officers and encouraged to learn through experience.

We could buy cars tax-free, so everyone did. I wanted a Ford Capri, popular at the time, but my sergeant said, 'Ruperts (officers) don't drive Capris, ma'am. Get a Fiesta'. So, I did. We received fuel vouchers each year, to subsidise travel back to UK and the drive home was a familiar route to all of us; departure by lunch-time on Friday, fast driving through Germany (the German autobahns didn't have a speed limit), Belgium and Holland to the ports, a quick sleep on the ferry and then home for a long weekend.

The best thing about the Army of the 80s was that it allowed me to learn from my mistakes as well as my successes, and as a teenage officer I probably had an equal number of each. Some lessons were simple, such as the time a senior took one look at my military bergen (rucksack) which had to be kept ready for short-notice callouts, and quickly re-did the whole thing to 'ensure I looked professional, in front of the soldiers'.

Some learning, particularly around women's roles, was two-way. One night, during Exercise Lionheart, I was on duty and walking across camp on my own when a vehicle pulled up and I was 'kidnapped' by men in black uniforms and taken to a small room somewhere on camp, where I sat, baffled, for four hours until a rather sheepish officer arrived to let me out. Apparently, part of the exercise that day was to have a group playing 'the enemy' and there had been instructions to the men on what to do, in event of capture. As a WRAC officer, I had not been included in the brief. The officer apologised saying, 'We weren't meant to snatch any women – the lads shouldn't have picked you up. Okay if we let you go and that's the end of it?'

Of course, I said yes and just headed back for breakfast in the mess. My boss called me in that afternoon and apologised that the WRAC hadn't been informed of the snatch squads because we weren't expected to be involved. Was I okay? I nodded and went back to work. But this episode started me thinking about applying for specialist roles in the future.

I was still getting used to driving my short wheel-base land rover. The large army exercise sites were often reached across muddy tracks that had been churned by HGVs. I arrived in the dark at one steep site, failed to understand that the axle width of the HGV vehicles versus my land rover was quite different and ended up with my downhill wheels in a one rut and my uphill wheels on a higher section. I can still recall the slow-motion tipping of the vehicle as it rolled downhill with me in it, only to end up – astonishingly – back on its wheels, apparently undamaged and with mud caked on the roof. As all the vehicles were heavily mudded (it had been a rainy week), my accident was not immediately obvious, but I found out later that I had actually done a bit of damage. It cost me a crate of beer and a lot of ribbing about 'women drivers' from the LAD (Light Aid Detachment, the vehicle repair section) who fixed it.

I had a second land rover incident that first year when I volunteered to drive a kayak trailer from Germany to the UK. I did well until I had to drive it onto the ferry, when I was ushered into the lorry lane. First, I had to back it between other lorries, which I managed, but then I had to drive it up a ramp. Somehow, I hit the top bar of the trailer on a low ferry bar. Another crate of beer, this time to the LAD in the UK, who welded the bars back on.

There were many tales of youthful clumsiness. Driving to an exercise in Hamburg, for reasons that seemed entirely sensible to 20-year-old me at the time, I decided to drive along the notorious Reeperbahn red light district, curious to see what it looked like. It should have been a covert, swift peek, but we broke down and had to call out recovery. Explaining the location for the pickup was excruciating and cost me quite a few 'extras'. These, short for extra duties, were the discipline tools of a military unit for minor offences. When I got back the unit adjutant invited me for 'an interview without coffee', meaning a disciplinary chat to discuss the offence and the number of extra duties I would take on in penance. Extras allowed the adjutant to fill unpopular duties such as being the officer on duty over Christmas or a holiday weekend.

Sadly, this tool has gone now and all offences, however minor, must be kept permanently on record.

Berlin was a city we all wanted to visit, and, in uniform, it was possible to visit the East. There was also the opportunity to visit Spandau prison, where Rudolf Hess was still incarcerated and to run in the Berlin marathon – at that time a fascinating run through each of the Western allied sectors and along the wall, so that you could hear cheering from both sides. I hoped to combine all three, having won a place in the marathon by running for miles after work each night through the woods around Rheindahlen camp. I had booked the military train, the Berliner, as it was called, which ran from the West German border at Braunschweig to Berlin. It ran once a day, taking about four hours, with an armed guard included as part of the security. But somehow, I got the timings wrong and arrived at the station after the train had left. I was so miserable that the military police who manned the checkpoint took pity and persuaded a French officer, who was driving into Berlin along the road corridor, to add me to his paperwork. As we approached the notorious Checkpoint Charlie, I sat rigid with anxiety. My name was typed onto his form in a different font and I could see it stood out a mile so I was convinced we would be stopped. But we got through without any problems and I made it in time for the marathon. Afterwards I travelled back on the Berliner. It was an iconic journey and I was lucky to experience it, because it ceased running in the early nineties when the Cold War ended.

My own blunders aside, as a young officer I had to resolve problems for the soldiers in my unit, and there were plenty. From closing a bank account without opening another, to having local women turning up at the gates with tales of soldiers' promises, to thinking they had money if there were blank cheques in the chequebook. Mostly, incidents were just humorous, but occasionally they were more serious. There were two notorious bars in Rheindahlen, the soldiers called them 'Pops' and 'Eddies'. When I was duty officer I was required to go and clear out any soldiers still drinking after a set curfew hour. One night I went in with the sergeant and stood in the doorway, as was protocol, while the seniors ordered soldiers back to barracks. One drunken soldier took a run at me, swinging his fist, angry at being ordered to leave by 'an 'effin woman'. I ducked, he missed, and he was hastily bundled out. Nowadays he would have been charged and it would have been permanently on his record. Back then, he came to see me in the morning, his face bruised. He apologised and the sergeant, who had disciplined him with a punch, followed him in. 'He won't do it again, ma'am. Are you content with the apology?'

I was. He was young, he had missed. It was done. There will be differing views on whether physical discipline is ever right, but later I would see careers held back, where a foolish youthful incident was still on a record.

At the latter end of my 3-year tour I was put in charge of the garrison telephone exchange. It was staffed by army and RAF service women, plus German civilians, who worked in shifts on rows of switchboards, taking calls from all over the world. The job was one for a captain and I was only a 21-year-old lieutenant, but there was a gap and I agreed to take it on. I was delighted because I got pay of higher rank, but after three months some of the civilian staff came to see me to say they didn't like my style. I was confused. I wasn't having difficulty with the service personnel, who understood my position, but the civilian staff wanted me to spend more time talking to them. Truthfully, I had been terrified of them. They were all older than me and I had no idea how to relate to them, so I had made the mistake of avoiding them. After their visit I started having coffee with them on breaks and even arranged a 'bring your children to work day' and the problem disappeared; my team were content again.

There were a few ugly incidents that would remain with me. As a young duty officer, I had to make a hospital visit to see a soldier whose hand had been nailed to the door of a nightclub by a group of drunken soldiers from a rival regiment. They decided he had insulted them and had left him there with the hammer just out of reach of his other hand. I was shaken by this level of barbarity; I hadn't yet learned about the tribal warfare that existed between some infantry regiments, or the extreme way some of them could behave when drunk. This particular incident was treated as a criminal act and the culprits were handed over to the German police.

More experienced officers were used to the extremes drunken infantrymen could go to. Feeling shaken, I mentioned it to a fellow officer who, without appearing remotely surprised, simply asked me what kind of hammer it was.

At the time homosexuality was not allowed in the Army. One day I was asked, as a female officer, to sit in while two male special investigation military police officers interviewed two service women accused of being lesbians. The role of the military police was to get the women to admit their 'crime'. It was the first thoroughly unpleasant thing I ever witnessed. The women, both competent soldiers, were made to describe their relationship in detail and both lost their jobs. That day, and the humiliation I witnessed, was among the lowest of my career.

There were plenty of relationships, both the forbidden and the permitted. Being a woman in the military was the Tinder of its generation. Most of the time, we liked the attention, just not from older officers and soldiers and not when any of them turned up late at night to proposition us. I also learned of the pull of RAF pilots. All the young female officers were invited to visit RAF Bruggen and were able to co-fly in the fast jets of our generation. I was sick in all of them, it wasn't glamorous, but I thought the pilots were.

All of us had to be alert for inappropriate advances. When I attended functions, I learned to leave at the 'right time' to avoid drunken advances, particularly from senior officers. I had flowers left on my bed, was sent love-notes and was often followed back to my room. Soon after I arrived, I was invited to an officers' party in Dusseldorf. I was promised a lift home by my host, but as the evening wore on it became apparent I was expected to stay the night. I borrowed a bicycle, hitched up my long dress and cycled 20 miles home back along the autobahn at two in the morning. Another time I was trapped in the corridor by a senior officer and, unable to talk my way out of his unwelcome advances, used my karate skills to knock him down. In the morning he had a black eye, but neither of us said a word.

The main escape was a stable relationship with someone of a similar rank. Generally, No meant No and we settled into positive relationships with the men. Many of my fellow female officers met their husbands while serving. But at times, it was the 'wild west', and the downside of this was that we were not taken seriously. We were treated politely but seen more as the forces' sweethearts than as professional colleagues. The term 'forces' sweethearts' was used as a reference to the great Dame Vera Lynn, who was widely known as the forces' sweetheart for giving beautiful, patriotic concerts for the troops during WW2. But we weren't singers. We were professional army officers. It was a compliment to her; not to us. However, I was learning what it felt to be respected and how it felt to be disrespected. More importantly, I was learning how to look after and respect myself.

For the most part I enjoyed Germany enormously. I learned what it was to be an officer, hosted a visit from the (rather grumpy) Princess Royal and volunteered for everything. On my 21st birthday the officers' mess presented me with a Barbour Jacket, a required item of off-duty officer uniform, along with a cake, presented to me by a young squaddie who happened to be a bodybuilder and who popped – muscles well-oiled and in a tiny pair of swimming trunks – out of a packing crate. I blushed scarlet as the officers around me hooted with laughter.

By the end of my 3-year tour, I had built-up a good rapport with the soldiers, acquired more trophies, plaques and photographs than I could display and made friends I would keep for life.

It was time to think about my next posting. Germany had been an easy tour, but as I was presented with that dream sheet of where to go next, I thought about fun versus work. Great adventuring, sporting or work success involves a lot of graft... and I found I liked graft. Years later, Mark Beaumont, the world class cyclist gave me an explanation for this. Type 1 fun, he said, is fun in the moment: drinking beer, chatting to friends, watching movies. But type 2 fun, things like climbing mountains, delivering projects or winning a race is not necessarily fun at the time, it means being prepared to delay the pleasure and suffer for the bigger prize. And as I discovered, type

2 fun can be addictive – each goal I achieved pushed me on to a bigger one.

I was determined to prove myself. I could already see I was a woman in a man's world, but what was hardest for me was working out what equality actually meant. I could see that men were usually stronger and faster than women (not always, I could out-run and out-lift quite a few of them), so demanding all posts be open to all women seemed a fantasy at that time. But we could do an awful lot more than administration. What we needed was equality of opportunity, for it to be about who could do the job, without discrimination on the basis of gender or any other attribute. Many men could see that too and were open to change and fair competition; it was just a few, the Red Lighters, who were openly obstructive.

At Sandhurst I had learned that in the Army the men were setting the rules and women were only allowed to play if we obeyed these rules. I could now see that if only men set the rules, then the rules will favour men. I wanted to see change, real change, which meant women sharing power, and I was determined to be a part of it.

In the end I didn't include another tour of Germany on my dream-sheet, though many did. It was fun, the hours were short, and the pay was higher, with overseas allowances. I wanted to do some graft. So, I volunteered for the Army's only conflict zone of the time – Northern Ireland.

Chapter Four
Northern Ireland

A boat is safe in the harbour, but that's not what boats are made for.

Anon

If my family had been worried by my posting to Germany, they were much more worried about me serving in Northern Ireland. But as I packed my boxes, I felt none of their apprehension. I was looking forward to a more demanding posting that I could really get stuck into. I was 22 and like most youngsters I felt immortal.

Besides, Northern Ireland was not a far-flung location; it was a part of the UK. Yes, it was a part that was openly engaged in civil unrest, but it was still close to home and because of that, and the fact that I had never been into a conflict zone before, I felt more excited than fearful.

What I didn't understand until I got there was just how deep the polarised ideologies of the region went; individuals were willing to kill for their beliefs and for

54

criminal gain, all in an urban setting. These events would cost the lives of local civilians as well as those signed up for the fight: The Royal Ulster Constabulary, terrorists, criminals and the British troops who had been ordered there by the Government.

Unrest had escalated due to power inequalities between the ruling Protestant Unionists and the minority Catholic Nationalists. Most nationalists were moderate and sought their ambitions (for a united Ireland) through democratic means, but a small faction, the Republican paramilitaries, were willing to engage in terrorism. Most protestants (who wanted to keep Northern Ireland part of the United Kingdom), were also moderate, but with their own small faction, the Loyalist paramilitaries, also willing to take up arms. Both sides had political front parties and were as keen to dominate the criminal drugs trade as to achieve political goals. Despite the religious dichotomy, this was more a conflict about power.

At Sandhurst I had learned the history – how British Troops had been brought in after rioting in August 1969, during a civil rights campaign in which Irish Catholics were demanding an end to discrimination. The police force, the Royal Ulster Constabulary, could no longer contain things and the British Government wanted to regain civil order. The Army was sent in, initially for a few months, and ended up being there for 30 years. Sensitive documents released recently by the Government have confirmed just how difficult they were finding it to withdraw the troops for fear of escalating violence.

The military remit was clear- to support the civil authorities (we were not in the lead as, for example, in Malaya). As soldiers, we are used to being the target of a foreign enemy but this was a new experience - being attacked from within communities we were there to protect. Historically, any force required to stay on after quelling the initial unrest is at risk of being seen as an occupying force and there was a very effective IRA propaganda machine that exploited this fear, turning anger on the British troops. A good example of the Troubles was in 1972, with the events that became known as Bloody Sunday, in which British troops shot 28 people during a civil rights march, killing fourteen of them. The facts of the day remain disputed (I wasn't there but I have seen the photographs - it may have been a civil rights march but it wasn't being conducted very civilly - the troops can clearly be seen under attack, sheltering behind vehicles before they opened fire). And it was followed by the almost immediate IRA revenge bombing of the Parachute Regiment HQ in Aldershot – it was the Paras who were involved in Bloody Sunday – in which 7 civilian staff were killed and 19 wounded. It resulted in a simmering hatred between the Paras and the IRA that continues today.

After Bloody Sunday there was a surge in membership of and support for the IRA and terrorist activities escalated. And although the worst atrocities were in the 1970s, by the time I got there in 1986, the Troubles, as this period came to be known, were by no means over..

From the moment I arrived there was an instant sense of difference from the friendly training grounds of Germany. Here we were briefed to be careful off-duty in what we wore and said and to avoid military insignia or identifiers on our vehicles and clothes. Moving in and out of our camps meant checking the conditions of the day first and avoiding some areas.

Military efforts were focused on shutting down the impact of the terrorist attacks on communities. The failure of the bombing campaigns of the 1970s and relative 'success' of hunger strikes, especially after the death of IRA man Bobby Sands in 1981, which garnered greater global sympathy than indiscriminate bombings, instigated a change to a dual approach by the Republicans, known as 'bullet & ballot'; ongoing violence mixed with political engagement, through Sinn Fein, the IRA's political wing.

Sinn Fein had two strong, charismatic leaders, Gerry Adams and Martin McGuinness. As a military officer, I found it possible both to be appalled by their modus operandi yet still admire the power of their leadership and the professional abilities of their propaganda machine. But what I was reading in the military reports was very different to what the media was reporting, not dissimilar to 2019, where unbalanced and at times biased reporting was assisting and reinforcing one side over another. In this case, the lie of the IRA as oppressed soldiers engaged in a popular uprising to force the unification of Ireland. I could see this wasn't true. The republican movements were non-democratic and rejected the political wishes of the majority.

Yet their propaganda machine and ruthless approach to dissent were both effective. The IRA and other terrorist organisations worked hard to present their terrorists as paramilitary insurgents, working in brigades, rather than as a criminal mafia. They described themselves as 'soldiers for the cause', their combatants were deemed to be on active duty and at funerals and on murals, they appeared in uniforms. And they ruthlessly suppressed any views that differed to their own. Not all Catholics sought a united Ireland, but they were unable to express those views for fear of reprisals.

American Irish were particularly susceptible to this narrative, blind to any evidence shown that the IRA were being armed, financed and trained by Libya's Gaddafi, then a lead sponsor of all international terrorist groups. Sending terrorists to the Middle East to learn their trade began long before the recent Islamic terrorist phase.

The strongholds of both sides in the conflict were marked with flags and colours: in Loyalist areas, there were Union Jacks, the colours red, white and blue or the Red hand of Ulster were dominant and murals displayed William of Orange and the Battle of the Boyne. In Republican strongholds, there were vast murals of men in black balaclavas, with rifles in the tricolour of Ireland. Even the paving stones in these areas were painted green, white and orange.

I learned from Northern Ireland how quickly conflict escalates: direct rule imposed from London, internment without trial, city curfews, barricades and no-go areas. In Belfast keeping factions apart required building a wall, the Peace Line, that separated hardliner areas such as the Protestant Shankhill Road and the Catholic Falls Road.

The military strategy, by the time I arrived, was intensive surveillance and infiltration of the terrorist groups while leaving open the door to negotiation. On the ground, it meant uniformed soldiers providing daily reassurance patrols. It was surreal to watch soldiers under attack or taking cover, while civilians carried on with their daily business, but that was the plan – to disrupt civilian life as little as possible. Politicians, as is common, conducted both overt and clandestine talks with the various factions, but progress was painfully slow. It was not until 1998 that politicians from all sides reached a peace accord – The Good Friday Agreement.

Conflict zones do not fade easily from the mind. The 1980s was only the middle phase of a 30-year conflict and my time in the Province would not see the worst of the violence, but it was bad enough for all who served there to remember their service in stark detail. There is an argument that the IRA, by starting their campaign in the 70s, put back progress in achieving Catholic equality. A similar argument was made about the Falklands Conflict; negotiations on returning the Falklands to Argentina were already underway prior to the Argentinian invasion, but after British lives were lost defending the islands, all negotiations ceased. I was still learning about the nuances of conflict resolution.

I lived and worked in Thiepval Barracks, in Lisburn. A city eight miles southwest of Belfast, Lisburn is on the River Lagan which forms the boundary between County Antrim and County Down. Thiepval Barracks was, and still is, the headquarters of the British Army in Northern Ireland.

Mine was an administrative post, but I had additional roles in connection with security and oversight of the WRAC. It included controlling access, threat responses and perimeters for the camp, visiting isolated servicewomen around the Province, and a standing task of attending court martials (military trials) which were held in the grounds of the notorious Maze prison – also at times the location of the famed Diplock courts in which serious criminal cases connected with the Troubles were tried by a single judge, with no jury, in order to avoid intimidation of jurors, or jurors deciding on the basis of political allegiance, rather than the case in hand.

I found it frustrating that the hierarchy still seemed more interested in my dress sense than my desire to take part in military operations. I was interviewed by the head of the WRAC when I arrived and she mentioned it immediately, asking if I would like any further advice. Bloody hell, I thought, they have a file on me. She also recommended I complete a WRAC-focused tour in my next job. Given that my view was that we needed to integrate more, not less, I knew that wouldn't be my choice.

We could leave camp, unlike the infantry based in higher threat areas. But the British Army uniform was seen by some as provocation enough, so precautions had to be taken. We didn't wear uniforms off duty – even travelling between units meant civilian attire and then changing, though some took shortcuts and just draped a jacket over their uniform.

The significance of the uniform was brought home to me on the day I had cycled out of the Barracks to go for a run. I arrived back in sweaty sports clothes and as I approached the garrison, I could see there was a civilian crowd at the gate. It seemed peaceful, so I pushed my bike through the crowd who politely parted to let me in. In the duty room, I learned that the crowd wanted a statement about an incident that had occurred. One had been prepared and I was asked to go and read it out to the crowd. I changed into uniform and, with a small team of infantry as security, stepped outside. The crowd became immediately hostile and I was spat on and shouted at as I read out the short statement. I wanted to say, 'I just rode my bike through here and you were fine then', but of course it was about the uniform and what it represented; the person inside the uniform was irrelevant.

One of my roles was to inspect the block where the servicewomen slept. I had to visit this accommodation in the evenings and double check with the duty corporal stationed at the entrance that all 'the girls' were in their rooms. I soon learned that if I stopped at the duty-room to chat for a few minutes, word would get around of my arrival and any illegally visiting 'guests' would have time to climb out of the windows and disappear. These bed-checks were resented, so much so that some of the Intelligence Corps women had already abandoned the arrangement and moved into shared houses away from the block.

I was frustrated by the lack of progress for women. Equality issues were improving slightly, but women were still called by their first names, whereas men were referred to by rank and surname. The military commanders also delegated discipline of servicewomen to the WRAC. Particularly if there were 'women's problems' involved, which were often communication rather than medical issues. Women were not all innocent; one senior had been taking extra days off each month and I was asked by her line manager to talk to her. She admitted she had no medical issues but knew her boss wouldn't question her if she mentioned 'women's problems'. We agreed on a trip to the doctor, to confirm she had no actual problems and a return to full duties.

But I did get involved in operations and I would publish weekly updates of bombing incidents, internecine killings and kidnappings. There were hijackings of buses and cabs, knee-cappings and disappearances. These became a legacy issue of the Troubles; many families are still seeking closure on what happened to their loved ones.

I would also go out with the signals teams to check isolated communications sites and more than once we found broken security locks and had to assume the cause was terrorism rather than vandalism. It would always get the adrenaline pumping.

Danger was never far away. Sometimes there would be coded warnings before bombings, but not always. There was a high threat of mortars being fired at camps, so patrols were frequent around the perimeter and undercar bombs were common, detonated for example by tilt switches or wired directly to the ignition. The infantry patrols faced snipers and IEDs (improvised explosive devices) and the helicopters that moved them around the rural patrol areas would come under fire.

Conflict zones heighten the senses and help us to focus on the important stuff. Normal became checking under our vehicles for explosives and suspicious wires before turning the ignition, varying routine and watching what we said, who we met, where we went. The tempo of real operations stripped down unnecessary bureaucracy and the pettiness of daily living (as well as offering adrenaline surges, which were addictive). When death is closer, I think we live more in the moment.

In this posting I came to realise how much the public ask of young soldiers. War zones demand split second decisions between life and death, for us as well as those with whom we interact. A soldier may just have seen a colleague die, been spat at or had petrol bombs thrown at their vehicle. It is our professional duty to get it right, to absorb war-weary anger and guerrilla tactics, but it isn't surprising that we tread a fine line and a few make mistakes or poor decisions and it's important to judge these against the level of conflict at the time. War zones offer very little time to make a nuanced judgment.

It brings me to the current military anger at the repetitive Bloody Sunday investigations. Some soldiers have been repeatedly investigated, and yet it continues. I feel deep pain at these ongoing, one-sided witch-hunts currently aimed at old soldiers, while amnesty is offered to terrorists. If we must investigate incidents from long ago for political reasons, it is organisations, not individuals that should be in the firing line (pun intended). The pursuit of a few soldiers by politicians and the courts is doing significant harm to recruitment, retention and morale in the armed forces. Orders were given, soldiers followed them. Individuals should not be taken to court if they followed orders – the judicial process should be aimed at those who gave the orders.

Inevitably there were deaths and injuries, and another of my roles was to visit injured soldiers in the special security wing Royal Victoria Hospital in Belfast, where I saw for myself the damage that an explosion, knife or bullet could do.

As a duty officer, I would receive a list of who was in hospital, their injuries and any plan to rehabilitate them, get them back to work or send them home. I would take messages from friends or family and share them, and it was also a chance for the injured soldier to share any worries or concerns that they needed me to pass on to their families or workmates. There were no mobiles at that time and even the use of public phones was restricted as we were in a conflict zone, so my role as the communication conduit was important.

Often, I would sit by the bed and just chat, especially with the younger ones, and if they were scared or upset I would talk for some time and then talk to the doctors. At other times, for those who didn't want to talk, it was just a quick welfare visit. This was the 1980s and still very 'stiff upper lip' so most of them would tend to say, 'Don't worry about me, I am doing fine- tell my mates not to worry, I will be back with them shortly' or, 'Tell my missus not to worry' (it was all men at this time).

Soldiers were not the only target; the police shared the security wing, so I had a chance to build a rapport with Royal Ulster Constabulary (RUC) members as well.

Women were still not authorised to carry weapons, for fear that we would become targets, but there were opportunities. The male officers who had to travel to the border areas would often ask women to accompany them as it looked less suspicious than driving alone, and on these occasions, we could take weapons for protection. On one drive we came across boulders on the road. There had been a recent alert about ambushes created by placing stones as roadblocks, so we took no chances and accelerated over them with a sickening crunch, after which we couldn't change gear. We drove for almost an hour in third gear, until we got back to the barracks.

On another occasion I was hitching a ride back to base in a military convoy and we had to stop to assist in setting up a cordon after a car bombing. There was a body in the mangled remains of the car and on the ground nearby a severed hand, still twitching as the blood drained out of it. I found it hard to take my eyes off it. I'm not sure it is possible to prepare for these moments, and it's certainly not possible ever to forget them.

One of the worst incidents of the Troubles was the murder of two young Royal Signals corporals, Derek Wood aged 23 and David Howes aged 24. They were in civilian clothes and a civilian car – Howes had just arrived, and Wood was showing him around. They accidentally got caught up in the funeral procession of a high-profile IRA man and some of the mourners, believing that they were Loyalists about to attack (as had happened at another funeral three days earlier) dragged them from their car, beat, stripped, stabbed and then shot them. It happened in March 1988, just after I had left, and it felt particularly close to home as it was in an area I had visited not long before. It could have been any of us.

Resentment against the Army ran high, not least because of the stop and search policy. It was as controversial in the 80s as it is now, but it was a necessary part of finding concealed weapons or drugs. Male soldiers couldn't search women and children, so trained women were needed. The job was done by military policewomen and the women of the Ulster Defence Regiment, which was formed to defend the Province during the Troubles.

These women were called the Greenfinches. Sometimes, there would be trawls for WRAC to assist the Greenfinches and I volunteered.

Training was an eye-opener; we learned how to avoid being cut by razors left deliberately under collars or in pockets to frustrate the search and how to react to being spat at and insulted. Time with the Greenfinches also gave me the opportunity to go out on patrols. On one patrol we were close to the Divis flats – a 20-storey tower block surrounded by series of twelve eight-storey blocks which stood at the top of the strongly Republican Falls Road. The Divis flats area was synonymous with deprivation, poverty and hatred of the police and the Army. As we patrolled, I heard a sharp crack. It was the first time I had come under live fire and I froze, like a meerkat, only to be rugby-tackled to the ground by one of the patrol members with more experience.

As we had to be careful about leaving the camp, most entertainment took place inside it. Famous entertainers of the day sometimes came to entertain the troops and I was one of the hosting team. I was hoping to host Rod Stewart, but I got the Barron Knights. Still pretty good entertainment, if not quite of the same calibre. I also hosted visits by the WRAC Director, who seemed genuinely interested in her young officers and never once mentioned my dress sense.

Life on camp was based around regimental socials and the on-camp, all-ranks supermarket, coffee and bar known as the NAAFI (Naval, Army and Air Force institute).

There were also enough bars on camp to allow for a cheap, if unadventurous, pub crawl. I was now a little more mature than my years in Germany and most of the time I stayed out of trouble, but there was one embarrassing incident where the young officers went off-camp to try the local moonshine, Pocheen (what the Pogues call 'the Good ol' Mountain Dew'). I didn't drink that much, but it was a bad batch and it made me very sick for days afterwards – I had to see the camp doctor and confess what I'd drunk. As a result of this I was disciplined and given extra duties for drinking unregulated alcohol. The other WRAC officers with me were disciplined too, but the men involved were let off and their offence dismissed as 'high jinks'.

It wasn't all work. Northern Ireland, particularly the Antrim coast, was beautiful and there were a few rare chances to go further afield and explore. There were also lots of opportunities for sport; I played hockey for Lisburn garrison, learnt to SCUBA dive and completed my ski instructor qualifications at Pitztal, the Austrian Tyrol's highest glacier. We had to use ridiculously long two-metre skis – none of the lovely carving skis we have now – and there was still no kit for women, so my skis were way too long for me.

When I turned up for my course, the instructor hadn't expected a woman and had arranged a selection of porn films for the evening entertainment. I took the graceful route and went out in the evenings, leaving them to it – some of the men opted out as well.

Perhaps not surprisingly, given this kind of scenario, women were still viewed, by some of the men, as fair game. One evening I was invited to a social event in North Howard Street Mill Barracks in Belfast. I jumped at the chance, not least because it meant a ride there by Humber Pig, the light armoured personnel vehicles used in urban operations at the time. There were about eight of us invited but I only realised at the pickup that we were all women. I was the officer in charge.

As we sped along rubble-strewn streets, a young boy casually lit and threw a petrol bomb. The glass shattered against the side of the Pig and the petrol burned, but the troops didn't react at all. We entered the armoured gates of the barracks, drove past the watchtower and were dropped off in a compound.

The social was to be a sit-down review, a series of short sketches, and the actors were the men of the unit (I won't name it). The women were allocated seats in the front row, alongside selected men and I sat next to a young captain. We were in a big open hangar and the stage was made of packing crates. I knew I was out of my depth with the first 'sketch', in which a naked man ran onto the stage with a live chicken and bit its head off. I looked at the other women – all of them with faces aghast.

It didn't get any better – as the crude jokes followed thick and fast the tension among us rose. As it ground to a painful finish the audience all stood up.

Suddenly there was a surge of men around us. As one grabbed me, I struck out hard, knocking him to the floor. Taken aback, the troops hesitated, and the women and I were able to run up the stairs to one side and into a room where we locked the door.

The eight of us stood, shaken and uncertain what to do next. Thankfully a few minutes later a sheepish commanding officer knocked on the door and gave us his assurances that we were safe and would be escorted back to our base. We walked with him through the now-empty hangar, back to the vehicles. What would have happened that night if we hadn't run? I don't know, but I'm glad I didn't wait to find out. As far as I know, none of us reported it. That wasn't the Army way.

I was in Northern Ireland for two years and it was long enough. As the end of my time there approached, I was presented, once again, with the dream-sheet. But this time my choices were limited. Career managers were making recommendations about what I *should* do next, suggesting UK posts in WRAC establishments.

I was 24 and I wanted to pick my own career path but only one path was being offered. And I was frustrated by the Army's attitude. The two men I worked with were often absent and happy to leave me to do all the work, yet they hadn't given me credit. My more senior boss had spent many days on the golf course and expected me to cover his absences.

I was also starting to see individuals being promoted not on merit, but because of their regimental affiliations and who they knew. Why? Why would this organisation choose to favour privilege over talent? I was still young enough to be asking this question honestly and with surprise.

During my time in Germany, I had approached the Signals about transferring but pulled back when I was informed that I would have to go back to basic training. Now I approached a colleague about applying for 'special duties' which involved a selection process. I completed the pre-selection successfully but was advised to defer for a couple of years so that I could gain experience. With hindsight, they were right; I had some maturing still to do. But regressive career paths, delays and tours with the WRAC felt too constraining for me at that time. I needed to explore the world. So, I resigned. In the end it wasn't the big stuff, it was the trivial that made me leave: the attitude of the WRAC and lack of opportunities for women.

Casual sexism, and even groping, was very much part of women's daily lives, but for me, groping wasn't as damaging as being automatically assumed to be incompetent. Each new posting meant proving myself, but the men weren't having to do that. Comments such as 'you are actually good, for a woman' were intended as compliments but, while this attitude was the societal norm, I wanted and expected equality in the Army.

Women did not speak up; complaining was never the Army way but being punished or asked to do tasks that the men didn't have to do was frustrating. I needed to leave to see if bias was less prevalent outside the Army and to learn to speak up. And I needed to get my head around class and privilege and why it was still such a dominant factor in the Army.

So, it wasn't hard to leave, I was ready. I was given a blackthorn walking pole and a Waterford crystal decanter as leaving gifts, but my main keepsakes were internal; it would take me a month back home to stop looking under vehicles and being hyper-alert to surroundings and I could never hear Danny Boy again without fast-forwarding.

Eight years later, in 1996, the IRA would bomb Lisburn Garrison, rigging a second explosion close to the medical centre minutes after the first, to ensure that the rescuers were caught as well. Thirty-one people were injured, and one soldier died.

There were many soldiers who lost their lives in the Troubles, so while I recognise the suffering on all sides, it is the uniformed services as well as civilians who I feel for. 30 years on, some of our media are creating a story of innocent civilians and evil military as the politicians weakly allow a few unlucky soldiers to be pursued repeatedly through the courts, but the reality was far, far more nuanced than that. The Troubles were not about fairness or rule of law for the terrorists, it was about maximising terror, criminal gains and power.

Chapter Five
University – and Joining the Reserves

If your dreams do not scare you, they are not big enough.
Ellen Johnson Sirleaf

I had scratched that first military itch and now I needed to be out on my own to start working out what life was all about.

I joined the Army for a professional career. But as a young woman officer in the 1980s, I was seen more as the forces' sweetheart. Had I joined, as some did, for a professional matchmaking service, it would have been fine, but I didn't and the attitudes to women that I encountered frustrated me. The Army had given me structure and financial independence, but ultimately, I found it too constraining.

An institution is a perfect first job. It made me feel safe emotionally, with little requirement for me to understand how to live independently. It was very easy to see why some soldiers find it hard to adjust to civvy street after years in the forces. You need coping skills to gain true independence, and I had to leave in order to learn those skills.

I took the option of a lump sum, rather than a pension later. Free of the immediate need to earn money, I went travelling, taking work picking fruit and then selling time-shares in the Canaries. I made my way through mainland Europe, Wales, Scotland and England working as driver, kayaker, climber, trail leader and SCUBA diver. I set up indoor shooting ranges and spent my evenings on target practice rather than drinking; away from the Army I became almost teetotal. I led ski trips in France and Austria and set up outdoor centres in the Channel Islands and in the Ardeche. I was in my element. During this year of ad hoc work, I lived in a tent, a school, a hotel and even a broom cupboard - briefly.

Eventually I started to think about earning a steady income. I felt ready for university and decided I wanted a vocational degree in sports, that would allow me to travel. I had experienced a few injuries by then and gone through rehabilitation and I was fascinated by the way the body worked. My passion for white water kayaking had led me to Nottingham, which had a slalom course, so I decided to apply to do physiotherapy at the university there.

I got in and started my 3-year course in September 1988. The course was sponsored by the NHS and it involved a full day, five days a week, so very different to a standard university course. At 24, I was considered a mature student and having served in the Army and then worked, I felt it. And I was surprised by how much I didn't

74

like being back in an institution. On my first day I wondered whether I had done the right thing. My course was almost all-female (two men out of 30 students) and I was surrounded by women younger than me; the atmosphere felt a bit like going back to school. I considered pulling out, but there was a great tutor, Simon, who suggested I stay for the first term before deciding. He could see I was struggling with the school-feel and he gave me a bit more flexibility than some of the others. I was very sad to hear, a few years after the course ended, that Simon had died suddenly.

At the beginning I was in university accommodation at Basford Hospital but, despite having single rooms, I hated the dorm feel so in my second term I moved out to a shared house with a bunch of semi-pro kayakers. House sharing wasn't easy either, after army living, so I moved again and rented from a friend who had a place near Nottingham. Finally, some space.

The first year of physiotherapy studies was mostly classroom-based and shared with medical students – the second and third years would involve more work placements. Graham, my first boyfriend at university, was a medical student and we got together in our first term, while dissecting human bodies. Very romantic. We got on well, we both loved SCUBA, hiking and music, but we weren't in love and before the end of my first year we drifted apart.

I felt separate from the other students, not just because I was older, but because I was no longer as worried about just fitting in. If I wasn't interested in an aspect of student life, for instance going clubbing, I was now willing to stand up and say so – to tread my own path. I realised I was more confident in my self - aware of what made me happy, where I wanted to focus my time. I found satisfaction through playing university-level sport and gaining SCUBA and kayak qualifications. Yet something was still missing, and I realised it was military camaraderie. The commonest time for veterans to miss the comradeship is around two years after leaving so the picture fitted. Leaving jobs which feel like a calling or a vocation can feel as if you are leaving part of yourself behind. If that role has involved conflict or adventure, then a bond of mutual trust and friendship is forged which is rarely forgotten. I didn't want to re-join the regular army, I wanted more freedom of choice in my life than was possible there, so what were my options? I looked briefly at the University Officer Training Corps (UOTC), a type of army training unit within universities that recruits potential officers from students, but I liked working with soldiers, not just officers. So, it was time to consider the reserves.

What most people don't know is that there are at least four different types of military service, all working together.

The regulars, what I had been in Germany and Northern Ireland, are the full-time professional soldiers and they can be ordered anywhere, any time in the interests of the service. We draw higher pay and benefits, including subsidised housing, health and dental benefits (although benefits and housing quality are eroding rapidly). Regulars move every two to three years, with some choice on location, but ultimately the Army decides. When you're single, moving is a motivator; but far less so once you're married or have children. Higher risk roles are usually carried out un-accompanied, Regulars are the reliable, resourceful backbone, yet seen as institutionalised and, in my experience, often less agile of thought and less productive.

The 'true' reserve has a civilian job and stand up full-time only in crisis. They train for around 27 days per year, at weekends and some do weekday evenings too. They receive a lower day-rate, but in return, can't be sent on tours unless they volunteer, or in extremis. Some expenses and benefits are available, but many are difficult to access. Good reserves put up with a lot and give a lot of time and energy. They can be unreliable unless mobilised, but are generally flexible and enthusiastic

The Full-Time Reserve Service (FTRS) is a hybrid of the two - either regulars who retire and want to stay on, or reserves who want full-time work. They tend to plug gaps for regular shortfalls or where a more expensive regular is not needed, for example in reserve HQs. The quality of FTRS staff makes or breaks reserve units and influences views about reserves. The pay rate is higher than a civilian equivalent role. In most businesses if you pay low – or high – you get what you pay for. But with army rank inflation, meaning the promotion of those who don't necessarily deserve it, to fill a skills gap – rules were being changed to fix the short-term problem, not address the actual problem - of why so many leave early. Result? Individuals who would normally have left at a lower rank could promote without qualifications, at higher pay, but not necessarily more responsibility. The Army has no independent human resources system, so there are plenty of examples of 'pay high for low value'. This can also block the system, because the individuals concerned won't move on, as they can't get the same pay outside the Army. It's a huge problem, with far too many people drawing middle management salaries for doing non-management or junior management roles.

Because of this it has become known as the 'users, cruisers and losers' contract. But the problems should not detract from the cohort who genuinely love the military and do a great job. FTRS roles need a strong management system to avoid being a low-achieving drinking club for those unable to function in the civilian world.

Finally, there are the civil servants in MOD posts and some civilian contractors. Civilians offer continuity to counter the knowledge-gaps created by the regular posting cycles, but they don't deploy and, as they are the only unionised group in the MOD, it can create complications. Catering, for example, used to be a military role. I remember when we were out all night looking for a lost cadet, I was able to call the military duty chef out of bed to rustle up tea and bacon sandwiches for the searchers (we found the lad who had wandered away from a local cadet exercise, at about four in the morning). I couldn't do that once the chefs were included under the civil service umbrella – calling out the chef would have been a non-contractual addition and as such would have involved endless paperwork and expense.

When I left Northern Ireland, I was automatically transferred to the regular reserves. Any full-timers who opt to leave before normal retirement age are obliged to transfer to this list, which means that you can be called back in to serve if a situation arises that requires it. In those days this meant in a war, although since 2014 army reserves can be called on when extra people are needed, for instance for an event such as the Olympics or Brexit. There's no training for the regular reserves – in fact the only requirement is a medical once a year. It's lucky the Army didn't look for me in that first 18 months after I left, I moved so often that they probably wouldn't have found me.

Being in the regular reserves wasn't enough for me now that I was settled, I wanted more, but I still needed to be part-time. True reserves sounded right. Formerly called the Territorial Army (or TA), they are, since 2013 when their status was changed to part-time workers, now acknowledged as the main army reserve. The AR has both mass augmentation units, for example infantry reserves and niche specialists who act as individuals or in small teams, to augment the regulars, for example cyber specialists.

The regulars have a nickname for reserves: STABS (stupid TA ba****ds). Reserves have a tit-for-tat name for regulars: ARABS (arrogant regular army ba****ds). There is low empathy on both sides, but the antipathy comes from the regulars. Reserves (as I witnessed when I was a regular) are often ignored or treated poorly. We regulars called them 'weekend warriors', 'the unreliables' and worse. They had a reputation for being amateur soldiers but professional drinkers. The general public didn't always have a high regard for the TA either, they were seen by many as a kind of Dad's Army who met at weekends to play at being soldiers.

This negative culture towards the reserves made me reluctant to join them. But the attitudes also frustrated me. It is a recognised need for teams to have substitutes, both niche specialists and bulk capacity, to bolster the main team. Sport, business, armies – all of them need reserves. Sometimes you need mass, which takes longer to get going, but is harder to stop. Sometimes you need niche precision, a scarcer resource and harder to replace. Reserves offer an option to change the dynamics of the situation.

Initially the hardest part, pre-internet, was finding details of TA units I might be able to join. Eventually I found a Signals detachment in Nottingham. This time, I felt none of the fear of my first army contact. I rang and was invited to come along and my first impression was of friendly people. I wasn't used to the degree of overfamiliarity between ranks (that wouldn't have happened in the regular army), but the culture was familiar.

Reserve commitment was explained to me; one weekend every six weeks, arrive on a Friday evening and get home on Sunday evening. There was also a voluntary midweek, two-hour drill-night and a compulsory two-week annual camp. Reserves were paid only for days they showed up, plus an annual bonus (known as 'the bounty') for meeting set standards.

Did I have to think about it? For a moment, if only because I knew I would be reluctant to tell my friends in the regulars that I had joined the TA. But in the end, I knew it was what I wanted at that point in my life, so I signed up.

I was quickly to find out there were roughly three groups in the Unit. The reliable group who ran the unit, the occasional who would turn up, but only for the minimum, and the unreliable, what I came to think of as the 'any number of excuses' group who gave the reserves a bad name. Friday nights were always painful, rationalising who said they were coming with those who actually turned up. Weekends for those in the TA are in competition with hobbies, family time, good sport, bad weather and work, and for some the TA took a back seat to these. But despite this the image I had been given of all reserves being unreliable was false, it was a mixed bag and there were those who were absolutely reliable and committed.

My military knowledge was ahead of most reserves, so I easily came top of the reserve captains' course, with little study. Recent ex-regulars like me could offer depth, but at the same time we didn't understand how to run reserve units. For example, when I was a regular, it was annoying but not important if the time and date of an activity changed. For reserves (who may have booked a day off work up to six months ahead), a change in date meant we couldn't turn up.

The knowledge gap between regulars and reserves was low in junior posts. By middle levels, if reserves do regular operational tasks, the gap is manageable, but by senior level, the knowledge gap is stark. Reserves compensate to some extent with broader life knowledge, but they still need regulars to lead on military process.

Initially I was an occasional. I turned up when required but I kept the reserves at arm's length, as do most ex-regulars. I was spending a lot of time on outdoor pursuits; I paddled big rivers, honed SCUBA skills, skied my way around Europe and I learned new skills like caving and mountain-biking. I gained experience and became a multi-sports instructor. I took personal risks - I remember the exhilaration of walking out into a deep river holding my breath, a large boulder in my arms as my weight belt, then letting go at the deepest part and floating up. But although these were simpler times for risk management, I didn't take risks with the youngsters I taught. My parents had let me and my brothers and sisters jump off our summerhouse roof onto mattresses and learn about how to land properly and cushion impact. That would probably be rated as inadequate parenting now, but it taught me valuable lessons about high-risk decision making. When my kayak group went off to ride a big river in Scotland in flood, I looked at the conditions and I judged the risk to be too high and didn't go. I learned later a kayaker died on that trip.

On my reserve weekends we worked hard. We used to arrive on a Friday night after a full day's work, drive for up to eight hours (the longest I remember was Trowbridge to Carlisle in one shift), complete a full exercise overnight on Friday and Saturday and then drive back the same distance on Sunday evening. But despite the breadth of experience on offer and the commitment of many reserves, the regulars who were attached to the unit tended towards a Brian Clough style of leadership. Brian was the manager of Nottingham Forest football club when I was living in the area and he was famous for his belief that he was always right. To the regulars the reserves' views were less valued or, more accurately, not even assessed. When I asked a reserve to assist with the plan for a VIP visit, the regular working with me said, 'Why are you asking a corporal?'

'Because he is the Lord Mayor of his city,' I said. 'He knows the protocol and I don't.'

I began to question why I'd been taught to be stand-offish with reserves. I could see that it started with a sense of pride in being a full-time professional while the reserves were part-timers. But when did it shift to seeing every reserve as less able than every full-timer? If we limit ourselves to the superficial stereotypes, we are likely to miss the richness of what difference brings.

As regulars our attitude to the reserves wasn't just about a perceived lack of knowledge, we sneered at enthusiasm, as if enthusiasm was a bad thing. If this culture had changed in the 30 years I have been observing, I would make less of a point here, but it hasn't. The 2018 military attitude survey was similar to previous surveys, it gave being undervalued and treated poorly by regulars as one of the top reasons that reserves are still leaving. Only one third felt valued or treated as equals by the regulars, a number that is slightly improving, but is still ridiculously low.

Seniority in the reserves didn't equate to civilian achievements, which is why we had Lord Mayors as junior soldiers. But some people who had senior civilian jobs enjoyed taking on junior military roles. It created a healthier hierarchy, but often puzzled the regulars. Reserves also retain the option of dipping in and out of the Army and being able to change their commitment, dependent on availability. These options confused the regular leadership, including me, initially.

When I joined the TA, I met Mark, when we were asked to set up an event together for the military unit. We started dating and at first kept it quiet, as relationships between ranks were frowned on; I was a Lieutenant and he was a sergeant. But outside the TA he was a senior BT engineer and I was a student, so it didn't feel unequal. I started staying over at his house, which was in a pretty village called East Leake, near Loughborough, and by the end of my second year at university he asked me to move in with him. He was my first serious love and it was a very happy time.

The years when I was at university were a time of rapid change on the world stage, and especially in Europe. In the November of my first year the Berlin wall came down. The following couple of years saw the Czechoslovakian Velvet Revolution, the more violent Romanian overthrow of Ceausescu and the break-up of the USSR. The collapse of communism started in Poland, then spread, leading to the end of the Cold War in 1991. It wasn't just Europe that was changing; the first Iran-Iraq war was ending, there were protests in Beijing's Tiananmen Square, there was revolution in Mongolia and apartheid was being dismantled in South Africa. Communism and dictatorships seemed vulnerable to the will of the people and the zeitgeist was reflected in a hugely popular song of the time, *Wind of Change,* by the Scorpions.

This rise in the power of public opinion was linked to a revolution in communications. It began, I think, with the arrival of 2G and digital to replace analogue. It allowed the mobile phone to move from novelty to mainstream, so that waiting in for a phone call or finding a phone box to make a call soon became a memory. A new tech industrial revolution started, for business and leisure. Gameboys and Nintendo offered seductive but passive alternatives to being outdoors and nations started to get fatter. I remember my beloved VHS video collection becoming redundant almost overnight and having to replace music systems, records, tapes and videos with the DVD.

In the West, health services and life expectancy were improving, threat of conflict and early death reducing. Western societies were able to focus on quality of life, not just existence. Yet this seemed to reduce the sense of responsibility. There was still plenty to prick our consciences; scientists found a hole in the ozone layer over Antarctica and linked it to use of aerosols, and while poverty, famine and conflict still raged in parts of the world, they were just further away from our own doorstep. It seemed that without common enemies to unify and level us, disparities of power, wealth and personal responsibility grew. And our respect for our leaders shrank.

In 1990, just as I was about to start my final year at university, the first Gulf War broke out, after the Iraqi invasion of Kuwait. Briefly, I considered re-joining the regular army, in order to do my bit, but it would have meant delaying my graduation and I wanted to finish university and move on. At that stage I didn't want to be part of an institution – either the Army or the NHS.

Weeks later, in November 1990, Margaret Thatcher resigned. She was a divisive figure but an iconic influencer who had been in power since 1979, all my adult life. I was at a work placement in a children's home in

Nottingham, attempting to work with a highly disturbed autistic boy who was hitting me as I watched Thatcher being driven from Downing Street in tears. All power ends in failure, when the people have a say. This was a British 'wind of change' moment.

I returned to work with the regulars for the summers of my university years. The first summer it was as a ski instructor for an infantry unit, on a dry ski slope. There was nowhere to go in the evenings, so I was invited to join the men in the bar. I politely declined since I was the only serving woman on camp. Each night I was asked and declined and it became increasingly tense, with comments like 'frigid' being made out loud. On the last night, I was expecting trouble. I had been allocated a room in a block with my name on the door, so I moved to sleep in the block opposite. I was woken around midnight and watched silently through a window as three or four soldiers kicked the door to my room off its hinges. This incident did go public in the morning because I had to explain the damage. Again, I was asked to let it go as 'just high jinks' and I did. I had forgotten most of these stories until I read similar ones from other serving women recently. Mine was not an isolated experience.

I was beginning to enjoy developing the roles I took on and myself in the process. I set up new reserves' summer camps to fast-track officers through training and got a commendation and I re-organised outdoor pursuit centres in Guernsey, France and Wales.

I always felt the need to protect and support others. Where did this warrior-protector nature come from? As a middle child, from a broken home, was it just that I needed to prove myself? At university, when asked to complete a leg of the Nottingham half-marathon, pushing a bed for charity, I volunteered to run the whole course. My norm was to over-achieve and to look out for others. Beneath the action-woman veneer, I knew I was still angry with my father, even though he had left many years before. But I pushed concerns out of my mind and filled my time with adventures and university was mostly a happy and carefree phase.

Towards the end of my course I did buy a house, in the village where Mark and I were living. I wanted to get on the property ladder, so I borrowed from family, bought the house with a mortgage and rented it out. I still struggled with the repayments each month, as interest rates crept up to 15 percent.

My three years at university had been a transition period for me. I loved the freedom to choose where to work, live, eat and sleep, what country to be in, what job to do and even what time to get up. Like many ex-military people, I would end up 'posting' myself about every three years for the next 10 years, it's amazing how quickly you get set in the pattern. But at the same time, I was well aware, by the time I graduated, that the world outside the military was far more complex. I loved the fact that in civilian workplaces, I was expected to work hard and deliver results, or leave.

After graduating, I applied instead for roles in the United States where, rather than the long and winding route of physiotherapy under the NHS, I would be allowed to specialise immediately in sports and orthopaedics. Besides which, having seen Europe, I wanted to see America. Frustratingly, mine was the final year to do a graduate diploma in physiotherapy rather than a BSc, which meant we did all the work for a degree and then didn't get it awarded as the change from diploma to degree hadn't yet been ratified, so I had to delay leaving for a year to do some additional modules which lifted my diploma to a BSc, allowing me to work in the USA.

Although I chafed at the delay, it was a valuable time; I worked for BUPA, with professional rugby players. The Leicester Tigers taught me about focus, vision and commitment. I had learned something of the first two in the Army, but what I learned from these professional athletes was about sacrifice – to be the best meant being prepared to eliminate bad habits - over-drinking, emotional spikes, poor diet and giving up time with family and friends, in return for gaining that extra one or two percent of performance. These were the type of people I wanted to mix with.

Before I left for the States there was a significant change for army women when, in April 1992, the WRAC disbanded. It made the newspapers, but other than career disparities to resolve, it made little role difference. I did notice a change in attitude from some men; now that women were sharing the same career path, they saw us for

89

the first time as rivals. And it was different in the military compared to my civilian employment. If I offered an idea or spoke up too loudly within a military setting, I was ignored or put down. This was very different to my experiences in the NHS or in outdoor centres. It reminded me of a 1950s dinner party where the women are expected to leave the room to let the men have serious conversations. Why were my ideas not equally valued by military bosses? And why did I still not speak up?

I could see that reserves and women could do more than boost numbers – they could add breadth of ideas and it was incredibly frustrating that they were dismissed by so many of the regulars. But I thought it would just take time for attitudes to change and I was willing to be patient, because for the immediate future, I had other plans.

Chapter Six
Spreading my Wings

*Instead of seeing the rugs being pulled from under us, we can learn
to dance on a shifting carpet*
Thomas Crum

    I planned to be away for a year, but I ended up
staying for five.

    Initially I was required to take a leave of absence
from the reserves but when, after year, I decided to stay
on in the States I had to resign. It was worth it for the
freedom to adventure and experience a different culture.
I wanted to see how other countries treated their military,
how younger nations felt about their past and to find out
about the American dream. How did an ethos of
welcoming migrants work within a society seen as inward
facing? How were Brits seen by other English-speaking
countries? Most of all I wanted to explore the fifty states
that made up America.

    I had done an internship in Florida in the summer
of 1991 and spent eight weeks treating the results of

gunshot wounds. Visiting soldiers in Belfast with explosive, gun and knife injuries had prepared me for the extent of the damage. The simple in and out wounds and speedy recoveries of Hollywood are pure fantasy; exit wounds are typically horrendous, as are internal injuries and the resulting long-term disability. After that reminder of conflict zones, I decided eight weeks was enough and applied instead to Reynold's Memorial Hospital in Wheeling, West Virginia. I chose it largely for the same reasons that I chose the Army and Nottingham – there were great outdoor opportunities and they said yes to my application.

I hit lucky in the US green-card lottery – receiving one of a limited number of green cards (allowing you to live and work in the States) issued by the US government each year. Millions from around the word applied for only a few thousand cards, so I was incredibly lucky.

I left for the States in September 1992. Mark and I had planned to go together, but as the date for departure neared, he felt less ready. I had a job offer and a green card, so I made the decision to go it alone and he promised to join me later. I packed just one box and took off.

I arrived in Wheeling, West Virginia and spent my first night in Pittsburgh with the head of the hospital's physiotherapy department. After that one of the other physical therapists in Wheeling let me stay with her for a month until I found a place to rent. My new boss loaned me his car for the first week on my international driving license until I passed the US driving test and bought a

Pontiac Le Mans – cheap because it was a gear shift, not automatic.

I loved Wheeling from the start. It sits in the northern panhandle of West Virginia, very closely bordered by Ohio and Pennsylvania, lying along the Ohio River in the foothills of the Appalachian Mountains, with a wonderful state park, Oglebay, on its doorstep. It was incredibly beautiful there, with all the outdoor opportunities I loved so much.

I worked in the main physiotherapy department of the hospital, on inpatient orthopaedics, with the friendliest, nicest bunch of people I had ever met. I felt instantly as if they were my family. They invited me into their homes, bought me housewarming gifts, took me to festivals and made me feel welcome in every way possible. I still think of all of them with real warmth.

Life there suited me because outdoor living was central to life and I was able to pursue everything from white-water kayaking to SCUBA diving. West Virginia, far from being a sleepy hollow, had so much to offer, from access to a wonderful little ski resort to summer rivers and mountains. Mark never did join me and I was sad about it, but I had a rich social life in the States, which I loved. Better weather meant open-air concerts and festivals and I went to see big-name pop acts of the time, drinking beer with friends off the back of a truck.

The standard of service surprised me; Americans were more assertive and expected more and generally they got it. Their equivalent of the AA would send you a complete itinerary for a road trip, with routes marked, suggested accommodation and restaurants. This was long before the internet and I loved those little packs arriving at my door before my adventures.

It was the beginning of the mass digital age. I sent my first text in America, albeit as an unworkable novelty (we continued to use more reliable pagers or radios when adventuring). With the ending of many long-standing conflicts, this was an optimistic decade. Bill Clinton was a charismatic, charming leader, Americans were welcoming, and I found it an honest culture; young, willing to share its emotions and mistakes and to open its heart to strangers. I saw a healthy pride in identity and work success was important, but not at the expense of family. Alcohol was there, but the 'drink as many as you can until you are pi**ed' approach we nurtured in the UK was far less common. Events were more inter-generational, class and gender free, with an enjoyable coffee-shop culture too.

I did have to rein in my dry wit, which baffled some Americans, and I learned to tolerate the two phrases that cropped up, in West Virginia, almost daily:

'Gee, I love your accent; I could listen to it all day.'

'What is with that Monty Python?' (Emphasis on the last syllable.)

From the daily pledge to the American flag, to singing anthems at festivals (the one I recall was Lee Greenwoods 'God Bless the USA', a patriotic song not dissimilar in sentiment to 'Rule Britannia'), America was unashamedly nationalist, in a similar way to the Welsh and Scottish.

Why is Britain, particularly England, ashamed of our flag and identity? Our past is no different to the pasts of many other countries, with the good and the bad, depending on your perspective. American history is also chequered, but it hasn't made them question their values or the dream that success is possible for all if you contribute and commit.

And they respected their military veterans. My sister, now also in the military, came to visit me and we went out to Florida to dive. There was a discount if you were in the military, so we confirmed that we were. As we settled on the boat in our denim shorts and t-shirts, the coxswain made a public announcement, 'Ma'ams, sirs, we have two veterans on board today, can I ask you to show them respect, in the usual manner'. I don't know whether they expected it to be the two twenty-something women in the group, but we got awkwardly to our feet and they gave us a long round of applause. Mortifyingly embarrassed, we never mentioned we were veterans again.

I was well-paid, loved the life, people, cars, road systems and above all the state parks and events. I completed many road trips, straddling the continent and I managed to visit 35 of the 50 states and some of Canada. I made wonderful friends through the Three Rivers Paddling Club in Pittsburgh; they adopted me and led me on many a white-water kayak escapade (and a few off the water too), from Mardi Gras in New Orleans to Niagara

Falls and the Grand Canyon. And the Wheeling SCUBA divers opened my eyes to warm water diving in the Bahamas, Virgin Islands, Cozumel and Mexico.

I had some near misses. Kayaking in Mexico I ended up the wrong side of a waterfall and had to take off my buoyancy aide to swim out and I came close to an avalanche a few times when skiing in the backwoods of Colorado, but generally I stayed on the right side of sensible. Although perhaps night-diving wrecks solo in the Caymans would not be included in most people's definition of sensible.

America wasn't perfect. I missed global debate, something I took for granted in the UK. I was surprised by how many Americans had guns in their houses and how few Americans, even those with college degrees, were aware of the world beyond those 50 states. I remember trying to debate the genocide going on in Rwanda at the time and finding that no-one had read about it. I also struggled with the support for the Republican cause in Northern Ireland. Mostly I stayed away from these discussions, but when we went to Boston for St Patrick's night there was an open mic debate in one of the bars. A young American stood up to ask for donations to support the 'oppressed freedom-fighters' in their stand against the 'ruthless death squads of the British government'. With a few (green) beers inside me, I took the mic and gave a counter argument. I did get a small round of applause at the end, but mine certainly wasn't the popular view.

It wasn't easy to come home after five years. But I was missing my family, friends and marmite and despite my strong bond with America, it was becoming tiring for my British soul having to explain British repression, 'We're just rather introverted' and whimsy, 'We really do find Monty Python funny' to a few of my baffled buddies.

I travelled back to UK via a few months in Australia, wanting to clear my head in my usual way through outdoor activities. When I got home, in the summer of 1997, I sold up in Nottingham, officially broke up my now-stale relationship with Mark and went to stay with my sister in Hereford and did some NHS locum work while I adjusted to life back in the UK.

After so long away I saw Britain differently, less at the centre of the world, more as a small country. I came back as Tony Blair, another charismatic and initially charming individual, took power. Times had moved on in my absence: there was a more diverse demographic, particularly in London. Britain was in the throes of social change, young women were feeling empowered, yet wearing a faintly ridiculous mix of platform sports shoes, baggy combat trousers, butterfly hairclips and carrying Tamagotchi digital pets. There was a girl-power mantra developing that I hadn't witnessed in America. A new UK generation was grabbing feminism and re-branding it in a more uplifting style, despite the fact that this early phase seemed to be mostly about mimicking the worst rather than the best of young male behaviour: drunk, loud and 'in your face'.

I arrived back just before Princess Diana died and witnessed the growing power of public opinion. The Establishment was wrong-footed by new media irreverence to their more traditional grieving. Even the Queen, normally the most loved of royals became temporarily branded as distant and uncaring in the aftermath. The public was also increasingly willing to speak out against national leadership. We had more tools to express opinion; phones enabled texts to be sent and the internet was now offering email.

I worked on a medical study for the military, evaluating 'gender fair' fitness programmes for recruits – a study I would find useful in later military projects. And I started to lead expeditions for commercial companies in Africa and Europe. But there was a bit of 'going through the motions'. When my sister sold her house and moved to Southampton for work reasons, I rented a lovely farmhouse just south of Bristol and continued to locum, trying to decide if this was the area where I wanted to settle. Eventually, I found a role in Bristol in a public-private occupational health initiative.

In the couple of years after arriving back from the States I had been unsure about what I wanted, and I felt unsettled. I missed the States a lot, and thought about going back, but at the same time my family was in the UK and I was by then in my early thirties and feeling it was time I found a more permanent base.

Things fell into place just as the millennium arrived. The hospital offered me a permanent job and within a few months I started to cover the business manager role, which I enjoyed. I had to move out of the farmhouse, so I began looking around for a place to buy and eventually settled on a pretty but dilapidated cottage on a hillside in a village a few miles outside Bristol. It was at the extreme of my budget, so to supplement my income I started to do some leadership coaching for an ex-military friend who held an outdoor franchise.

I took on some work in private security too. In those days very few women did this kind of work, but I enjoyed it. I was trained in security and martial arts and I liked getting back to that sense of adrenaline and hyper awareness that I was familiar with from the military.

I went to guard a big event for a mining company who were holding their AGM in a London hotel. They thought there would be violent eco-protesters and there were. I was guarding the stage when a group of protesters rushed forward. I gave them my most steely stare and braced for contact, but they backed off. For a second I congratulated myself, until I noticed the two burly ex-SAS lads who had materialised just behind my shoulders as back up, Thanks lads, no injuries that day, other than to my pride.

One of the reasons I came back from the States was that deep in my heart I knew I had unfinished business with the military. So not long after my move to Bristol, I signed back up to the reserves and re-joined the Royal Signals. In the time I'd been gone my military friends had been to war, in the first Gulf War and in

Bosnia on peace-keeping duties and increasing numbers of ex-military people were writing books, soldiers' tales, like Bravo Two Zero and command tales from the bosses. The MOD had attempted to stop the SAS writing books by forcing them to sign up to confidentiality clauses in 1996, but it was harder to stop this when chiefs were doing it too. Meanwhile the Army was trying hybrid units of combined regular and reserve personnel which seemed ideal for me.

After living in America, which was more egalitarian, I was less willing to accept day to day sexism. By the end of my time in the US, I had held a senior role as Director of an Industrial Medicine Centre. In my first senior meeting I was the only woman in the room and had anticipated being ignored – until I was asked my view. Suddenly, I was expected to participate and the power that gives is immense; by being included, I felt I had an investment.

Now I wanted to be invested in my military career. This meant getting the hierarchy to take me seriously, so I applied for a more senior role as company commander of a Signals sub-unit. When the appointment I applied for went to a man with less experience, I had a strategy. I called it my fight, fright or flight response (the choice of fighting the decision, being cowed into submission or taking flight and leaving). I chose to leave. Not the military, just the Signals.

Years later, I met the officer who had selected the male candidate over me, and he expressed his sorrow that

I had left, as the chap hadn't worked out. He said he 'couldn't work out why they had picked him over me'. I could. Nowadays they call it unconscious bias. I think Caitlin Moran calls it a penis premium – a man is assumed competent unless he proves otherwise, and a woman assumed incompetent until she proves otherwise. Some men (and interestingly, some women) will always pick men over women for leadership roles. This bias is frustrating and costly; the energy it takes to separate appropriate rejection (the other candidate was better skilled) and inappropriate rejection (bias) is significant. Hence my fight, fright or flight as options; sometimes energy is better channelled into seeking other opportunities than fighting bias.

I had applied for intelligence before but been deferred due to my immaturity. Now I had more experience and it felt like the right time, so I applied again. The first step was to pass the selection which took place at an army camp in the middle of England.

I hadn't done a military selection in years. I got blisters. I was cross. Surely, I had more experience than that? I taped my heels and suffered through the rest of the weekend. One of the tasks we had to complete was an assault course. I was good at these; I had taken the time to master the tricks of each obstacle over the years. I was also fit. There was an infantry candidate who pushed in front of me on the start line, saying he didn't want me to hold him up. He then suggested that I could follow him around if I was unsure what to do. That assumption of incompetence again. He did set off faster than me but fell off the first set of parallel bars, where the trick is all about momentum, into the mud below. I completed the course at the front of the pack. However, I knew I had other areas of weakness. I could be hesitant when asked to 'big myself up', so I had been rehearsing techniques, but rehearsal is not the same as performance. As I entered the room for my interview, I saw a lone chair that had been placed in the centre of the room, facing four or five interviewers. I am tall, but my feet didn't quite touch the ground in this seat. I felt like Alice in Wonderland. I was ready for those 'why you are right for intelligence' questions but when I was asked the difference between information and intelligence, I froze.

The chairman, who would become a good and lifelong friend of mine, looked amused and said, 'You might want to start with your background in analysis and how you might use that to process the information'. Grateful, I answered the question.

I was paired with a history professor who was also trying to transfer. We were given the task of breaking into a guarded building in the dead of night. We worked out our plan – to enter through the un-guarded side meant crawling past cows, and through cowpats, for about two hours, but we did it. No-one had expected that level of determination. Later we had to complete a series of krypton factor-style tasks. I was able to identify the signs of disturbed ground, and I had the skills to map-read, but when we had to decipher a code, I was stumped. My partner said, 'Oh, they've used a simple substitution cipher, it will only take a minute' and for him, it did, although that part was meant to take us an hour. We finished the exercise in record time, and I think he and I were the only two who passed that weekend.

I had chosen the right sector. I felt at home in the intelligence world, where my intellect and enthusiasm were given free rein. That didn't mean it was easy, I had been away from the military and needed to catch up, but I was invested, and I became one of the committed reliables.

Reserve officers did the same intelligence training as soldiers. This meant a long drive to Bedford and two weeks of intense, eighteen-hour days. I had never been to the Intelligence HQ, where the officers' mess is in a former monastery - the Priory, which has a reputation for being haunted. Getting into the Priory is one of those things where the system works when you know it. I didn't. I arrived around midnight on a Friday and knocked on the door, but no-one answered, and all the doors were locked (this is common at weekends on military sites). I needed the code to the door as the room keys were inside and I didn't know at the time that the guardroom could have given me the code. So, I found an open window, squeezed in and found myself in the men's toilets. It was dark. It was midnight and the place creaked and made strange noises. I moved into a bigger room and, groping around for a light-switch, I bumped into a suit of armour. For a good few seconds I was convinced it moved and I stood there, terrified. I still hate that suit of armour now, twenty years later.

The staff running the course were outstanding. They were all regular and genuinely invested in training reserves. For a long time, Intelligence HQ used to send its worst trainers to the reserves. When it decided to send its best instead it paid dividends. Despite the long hours, I felt part of something, and I knew I had found my home within the military. The trainers laid it on thick; officers were expected to come top, so I worked hard, and I did. It wasn't that it came easy, but I knew how to study and put the hours in.

We had to give an introductory speech on 'something you won't know about me'. I went last and by then there were some hard acts to follow. One was a rocket scientist; another had a rubber fetish. How could I be memorable? So, I told them about the time I had been bodyguard to a group of male strippers in a club where there were baying female rugby clubs and hen parties in the audience. The strippers told us hands on chests, arms and gentle bum touching was fine, but grabbing of genitals was out. I was given the role of standing on the side of the stage to stop anyone clambering up, so I got a very close-up view. The finale was a huge man wearing just a cloak and what I will assume was a penis appendage which lengthened his manhood to around his knee. It wasn't easy to keep my 'serious guard expression' at this point.

Needless to say, this story went down well with the others on my course.

Once I was in, I volunteered for anything adventurous. I took my troops to learn new skills including abseiling from helicopters and completing the Three Peaks Challenge – climbing the highest peaks in England, Scotland and Wales. We also tried the underwater helicopter escape training pod known as The Dunker. In this exercise you were dropped into the water in the dark, in a helicopter mock-up. It turned upside down and you had to find your way out as the water slowly rose over your head.

I also led annual ski expeditions for the Army to expose troops to mountain conditions. On one occasion, we were descending to safety on a piste after the sudden onset of bad weather. One of my students was starting to say it was too dangerous, even for soldiers, when a school group of 5-year-olds skied past, oblivious to the wind and snow, following their teacher. It was a normal school day for them, and it put the risk into perspective for my soldiers, some of whom had never previously experienced a full mountain white-out.

On another trip, I was leading a mixed-sex group and I was made aware of an awkward group dynamic. It was my duty to make sure that any potential inappropriate behaviour was stopped. I was approached by the men in the group, asking me to speak to the senior officer attending as he was only talking to the young women in the team. I asked the young women if it was also a problem for them. They said yes, it was very uncomfortable, and it wasn't their faces he was talking to.

I had an excruciating conversation with the senior officer, who seemed genuinely unaware of his behaviour, and ended up skiing with him alone as the only way to mend the group dynamics.

I loved what I was doing in the reserves, but I was aware that I needed to work out the right balance between helping myself, helping others and asking for help. How much selfish behaviour was necessary to get ahead? I didn't want to stop helping others, but I wanted to look after myself and I wanted to succeed.

I had become more assertive in America; I had found ways to ask for and be remunerated for a director job. Encouraged by the culture around me, I believed in my abilities to succeed. How had I lost that again and reverted to holding back?

I thought a lot about the different male and female approaches to work, and to life. When I had worked in the NHS, common conversations between women were about balancing paid work with child-care, housework and family-management. In male-dominated workplaces conversations were more about hobbies and ambitions. There was collaboration in both groups, but a sense in the male environments that when the fight for the top came, it would be dog eat dog, while the female-dominated groups collaborated for longer and sacrificed to the team more. It was not that women were less ambitious, but our approach was different. We gave power up by working more unpaid hours and having a broader focus. I am not suggesting women switch to being pseudo-men and adopting their approach, but we need to value our time as equally precious and decide what our priorities are.

My passion was for making a difference. I wasn't as interested in the seductive powers of pleasures like food, possessions or indoor entertainment, for me fulfilment was via the outdoors and projects. Most of us need to find a purpose to be happy. I had mine, but I needed to understand personal power and the nuance of how to influence.

America had taught me so much; to be more open, to love my life, to seize the moment. When I came home, it took a while to settle but eventually I was starting to work out the missing parts – find a relationship, develop this interesting military role and carry on the combined business-clinical role in the NHS, supplemented by coaching and expedition leader roles. In the nineties I adventured my way around the world as a civilian. Now I had found a military home, I was ready to go on military operations.

Chapter Seven
Call Up

When you are going through Hell, keep going
Winston Churchill

The primary role of reserves is to be called up 'in extremis' which means, effectively, in times of war. And for me that call came early in 2002, shortly after the twin towers came down in America. That was when the Ministry of Defence decided on its first large-scale call-up since conscription had ended in 1960. All 12000 reserves, both regular and TA, were warned for action as the government anticipated the conflict that would inevitably follow the attacks in the States.

Around a third of 'true reserves' went willingly. Another third were keen to go, but waited for employer support and the last third were reluctant. Many of the regular reserve found ways to avoid call-out or were simply too hard to find. It was relatively easy to 'beat the draft' by getting employers to write letters claiming severe hardship, or by failing medical or dental inspections, or simply by not answering the call-up notice.

The reluctant third were mostly those who were coasting along in the 'drinking club' category. Many were given the option to resign, but if they stayed in, they had to mobilise.

The call-up would last for 10 years, to 2012, spanning the Iraq war and subsequent 'stabilisation', which began when the United States, supported by Britain, sent troops into Iraq on March 20, 2003. At that point the British Prime Minister Tony Blair was at the height of his power. His style was charming and reassuring in public, while in private he consulted a team of spin-doctors to control the narrative. While Blair had charisma and the conviction that the benefits of a strong US-UK alliance were more important than a clear legal remit to engage in Iraq, parliament and the public were less clear and there was a deep political divide on whether Britain should enter this war. Within the military there was also quite a debate, but the 'ours is not to reason why...' was essentially the only way forward.

It was eventually authorised by Blair over concern that Iraq's President, Saddam Hussein, held weapons of mass destruction. This was not the same reason as the US, who went to war to achieve regime change on the grounds that the Iraqi government supported the Al-Qaeda terrorists who carried out the 9/11 attack. The invasion and the subsequent 9-year requirement to stay in Iraq that followed was controversial, not least because it was never shown that Iraq did still have weapons of mass destruction.

As debate and argument raged about the rights and wrongs of the invasion, the TA were readying themselves for war. It created a fair bit of press interest and as the boss at the time of the detachment near Bristol, I was asked to take a group to meet the press. They were told they couldn't film our faces and weren't happy. The head journalist stomped along the line of soldiers waiting to meet him and walked right past me, although I had my hand out to shake his. He approached my (male) sergeant-major.

'Are you the one in charge?' he said without any preamble. 'Why can't we film faces?'

The sergeant-major waved a thumb in my direction with a smile, 'Better ask the boss. She might be a little less helpful as you just ignored her'. It was all apologies after that, but it brought home, once again, the way most people would still automatically go to the man. Sexism was not just a military issue.

Intelligence units were some of the first to be called on, and nearly everyone did their bit. By the end of this 10-year period, many reserves were doing the same number of tours as regulars and they had the medals to prove it.

Reserves needed the support of our employers in order to go. And most employers were cooperative, not least because a well-defended UK offers the best chance of national stability, which is necessary for businesses to thrive. But large employers may cap the percentage so that they don't lose too many employees at once and smaller companies can struggle when losing a team member. So, the MOD has to think carefully before robbing businesses of their human assets. And it must compensate employers during the reserves' absence, which can be very costly.

In 2002 the Army hadn't decided what it wanted, and it showed in the messy processes it applied to mobilisation. At that stage it didn't know what numbers would be available, how or where it would use reserves or for how long. We could potentially provide battle casualty replacements or extra mass to bolster regular numbers overseas (in all probability in Iraq at this stage), or we could provide niche support on the front-line or at home.

I was a true reserve, with a civilian career in the NHS at that time. Not having children made things easier but living on my own meant I would have to rent out my house or leave it unattended. There was only one intelligence reserve unit at that time, and it was practising 'intelligent mobilisation' by talking to reserves and working out when was the best time for each of us to go. I was deployed as part of the second wave.

Shortly before the call-up came, I had been ill. I was in my mid-30s and for nearly two decades I had been living an adventurous life. I felt like Rutger Hauer in his great speech in Blade Runner, when he says, 'I have seen things you would not believe'. But I had reached a time when chasing the next brightest light was not enough; I needed some roots.

I had tested my limits by, almost simultaneously, buying a house, breaking up a relationship, moving areas, re-training in the reserves and starting a new civilian job. For the first time in my life, I over-reached and made myself ill. I was always taught that being sick was weak, that we warriors had to deal with our issues ourselves and not ask for help, so finding myself unwell was something I struggled to come to terms with.

I was suffering from sudden debilitating fatigue and a virus and in the end, I had 12 weeks off work. My family said I had just taken all my sick leave in one batch, because I had never taken a day off, right through school and my time in the military. Being unwell though was not the failure I had imagined. It taught me a lot; that we are not immortal, that our thoughts and deeds are not separate and that we have only so much time and need to use it wisely.

That time off sick and the counselling I undertook as part of it, helped me to get back on track. I got to know myself better and accepted that some personality traits – like being an anxious overachiever – can never be overcome, only managed. I will always have a tendency to protect others and to be an excessive giver, but I can manage this by capping what I give away for free to 10 percent of my time. This felt, and still feels, about right.

I also learned that asking for help was easy once I tried it. Feeling vulnerable gave me a new perspective; I took responsibility for my relationships and I made up with my mother. She would take her life only a few years later, so I was glad and grateful that we had resolved our differences. Her suicide was not a cry for help or an act of desperation, she was very old and frail and had the strength to decide when and how her life would end, and I understood her decision. I wish she had felt able to talk to one of her children about it first, but I wasn't surprised that she didn't; it was from her that I learned about not asking for help.

As for my father, I found him an angry man who seemed to take little responsibility for the poor decisions he made and then he took his anger out on others. In counselling I realised how scared I had been of his anger as a child and how often he had been angry. But I forgave him too, although I chose not to rekindle a deeper relationship.

The time I spent ill was valuable. I was stronger, happier and more philosophical for having been through it. I finally felt at peace with my family and I got back my sense of joy at the wonderful moments in life – I think of them as kingfisher moments, those flashes of brightly-coloured brilliance – in which we experience extraordinary things.

During the two years before this illness and pre-mobilisation I had finished off my intelligence trade training. Intelligence is not what most people would imagine. It's not James Bond, evil super-villains and drinking cocktails in glorious overseas hotels (not unless you are an RAF pilot, the military joke goes). It is analysis, patterns, working out the right people and the right questions to ask, collating the answers and looking for the golden nugget which will help a military commander to understand what is going on - more quickly than his or her adversary. The military have trained analysts all around the world, in global bases trying to keep that competitive advantage. It's a skill that takes practice and there aren't enough full-timers, so the intelligence reserves are a vital reinforcement.

One of the skills I had to practise during my training was foreign vehicle recognition. I am no mechanic or military spotter, but I was the first one to get full marks on the test. The instructor said he was surprised; he hadn't thought I was interested in vehicles. I said I wasn't, I was interested in passing tests and, as there were a finite number of photos used, I had memorised them. Sadly, the internet has spoiled this particular ruse, since there are now an infinite number of photographs.

By mid-2002 I was ready to be called up, but the Army was still dithering. Eventually I, along with many others, got a provisional date and arranged cover at work, only to be stood down with two weeks' notice and told I would go six months later. The NHS had already arranged cover for my job. Generously they offered me another instead, but it wasn't one I wanted.

I decided to turn this delay into a positive. Until then I had lacked the courage to go self-employed, but here was an opportunity. The Army initially offered no compensation for the change of date but I insisted on four weeks paid time to find a contract and used the time to take a group of University Officer Training Corps-students (from Bristol) on the hike along the Chemin de Liberte, the route along the Pyrenees from France into Spain that marked the toughest of the wartime escape routes for allied airmen and Jewish refugees. It was on this hike that I experienced a near-miss lightning strike. Ideally when exposed outside, if there is threat of lightning, you hunker down safely somewhere but in mountains that isn't always possible. We were right on the top as a storm came in and the lightning was upon us very quickly. The group was spread out into small clusters when the lightning forked and struck the ground with a loud bang that shook everyone. As we regrouped one of the students seemed to be in shock and confused, which worried me. The weather was still appalling so we closed up and headed down quickly to shelter in a closed gully area, where thankfully the student recovered quickly with no lasting effects. The incident was a real reminder of how quickly conditions can change in mountains.

After the expedition, I found a role with a private physiotherapy clinic, while at the same time I worked as a freelance leadership training consultant for three different leadership companies, one of which, Leadership Challenge, was run by an ex-army friend of mine from Windsor. I loved the work, it was a lot of fun, and I managed to combine it with my private work, renovating my house and my role in the reserves where, as a Major and in 'sub-unit command' I was now running the intelligence company in Keynsham.

When the time finally came, in February 2003, I went first to the mobilisation centre in Chilwell, Nottingham. This was where all 12,000 reserves had to be processed at the start of our service and again at the end. Hundreds every week passed through a chaotic processing machine which, in the early days, was an under-resourced and ill-prepared sausage factory.

Most of us were given less than the mandated 21 days' notice to turn up – I think I had nine days to sort out my job, house and everything else – and given that we didn't know where we were going or when we would be back, I think most people handled it pretty well. In our single week at Chilwell before heading to our different army roles, we completed pre-deployment training, were issued with equipment and weapons, had health and dental checks, including vaccinations, and completed all the inevitable administrative paperwork. This included having to personally pay extra insurance in case our kit was damaged in a war zone. Is there a civilian equivalent in which you are expected to pay for damage to work equipment while working, when you have little control over the situation?

Nearly everyone in the centre was going to Iraq and I expected to go too, or at least to Germany. But at the eleventh hour I was told I would be staying in London. I was disappointed. Most reserves, if we are going to risk our civvy careers, want to deploy overseas, but this is the nature of the Army – we go where we are sent 'in the interests of the service'.

The sausage-factory found it impossible to deal with our little London group. Each queue we joined insisted we take the full list of items for Iraq.

'Anthrax injection?'

'I'm going to London; I don't think I need it.'

'Just stand still and stop with the questioning...'

'Ok.'

Weapon, body armour, new uniforms, I had it all. I had a weapon in the armoury in London and a set of body armour for six months because I was unable to hand it back. I wonder how many other sets of body armour could have gone to Iraq, where they were so badly needed, if our administration had been better organised. In March 2003, Sergeant Steve Roberts of the Royal Tank Regiment died, partly due to lack of body armour.

If Chilwell had been chaotic, the Joint Headquarters in Northwood, London, where I was sent next, was worse. The Northwood HQ brings together the Navy, Army and RAF and is the base from which overseas military operations are controlled. The site, which lies behind heavy metal fences topped with barbed wire, can house around 600 personnel.

We were mostly working in the underground bunker which dated from around 1939 and had been used during World War ll. By 2003, when I arrived, it had been refurbished as part of the concept of bringing tri-services (RAF, Navy and Army) all under one roof at the operational level. Much of the sensitive work was done here and it felt more like working on a submarine than anything else. We'd descend through security pods and go along a maze of corridors to reach the bunker. For six months I was on night shifts, so I went down around 6pm and stayed until 8am with little more than a quick trip up during the night for meals.

We did give briefings in a nice big shiny central ops room - think big TV screens, multiple clocks showing the time in each conflict zone and media feeds from many sources including BBC world services and Al Jazeera.

The posting did mean endless saluting – the joint HQ was full of officers of all kinds of ranks from many countries, so by the time I'd got from one part of the building to another my arm would be in autopilot, saluting at almost everyone I passed. The barcode ranks of the RAF were hardest to read, so I'd find myself squinting at them, ready with a hasty last-minute salute if the person walking towards me proved to be a more senior officer.

What wasn't remotely state of the art at Northwood were the arrangements made, or rather not made, for the reserves. The whole thing had a distinct element of dark comedy. When we arrived, there was no room to accommodate us, so a condemned block was hastily re-opened. Normally, on operations, those on night shifts and day shifts are in different areas, to allow those not working to sleep, but there was no plan for this. I was placed on permanent night shift and had nowhere to sleep during the day without disturbance. After some pressure, the officers' mess reluctantly offered rooms, but refused to delay a scheduled carpet refurbishment. All day, every day, there was the sound of carpets being ripped out and constant drilling. Eventually I moved out to sleep in my car for a month in a disused area of camp. Blissful peace.

Along with most others, I had problems getting paid. I asked if the pay office could open early so that I could go in at the end of my nightshift at 8 am. This was deemed impossible and I ended up spending nearly 24 hours awake one day just trying to get a form signed by all the right people. It is the way it is in the military. Anyone who has served will empathise with this tale. There is one process for all of us to follow and no flexibility.

My role was challenging. Over a third of us arriving there were reserves and we all arrived at once with varying degrees of readiness, not least because we didn't have access to the computer systems as each different system require the user to have attended a different course, especially if we needed access to US ones. Roles were randomly allocated so there was very little time to prepare. We had huge volumes of data and printed files to assimilate and summarise, to identify changing trends within Iraqi military capabilities.

This was the era when the media began to drive public opinion. Journalists were embedded with the military in Iraq and they could send photos and reports direct from the war zone instantly, so we had huge problems keeping ahead of them when, for instance, we needed to brief VIPs and military chiefs before a story broke in the papers. It was also when the military started to change its relationship with journalists and data.

The expected resistance from the Iraqi military didn't materialise, their formed military units folded quite quickly, but the threat from insurgents; those who could strike and then melt back into the civilian population, was far greater than anticipated (and it would continue for the next eight years).

When things quietened, after the initial invasion and the taking of Baghdad, I was given a new role of evaluating our contribution to the reconstruction phase. I was amazed to see how little planning there had been for stabilisation after the fighting phase – it was as thin as the subsequent inquiries have said it was. One night I was on my own covering the shift when I answered the phone. It was a civil servant, needing a briefing. I asked if it could wait until morning.

'It's for Number Ten', the voice said, rather irritated.

'Number Ten where?' I said, before realisation dawned. I drafted the input they needed very quickly after that.

As things calmed and our role became unnecessary, we reserves asked for our end-date. None was forthcoming. After pressure, the boss admitted he wanted to allow his regulars time to take leave and attend the summer ball before he was willing to let us go. It was not the most 'in extremis' reason I have been given for serving on.

Iraq wasn't a popular war, but I was still proud to have done my part. And on my last day, July 22, 2003, there was some closure. Saddam Hussein's two sons, Uday and Quasay, were killed by US forces in Mosul. That was worth waiting for. Some people are better dead. I would like to see it differently, but I saw what this cruel and ruthless pair had done.

When I went home again, I took a break for a few months from military work. I bought a little sports car, an MX5, did some house renovations and settled down. And I met a new partner, Newall Hunter, an adventurer and a cyber specialist. We were a good fit, and our partnership would lead us on some great and challenging adventures. Among many trips together we would climb Kilimanjaro, complete a tough road trip around Kenya, take a monster truck across the centre of Iceland, go ice-climbing in Scotland and ski in Morocco.

I planned to take it easy for a while, in terms of my commitment to the reserves, but a year or so later, I found out that an old friend was now commanding the intelligence unit and I agreed to go back and take on the lead role training intelligence recruits in London. It was a major commitment and for the next two to three years I put in at least 100 days a year, driving one evening a week and one or two weekends a month, the two to three hours from Gloucestershire to Uxbridge, where I parked and took the tube into Liverpool Street, turning up in time for an evening shift from 7pm to 9pm. Afterwards I'd have a quick drink in the TA centre bar and then reverse the process often getting home after midnight, although occasionally, if I wasn't working the next day, I'd go for a few drinks and stay over.

I had a team of highly committed reserves working with me to give the recruits the basic training, which is a prerequisite on joining the Army, before you move on to trade (in our case intelligence) training. Mostly we were teaching the simple skills like how to sleep under canvas, use military ration packs, march and salute. When I joined and learned these skills at Sandhurst, we were all young and fit, but now, around a third of these recruits needed remedial fitness training just to hit the basic test levels. We added in a little trade training just to keep them interested, things like observation and briefing skills and military equipment recognition.

At that time blogging was just getting going. The recruits were asked not to share what they did in training, but one recruit thought she would ignore this and get away with it by blogging anonymously. My warrant officer lead, a canny individual, read her posts and saw that she mentioned she had a tattoo on her foot. He arranged a foot inspection and she was held back from future training, not for the tattoo, but for giving out information without permission.

As I settled back into civilian routines, I was asked to give talks about how poorly the Army managed the mobilisation. There were probably a dozen or so of us selected for our tales (mine being the delayed call out which was so badly handled and then the accommodation issues at Northwood). I mixed with many who had the same tales and our conclusion was that people are not valued by the military. It is, I believe, the main reason that numbers are so low now and decreasing further. Despite this, I still wanted to serve, but I realised I had to move on from the Military Intelligence Unit in London, seeking roles in the wider military and being more selective in offering myself up for service. I knew that if I stayed in the training role in the intelligence unit, I could not progress my military career, plus the travel effort was hurting my civilian work. I made a conscious decision at this point to seek roles that would build my military career. But the Army was changing – the churn of tours to Iraq and then, soon afterwards, to Afghanistan was intense and the attitude towards those of us in the reserves was less about who you were and 'intelligent mobilisation' and more about just getting you to sign up for the next tour in order to get sufficient numbers mobilised. As a result, I was offered little advice from the military about which roles I should take, and this would come back to bite me years later.

The toll on my relationship could have been worse, but at this time Newall was away a lot too. In 2003, around the time when we met, he began the challenge of climbing the seven highest mountains, one on each continent and trekking to both poles, something he would complete in 2016 when he became only the 15th person to achieve this extraordinary adventurer's grand slam.

Alongside this he also managed to completely renovate a house.

Newall had his own interesting tale- his father was one of the early pioneers of RADAR who ended up working with Barnes-Wallace on the 'bouncing bomb' project as captured in *The Dambusters*. He was a brilliant man with a photographic memory, a science pioneer who was called up to the RAF as part of the war effort and then joined the civil service. Sadly, he died suddenly of a heart attack when Newall was just 14. Newall was dyslexic, so he struggled at school but was lucky enough to have a great teacher who recognised it was dyslexia and not lack of intellect holding him back. He let Newall spend time designing engineering projects and encouraged him to go to Bletchley Park in 1981 which at that time offered specialist degree courses. Newall would also end up working in RADAR.

When I met him, Newall told me he wished he'd had the opportunity to serve in uniform but felt he'd left it too late. I was able to put him in touch with a specialist communications unit who were happy to take him on, based on his civilian skills. That unit sent him to complete the professionally qualified officer commission, which involved attending Sandhurst for four weeks in the autumn of 2006, over 20 years after my training.

There is a story from that time which still makes us both laugh. He was standing on parade, having borrowed some of my uniform; a rank slide, a beret and a particularly shiny Sam Browne – the leather belt that goes

124

around the waist and over the shoulder and is now used mostly for ceremonial occasions (named after the one-armed British Army Officer who came up with the design to stabilise his sword after he lost his left arm fighting in India). The sergeant-major in charge, well aware that the people on this course had no previous army service – it was known as the tarts and vicars course – was confused by Newall's adventurer's physique and these items which denoted military experience.

He stopped in front of Newall.

'Nice Sam Browne, sir, where did you get it?'

'It's my girlfriend's.'

At which point, the sergeant-major was stunned into silence, followed by general laughter. This was a rehearsal; when the actual parade took place the same sergeant-major was accompanying an inspecting officer and this time he was ready.

'It's a real Sam Browne, ma'am. It's his girlfriend's.' Then he whispered, a little too loudly, 'I haven't checked, but he is probably also wearing her underwear.'

Chapter Eight
Army 2020

When someone shows you who they are, believe them the first time
Maya Angelou

After completing the training tour and mobilisation, I was ready to take my senior military exams. I had come top in the junior exams but the premium I'd had from being a regular was now gone. This next stage would be combat-focused, and I was not a natural military tactician.

The course was modular, over six months, from April to September 2007, a mixture of coursework to do at home and some weekends at Shrivenham, the UK Defence Academy near Swindon, where we also did our final two-week course. There were about 60 of us on this course, split into groups of 6 to 8 and with two staff members, one regular and one reserve, per group. These staff could be any cap-badge and they set the tone. By cap-badge, I mean the service that each of us are affiliated to, shown by a badge on our headwear; usually a metal badge for soldiers and a cloth one for officers. So my cap-badge is the Intelligence Corps. I knew if they were combat arms – those troops who participate in direct, tactical ground combat – it would be painful because they tended to be the most misogynistic and dismissive of women. Sure enough, both my directing staff were combat arms: an army air corps pilot and a yeomanry (upper class, armoured reconnaissance) officer. On the plus side, I had an interesting syndicate: a Member of Parliament, another Yeomanry officer and a German exchange officer, amongst others.

I was the only woman and from the start, if I got a question wrong, it was patronisingly mansplained, while if anyone else got one wrong, there was a light chuckle and a gentle explanation to assist him. I wondered if I was imagining this, until the German officer asked me during one coffee break if this level of gender bias was common in the British Army. On another occasion when I took a drubbing there was a visiting observer in the back of the room. The observer held me back at the end of the session and asked if I wanted to complain. I was still not ready to speak up, so I said no.

I was a major and I needed to pass this course with a good grade in order to earn promotion to lieutenant-colonel. I passed the course but was damned with faint praise in my final report. Some of it was potentially true (I am not a natural tactician) but nor were many of the men in my syndicate and that weakness was glossed over in their reports, so it was not a level playing field. This report would delay my promotion by about two years, so I should have spoken up, but I still wasn't ready to make a fuss.

The year before this course I had been appointed to a role in Whitehall, working in defence intelligence. Looking back, what we were doing was incredibly basic; computers were really just getting going and were very limited in their connectivity and data collation abilities, but it was challenging and enjoyable at the time. It was a part-time role, usually one day a week, over the next three years. During that time, I juggled this role in London with building my leadership training business. It was a happy time, I had my weekends back and Newall and I were doing lots of adventuring together, climbing, skiing, mountain biking and so on.

I hadn't worked much at the strategic end of intelligence until this period and I found it suited me well. Strategic work focuses on the entire organisation and most military people start at the tactical, short-term, end – looking at just one part of the business – as do most junior staff in any organisation. As part of my role I visited Washington DC, Germany and other parts of the UK and I began to understand the UK military-government interface, looking at defence as a holistic concept in which the government, as well as the military, will have a view about aspects such as budgets, roles and priorities and in which senior military people will communicate with civil servants and armed forces ministers to create a whole force concept. This, in turn, is the understanding that it is not just the full-time regulars who can or should provide the fighting power; there is a need for diversity and for regulars, reserves and civil servants to work together to deliver a truly effective fighting force.

In this job I was making the transition from middle to senior posts and I was starting to see more clearly the Establishment bias. A chosen few can do less work, yet still score higher, or can be promoted without doing any of the required courses the rest of us must do, while others, of the 'right' class, are favoured for promotion, roles and awards. These things are wrong and do us no favours. Yet I saw them all the time.

The background defence pressure at this time was from the Strategic Defence & Security Reviews (SDSRs). I was heavily involved in Army 2020, the SDSR which mandated the restructuring of the Army – first announced in 2008 (and then altered and refined several times over subsequent years) to be completed by 2020. It had a reserves' element called FR20, or Future Reserves 2020. The headline was that the government wanted a significant reduction in regulars, with more roles for the (cheaper) reserves. Many regulars saw it as 'reserves taking our jobs' and later, in 2012, a section of them would hatch a plan to fight it, which meant two opposing plans in Army HQ were being developed at the same time – never a good idea, to achieve real success you need unity of vision.

Most reserves were supportive and keen to be included in the planning, to make it viable and personally, I agreed that the Army was in need of re-structuring and could integrate its reserves much better, but needed to retain a strong regular presence at the centre because reserves can never be the A team; they must always be back up.

One thing everyone was clear about – this plan wasn't about offering better defence; it was about budget cuts. These cuts weren't just about cheaper human resources, although that is my focus here. The planners also had to factor in sneaky changes such as including war pensions in future budgets. Since the Army still hadn't balanced the books from previous deep cuts, these further cuts were going to hurt.

The Army was aware it was losing ground against the rapid societal and technical change that was happening. It needed to find a way for regulars and reserves to work together (that whole force concept), to harness new technologies and defend against old and new adversaries. This should have created the opportunity for joint regular and reserve committees to work out how to combine previously separate systems. But only a few, like Intelligence, did this. In the main the decisions were made by regulars, without consulting reserves and so 'whole force concept' became translated as, 'reserves will adopt regular systems'- another example of if you aren't setting the rules, you don't have the power.

It started with career management. Suddenly, reserves had a new language to learn for report writing, quota systems for promotion, orders of merit and career panels which were heavily regular, male and infantry dominated. Panel processes were opaque, their results, which were public, were skewed towards those same regular males, typically infantry candidates. Even the service chiefs were noticing that women and other minorities were not making it through the middle and senior boards at equal pace. Sir Peter Wall, Chief of the General Staff until 2014 even mentioned it in his farewell interview and it has been mentioned at least annually every year since.

What I saw was that there were some who were better than me who were not fulfilling their potential, but also many worse than me who were getting selected for promotions and for certain jobs. Some of it was down to self-belief. I suffered, as did many women, with difficulty speaking publicly in majority male environments. When I watched Theresa May, or Hilary Clinton, I could see that they did too. That culture in which many women were raised, which told us that we didn't have the right to be there was hard to shake off, and the enemy could smell blood. As historian Mary Beard has said, many women are 'overcoming deeply ingrained behaviours' in order to speak up.

I was also concerned about attitudes to the reserves. After their efforts, and successes, during Iraq, it should have been the time for a cultural shift in regular attitudes, but it wasn't happening. Reserves made up over 10 percent of roles in Iraq and a lot more in UK. Yet instead of a breakthrough in attitudes, views were about to become more entrenched against the reserves as the government moved to downsize the regular army further. Instead of seeing how diversity might improve fighting power in a digital age, the Army seemed to turn inwards and stall, with reserves frozen even further out of management decisions.

This was frustrating and saddening, good reserves can enhance and expand the force, and this was the time to use them. As I reached more senior roles, I wanted to explore why the cultural, negative monotone view that reserves were not worth integrating, training or using as valuable resources persisted, even after the successes in Iraq. If we were now to drop back to the old attitudes, not giving opportunities for reserves to 'come onto the pitch' and play a match, they would not be ready when we needed them again. Hence the conundrum that many regulars don't rate reserves because they are insufficiently trained yet deny reserves the opportunity to gain that training. While gender and ethnic bigotry were starting to reduce in the middle ranks, for some reason, discrimination against the Army reserve was particularly bad in this group. Why was this? I needed to understand it.

It is of course part of a wider societal conundrum- to fully integrate minorities requires an attitude shift. For the two minority scenarios I know best, those of reserves and women, I still see the same derogatory comments about STABS and women on LinkedIn, in the broad sheet media and on the less salubrious online military forums. And there is an ongoing debate about what to use as an acronym now that it is the AR and not the TA. None of the suggested titles are any more complimentary than STABS. How can we change attitudes if our senior leadership keeps tolerating anti-minority sentiment?

I knew a lot about reserves, not least because at this stage I had been one longer than I had been a regular. There are genuine gripes for both parties, but we have more in common than not and, like it or not, we need each other. I could see both sides and as I progressed my reserve career, I felt ideally placed to investigate the conundrum.

Except that after my Shrivenham career course, I hit a roadblock and for the next 18 months I was denied promotion. By now wary of the promotions system, I had started to keep a record. As a transferee, they advised me to 'gain more intelligence experience', as an ex-regular, I was to 'learn about reserves', as a reserve I needed to 'learn more about regulars'. With the new regular system, I was to 'focus on breadth'. It became obvious that certain types were clear favourites whatever they did, and these were just tricks to hold non-favourites back. This appeared to be the regular way – promote your mates – and now it was becoming the reserves' way too. As an analyst, I looked at who was getting through quickly: certain infantry, cavalry, a few engineers, nearly all men. The low percentage of women getting through were either the very rare highflyers or married to those same favoured few.

It is understandable and necessary for a career pyramid to have the few best at the top. So, these posts should be highly competitive. Except that in the military they are not, they are mostly pre-ordained. In the old reserve system, we were selected locally, and bias was fairly obvious and could be challenged. Now the system had been centralised it became opaque and hard to understand.

I was applying for posts, scoring well, yet kept seeing male colleagues pip me to the post. I knew other candidates and I knew that these results were not based solely on merit. I have never conformed to risk-avoidance strategies, so sometimes I make mistakes. But feedback on results was not offered and if requested, it was given reluctantly and was vague. 'The board were unanimous' (about what?), 'he had more experience' (in what?), 'they knew what they were looking for' (you mean 'who'). Vague feedback is usually an indicator of bias since if it isn't specific then the selection has probably been governed by instinct.

The unwritten military rule is that it is career-suicide to complain, but without getting through these 'shadow-boards' I wasn't going to get a post or experience or promotion. Shadow-boards was my name for the boarding processes under the whole force concept. It was hard to find out who the membership was, their affiliations or why they selected the candidates they did. What I did know was that the senior board members were all male and mostly from the same public-school backgrounds and they were not required to declare any conflicts of interest or explain their selection processes.

Frustrated and baffled, I started to ask questions, seeing individuals with no better career profile move ahead of me. I had a lot of qualifications and experience, so what criteria were they looking for? After repeated failures, I found my own way to beat the boards, by lobbying a board member with my CV.

Suddenly I was successful and three months later, in 2009, I was told I would be promoted to Lieutenant-Colonel. I was also told that my lobbying had, 'Made no difference at all' and, 'You would have won your promotion without that phone call'. I remained unconvinced. And there was one final sting: it turned out my boss, a regular Lieutenant-Colonel who was in command of the London Military Intelligence Unit at that time, had offered an extension to the man already in post, with the result that my promotion was delayed by a further six months. One step forward, two army boot size steps back.

While I was still at Whitehall, I went to the Falkland Islands for a couple of weeks, in April 2009, in support of a military exercise. It was a truly memorable trip. The common description is four seasons in one day and in the two weeks we were there we certainly had spring, summer and winter. We were delayed leaving the islands due to heavy snow. The two main islands were bleak and windswept, a little like the Shetlands, and mostly flat with occasional rolling hills. We went to see the site of Goose Green where Lieutenant Colonel H Jones died on May 28, 1982 (his son is now a very senior officer in the military). And then there were the wonderful windswept South Atlantic beaches with their colonies of penguins. The restricted access for people to some areas, as there was still a threat of landmines, allowed the wildlife to thrive and the islands were havens of biodiversity.

My role was to lead part of the permanent intelligence detachment within the main Falklands HQ. I got to know two great intelligence characters on this trip; one, Dan Duell, who sadly died not long afterwards in Brunei and the other, who I will call Smiley, who would work alongside me for the next ten years and who became a great friend. It was a year or so after we met that Smiley and I were walking through Uxbridge one evening with some of his special forces friends when I ran ahead to an ATM to draw out cash. As I did, a group of 3-4 thugs approached from the shadows and demanded money. I smiled. The thugs were puzzled until I pointed out the super-fit men now running towards us. The thugs ran off. That was my definition of 'friends with benefits'.

While I waited to take up my new posting, I took the opportunity to get out of the London hub. I knew I needed to gain the right kind of experience if I was to progress in rank (the next step-up would be to Colonel), so I undertook a six-month project based in the main regular intelligence HQ in Bedfordshire. I was interviewing all the intelligence units in the military to update their roles and capabilities in a journal. It was a useful but limited project although it did start to raise my profile.

When I finally took up my promotion, on April 1, 2010, I was given my first senior military role, as Chief of Staff of a technical intelligence team. I was excited and couldn't wait to get going. I was working with a small team of specialists for a unit I will call the Technical Intelligence Unit, or TIU. When I first met them, I felt a little daunted. I had a science background too, just not at the PhD level of this group. The TIU provided scientific insight to the military. On my first weekend, they conducted a study on the effectiveness of dowsing (dowsing didn't work) against other detection systems for finding Improvised Explosive Devices (IEDs). I loved their innovative approaches and their intellects were obvious. When I hosted a senior officer later that year, I said that if we made TIU bigger, we could really 'bring the outside in'. He agreed and, in effect, the unit that I would go on to command a few years later was born, although I didn't know that then. That senior officer I met would also go on to play a significant role.

About six months later, an exciting opportunity came along. Just before Christmas in 2011, I saw an advert for a job assisting an officer putting together the plan for delivering future structures for military intelligence as part of the Army 2020 plan. The work would start immediately and last for three months. This seemed a perfect project, it would be high-profile, and it sounded interesting. It would be a task I would have to do alongside my job as Chief of Staff of the TIU, but I knew I could manage it.

I went to meet the officer in charge at an RAF base on the east side of the UK, home at the time to the Army's one military intelligence brigade. I had met him before; he was the senior officer I had met in a bar in London and who I will call PSmith (after the character in the novels of P.G. Wodehouse). He was my first senior mentor and he inspired me. In return I invested time and energy. The project lead for the future structures work was his wife, who I will call Madeleine, a senior officer in her own right.

Mine was not an auspicious beginning. On my first visit to meet her, still weary from a 4am start, pulling into the line of cars outside the guardroom I scraped my car on another and spent 20 minutes exchanging details with a very understanding fellow driver. But despite this, the meeting went well. Madeleine was high energy, incisive and open to new ideas and we got on well from the start. She was equally frustrated by some of the entrenched negative attitudes holding back the whole force concept and we bonded over identifying ways in which to change that. I got the job and Madeleine and I formed quite a double act.

There was one other senior player, a reserve specially recruited for the task. He came from the Royal Signals but took over temporarily as Reserve Head of Intelligence as we lacked the right person to fill the role from within intelligence. I will call him Bruce. He was a quiet, slight man with a sense of gravitas, a straight talker and an excellent strategist. He shook hands and cut straight to it. 'Diane, we need two more reserve battalions as well as to grow the specialist role. I want you to be bold'.

I liked that simple direction.

I knew I could learn from PSmith, Madeleine and Bruce. They were a rare trio in that they weren't too worried about rocking the boat if it helped to knock a few barnacles off the bottom. At the time, intelligence had three regular and two reserve units. In addition, the main London-based reserve hub, 3MI, had TIU attached, plus there was a smaller northern one, 5MI, which had formed a few years earlier but had never really got going as it was badly located.

It wasn't going to be easy; just getting to the HQ took nearly three hours and the only way I could fit the work in was to compress my efforts into two, back to back 15-hour days, staying over at the camp. The rest of the week I worked off a laptop. As a true reserve, I had other career strands to maintain so it was going to be a tough juggle; I was still working in a private physiotherapy clinic in Gloucestershire in addition to running my outdoor education business. I was also working on an MSc in coastal zone management with the Open University. I had always been fascinated by the oceans and conservation and one of the things I felt I might like to do – one day – was to work in environmental management.

As the reserves' lead for the project, the first thing I needed to know was the 'what'. This was, and still is, an area of weakness for the military. What does the Army actually want? This time the senior architect of Army

2020, General Sir Nick Carter (who was Deputy Commander Land Forces and who became Chief of the General Staff – the Army Head – in September 2014 as I started up my new unit) was clear, he wanted to retain essential parts of the regular army while enabling reserves to deliver the less time-critical bits. He wanted a genuinely whole force approach – integration and access to industry and government departments and sensible infrastructure solutions. He must have done something right- he went on to be Chief of the Defence Staff (CDS).

Our plan had to show how we would cover current tasks plus new ones and where we needed to be. It was bold but it wasn't impossible. We had only six weeks to submit, which is why I had been taken on, so our approach was to build a business case concurrently with the plan. Where some regulars focused on fighting the cuts and chose not to consult reserves, intelligence consulted widely and focused on requirements and in doing this, the plan wrote itself.

Military Intelligence (MI) was already over-stretched, so didn't suffer such severe cuts as other sections of the Army. But reserves were still going to need to cover tasks traditionally allocated to regulars. That wouldn't be popular so our plan was to increase capacity by spreading the geographic footprint, co-locating our reserves with other relevant organisations (police, fire, government and related industries) and making sure TA centres were in professional areas, likely to attract quality recruits. We produced a plan to expand the current two reserve battalions (3MI and 5MI) to four, one to support each of the three regular units (these were 1MI, 2MI, 4MI), plus 3MI to support the various HQ, and an additional group of deep specialists – so five reserve units in all. We took the time to find sites which met the criteria: London, where we already had a base, plus Bristol, Edinburgh and Manchester. The specialist group, based on an expanded version of TIU, would be co-located alongside other 'specialist odd-balls' near Newbury.

Project management needs both visionaries and implementers, they are inter-dependent. Bruce and Madeleine were excellent visionaries and orators. They presented our case well and it was accepted. It wasn't universally popular, even within intelligence, but we had senior leadership onside. As part of the plan, the MOD changed the name and status of reserves to the Army Reserve (rather than TA) with pro-rata pension rights and some other benefits. The expectation, for all of us, was that the reserve culture would become more professional and flexible.

Then Bruce and Madeleine left in quick succession. Bruce leaving was a shock, he was a reserve and we expected him to stay on for longer, but he was offered a more senior role elsewhere and he made a career choice to leave us early, leaving a gap. Madeleine was simply posted earlier than expected and went on to an important posting. She didn't want to go and tried to delay but she was told she would be damaging her career if she didn't. PSmith was still there, and on board, but with two of the visionaries gone, I had the choice of leaving as well or taking the reins. Had I learned enough to lead such a large military project? It meant adjustments with my civilian roles, delaying the growth of my leadership business and turning down an option to join the physiotherapy business where I worked part-time. But Newall was away a lot, pursuing his grand plan. He had summited Everest in May 2011 and was planning his next trip to the North Pole, so I would be able to make time to do the A2020 project. In the end I decided to go for it.

I knew I'd taken on something big. But I didn't know then that my initial three-month job would end up lasting for five years, involving an organisational re-structure and then delivery. I would go on to establish the two new reserve intelligence units and re-structure a third, as well as to set up and command the deep specialists, one of the strangest groups in the Army. It had not been my intention to lead this charge, but when Bruce and Madeleine moved on, I felt strongly that someone had to see the project through. And as the project developed, I realised what I was doing was more than about broadening my knowledge. I wanted to give back to the Army and particularly the Intelligence Corps.

What I still wasn't ready for was the determination of a small cohort of Red Lighters within the military to try to scupper the plan. Would senior individuals really favour their own cap-badges over innovation? It seemed so, and as we progressed, they tried to trip us up in every possible way.

Despite that, when the intelligence vision was finally delivered, the project had retained all the key elements we sketched out in those early project meetings. There were compromises because delivering big projects within the MOD is challenging, but we made it and we delivered outstanding results. Two reserve intelligence units became four, based in excellent locations, and the group of deep specialists became fully operational as well.

If I had known that by the end I would experience the highest moment in my career, receiving an OBE for the success of the project, and the lowest, having my rights read to me at a military police interview, would I still have done it? I'm not sure. Because in the end, despite everything, those shadow-boards still found a way to say no to me.

What I could never have known, as I set out, was that the project that was my greatest achievement would mark the end of my military career.

Chapter Nine
Fighting my Corner

Those who say it cannot be done should not interrupt the person
doing it
Old Chinese Proverb

Over the next eighteen months I had to beg and borrow the staff to make up the team I needed in order to put the blueprint into action. The Army had told all cap-badges to deliver the A2020 plan but offered almost no additional resources, even to a cohort like intelligence which was to double in number. And the miserly resources we did get allocated were to be deliberately delayed until the size of the regular army had been reduced, which would take years. The result was that we had to apply for each post individually, with an in-depth business case to justify it. I needed three core team members, but initially I got only two. One was my old friend Smiley, the other a former infantry officer who was transferring to intelligence. Eventually I managed to get a third when Madeleine persuaded a high-quality former regular to re-join as a reserve on individual training days. Those three were my core team and all were excellent. But it took many months to get them, and even when I did, I needed to supplement them in busy times, so we put out requests for willing volunteers. Most of these were reliable and high quality, but I learned that the first to volunteer were not always the best and I had to let some go.

For that year and a half, we had to feed the bureaucratic monster that was army headquarters with numbers, costs and infrastructure needs; what the Army calls 'scrubbing' the plan. And we had to integrate our plan with others.

Over a period of months, two delaying agendas appeared: the predictable budgetary one and a subtler anti-reserve one. I could see the people at the top and bottom were keen for change, but there was a stubborn centre, mostly made up of the old establishment. Every organisation has a few people resistant to change, the Red Lighters I first learned about when I was at Sandhurst, but the Army had far more than a few, and this stubborn centre had a concerted plot to derail A2020 by delaying the downsizing of regular posts, which meant that the funds would not be available for staffing new reserve sections.

There was another problem. To make it easier with schooling, the Army posts most of its personnel over the summer, which means losing a chunk of corporate knowledge all in one go. In the summer of 2012, we lost the two chief staff officers in the brigade. My core team had to be based in the one intelligence brigade because it was from there that the A2020 plan for intelligence would be delivered. And this meant working closely with the regular chiefs of staff. These two would never normally have been posted at the same time, but just as one was posted the other decided to leave the Army.

Hard on the heels of this, in September 2012, PSmith was posted, just nine months after I started. This meant I had lost all three of the original project seniors and this last was a near-fatal blow. PSmith had declared the reserves' growth his main effort (an important military term meaning this project was the main focus of the brigade's time) so I lost my top-cover, the person who could deflect blows from above. I didn't know if his successor would offer the same support.

PSmith's replacement wasn't posted to the Eastern location, since the intelligence brigade was due, imminently, to leave and move south. He would go direct to the new location, near the Army HQ in Andover. This left the newly arrived senior staffer (chief operating officer in civilian parlance and the spokesperson for the Brigade Commander), who did work from the old location, with a little more power than usual and he made his presence felt. It didn't take long to discover that this new staff officer would not only refuse to support the reserves' plan, but, in my view, would actively attempt to derail it. He was a man I will call Lieutenant Blue. He arrived on attachment in the autumn of 2012 to refine the A2020 plan and then became the new head of staff. Blue had apparently been through the mill after a tour in Afghanistan. But for me, his main issue was that he wasn't prepared to listen to reserves (or women). At the first meeting, supposedly a preliminary, he announced to a packed audience his final plan – there would be no shared planning and no discussion. He said he didn't need input and if anyone wanted to disagree: 'Come and shoot me down later'.

I had grown the intelligence reserves from two units to five by this time, which meant we had 1346 people to find or retain (we remembered the number as it was the date of the battle of Crecy). It was actually a few more when we included the wider intelligence reserves posts – we would eventually get up to 1415. Blue was unable to reduce the number of reserves as I controlled that at the time, but what he did was to give up all my support staff and remove the reserves from key HQ posts, all really critical to growing the whole force concept. I managed to hold onto the training team, and I was able to hide some of those key HQ posts in it, but I shouldn't have had to do this. If PSmith had still been there, he wouldn't have allowed this to happen, but I didn't have the power to stop Blue, so he went ahead. I felt as if he'd brokered a deal with the other cap-badges to build his reputation, and that this was as much a driver than a commitment to the interests of intelligence as a whole force concept.

His view was that the previous plan was 'too fat' (in other words, there were too many people allocated to the HQ) and that regulars could manage reserve issues, both of which I believe to be poor assumptions. The way reserves are employed, used, recruited and promoted is quite different to regulars and the two systems (regular and reserve) used to be separate, for good reasons. The Army decided to merge the two under the whole force concept, but the entrenched middle of the regular army, people like Blue, seemed to interpret this to mean that reserves would simply adopt regular systems which were not designed for reserves. This created a lot of issues which could have been mitigated with a few key reserve posts in HQ, but Blue gave those posts away.

At this point I hoped the worst was over, but the initial culls turned out to be just a first move. This was the beginning of a new, more secretive style of leadership; the era of openness had been lost with the departure of PSmith and in early 2013, weeks after he arrived, Blue suddenly ordered my team to leave. It was hard to know whether he just didn't care about my team, or actively wanted to shut us down. I suspect that it was the former, we were 'just reserves' and it seemed he didn't want us in his HQ.

It was tempting to walk away, but I owed it to the team, and to the original plan, to see it through. During the many difficulties and trials we faced, I was reminded of the Confucius saying, 'If you do something, know that you will be up against those who would want to do the same thing, those who would want to do the exact opposite ... and the immense majority of those that don't want to do anything'.

With Blue on his own mission, I had to salvage things fast. The Army HQ near Andover, in Hampshire agreed to give us space, when I explained our situation to them, which was a relief. At least we would have a new base. While clearly ambivalent about the team, they were reasonably pleased to have Smiley and me move down there as they didn't have anyone else who understood the intelligence reserves' plan and Bruce's replacement (I will call him Mason), was unable to help; he didn't attend most of the key meetings as he took a civilian job in Africa, leaving us in the lurch for A2020.

Our ejection from the East Coast HQ was so sudden that we didn't even have time for a traditional farewell. Luckily, we had already celebrated. When PSmith left, we had produced an excellent photo image of the team, superimposed on an *Ocean's Thirteen* still. I have it in my office at home, a fitting tribute to a fine team who designed the original plan and who showed that the whole force concept could work and be enjoyable.

The speed of the change was nearly fatal because Andover couldn't take all of my core team. They would need to be geographically split up. Once I realised what was happening, I was able to place each of my key staff in 'good homes'. One went to Chicksands, home of intelligence, one to Army HQ and the third to a different role, for career reasons. I also went to Army HQ and we continued to co-ordinate to keep the plan on track, but at this stage the regulars were back in charge of the plan, as opposed to the original regular-reserve collaboration, and there was little thinking in their decision-making about the way any changes they made would affect reserves.

The Andover HQ was full of middle and senior ranked officers sitting at computers for long hours. It is a necessary part of soldiering, but it isn't fun. Signs on pillars guided us to our desks, in otherwise identical open-plan offices.

I could see from the start that most of the staff were indifferent to A2020. Success was going to be governed by the efforts of a few positive outliers weighing up against the obstructions of the negative outliers, but we were due a change at the top of intelligence and I was hopeful that the new head would be supportive.

I now had an easier commute, since Andover was closer to home, but a huge challenge – without someone supportive like PSmith my job would be so much harder. Not only was Blue not sharing information and refusing to include reserves in his decision-making, but I was also going to have to build the new units while guarding my successes. Intelligence did very well out of A2020 both in terms of gaining numbers and getting decent places for our army reserve centres. Other cap-badges like my former cap-badge, the Royal Signals did less well and some were now sore and smarting and determined to claw stuff back, so the team had to remain on alert.

The Army HQ is staffed by a mix of regulars, civil servants and full-time reserves. The regulars are professional soldiers who move every three years. A tour at Army HQ is essential for career progression; they fill 'staff roles' like plans, procurement and budgets which many are not trained for, so each department has some civil servants who have more expertise in these subjects and who have typically been there longer and can advise regular officers. These regulars were of mixed quality, all responsible for big project issues, some with little experience and others with no sense of investment. The few who were the change-leaders stood out and they were the ones I sought out for my team.

Shortly after I arrived, having submitted all those A2020 numbers (as had many others), the Army announced it had the sums wrong and cut a lot of full-time reserve posts. We had to write business cases for keeping the remaining posts or wait up to two years to get the staff we needed. The culture was very much 'too much to do with too little time' and just following orders. There was little space for innovation and no appetite for asking reserves what optimal might look like. I was to find it an excellent learning ground.

The friction caused by the A2020 losses and gains was being fanned by an earlier re-arrangement of capability groupings (the directorates) in which Intelligence was paired with Communications. However, there was a size differential: we were tiny, with no capacity to staff the directorate and heavily committed on operations, while communications was much bigger. Most of the communicators were graceful, but there were one or two angry at losses and out to even the score. Re-writes of the A2020 strategic plan and numbers appeared that had stripped out intelligence needs and replaced them with signals-friendly versions. I tried changing the paperwork back and asked the Signals officer who was doing the re-writes not to change anything without letting me know, but when neither of these strategies worked, I had to speak up.

When disputes occur, if they can't be resolved between you, the next step is to complain up the hierarchy, which for me meant full colonels and the brigadiers above them. Neither of which liked being bothered by trivia. You had to go to them with a BLUF (bottom line up front) verbal or written brief of what the issue was, possible courses of action, consequences if nothing was done and then recommendations. The senior officer decided what to do and we all then followed the new plan.

Thankfully I was listened to and the officer concerned was given a slap on the wrist. That should have been the end of it, but the irony – very typical in the Army – was that I was 'difficult' for having raised it. This was in part a rank issue; some had expected me to sort it through my own chain of command. But Mason was away, and I was convinced Blue wasn't interested in reserves' matters, so I didn't have any top cover.

I wondered whether my style at this senior level needed more subtlety, even when there was deliberate sabotage in the mix. I was always driving at the front of change and keeping the plan on track, but after that episode I felt I needed to find ways to achieve success without ruffling so many feathers. I have asked myself many times if I could have found a graceful way to keep a project on track even when there were others who were trying to derail it. With hindsight, though, I am not sure there was a way. I have talked to a few entrepreneurs and company CEOs since and the majority view is that to be in senior posts where you are making a difference and implementing change will always ruffle feathers.

Part of the government-savings plan, in tandem with the reduction in size of the regular army, was to sell off prime real estate, which meant closing army bases and squashing army units into ever smaller spaces. This included reserve centres as well as regular sites. Of course, the government wanted to sell off the highest value sites, leaving regulars and reserves in less pleasant locations. Regular army locations were less contentious than the reserves locations. The location of an army reserve centre is vital to recruiting, as reserves must travel to the centre in the evenings and at weekends. If it's miles out of the way, it's going to put them off. My A2020 team worked the problem out early, worked out what made a good location, took the time to travel around the country and check that the locations we chose would meet our needs and pitched for the ones we wanted.

But this meant a lot of moving for intelligence bases. Four of the five new reserve intelligence units needed to move sites. The leaders of all the cap-badges had all stated where we wanted to be and, not surprisingly, many picked the same places. The Reserve Forces & Cadets Associations (RFCAs), who manage the reserves estate wanted to retain all their sites, but that meant persuading people to be based in unpopular ones. This is how our Northern HQ had ended up in a lovely building, but a poor recruiting area. In contrast, regular locations were managed by the Defence Infrastructure Organisation (DIO), made up mostly of civilians or retired military. Neither organisation had any intention of being hurried or pressured by changing needs. The government however was keen to see quick change and place more reserves on regular sites. This made financial sense since regulars use bases from Monday to Friday in the daytime and reserves use them at weekends and in the evenings. The Army chiefs were also trying to move their people back from Germany and wanted to decide where they would move first. Reserves wanted their locations to be in the centre of towns – regular bases can be out of town, for reasons of vehicular access as well as cheaper real estate. And those who already were in prime real estate were not going to move without a fight.

With two different funding mechanisms, competing agendas and a history of the MOD having already sold off bases and housing stock for short term financial gain, it now had to face some of the longer-term consequences.

To unravel these needs, a series of meetings were arranged. New units like intelligence wanted 'in' to real estate quickly, old units that were closing wanted to hold out as long as possible. And no regular wanted to give up space on their bases for reserves. These meetings were like a trading floor. Each of us shouted out our needs while an adjudicator scribbled a note. At one tense meeting, the

RFCA tried to persuade me to take a TA centre in an impoverished area of Glasgow. I had done my research, since one of the sergeants in my team came from that area. He had said, 'You would be able to spot your recruits arriving, they would be the ones being mugged by the locals'. I was trying to say no with a little more subtlety than before and the RFCA was getting frustrated. The new head of army reserves was sitting nearby, and he started to chuckle at my struggles, but I didn't lose that day.

After many months of thrashing it through, we reached the final session. It was now a huge sheet of locations, caveats and sequencing. A very senior army officer arrived to have his Jean-Luc Picard moment (the firm but fair captain of the Enterprise, in *Star Trek: The Next Generation*), finishing with a, 'Now make it so'. He asked for final comments. The man from the DIO, who managed regular locations stood up. He gave a long speech, which amounted to, 'That's a great plan, General, but that's not how it will happen. First, we have to visit all the sites, update the site data, value each of the sites (it's not about the money, right?), then we can map all the requirements of new units and let you know if the plan is viable. The first stage will take about two years. Then we can look at when the moves start'.

This triggered a free-for-all. New units already had recruiting targets. We didn't have two years, we had about two months in which to establish our new bases. The basing plan became like a scenario from *Pirates of the*

Caribbean: more what you'd call guidelines than actual rules. Local negotiations became the norm. It was survival of the fastest. My team of three and I had to watch the 'master basing list' on a weekly basis for any hint of change and we worked to get our core new units onto sites as quickly as possible. Even one person in the new location meant you could 'hold the ground'.

In most cases, we ended up where we wanted to be, apart from one or two places which were compromises. There was one stage where all three new HQ sites (Bristol, Edinburgh and Manchester) were being managed by one poor regular who did an incredible job holding the plan together.

With Mason in Africa, I had twice the work. This was something of an own goal, since PSmith had hinted to me that Mason might not commit and yet I had championed his case. Thankfully I had experienced deputies more than willing to skirmish as needed. One of the challenges we spotted early on was that only one individual had been allocated to write the final implementation orders that would trigger the funding release and he was planning to take three weeks off to get married just as the orders were due for delivery. Intelligence had the most new units but with cap-badge nepotism we knew we had little chance of being at the front of the queue. So, my team helped by drafting all our final orders so that they were published on time. This was a real success; we were at the front of the queue and we managed to get all the MI units and the specialist unit in the first wave. We staggered them slightly, by our own choice, and in the end, this proved a real battle-winner and was worth all the hard work.

As Intelligence Corps reserves were doubling in size, we knew we would need to double the trade training places. The Army accepted from the start that basic training places would need to increase, but every soldier then also needed to move onto skilled trade training and Blue's view seemed to be that 'just because we are doubling in size doesn't mean we need more trade training places'. Well, it almost certainly did. But my team had been unable to persuade the regulars to provide additional places for reserves to train, so we set up a reserve team to take it on. This brought us into contact with another unsupportive regular. He was a relatively senior officer who seemed to believe reserves should listen and not speak. He had halted progress on reserves' issues due to 'other priorities'. I'll call him Captain White.

I went to see him to discuss the lack of progress in moving issues for reserves forward, but he decided to focus on the name of the new training team, rather than its function. He was keen to remove the R for reserve from the title and he had a verbal fight with one of my A2020 core team in which he said that we needed to respect his experience and let him decide the name of the training group. He didn't win this, and soon after the management of the reserve training team was handed to our London hub by Blue, who was keen to drop it from his brigade. The London hub did an excellent job but

White, who had been side-lined, didn't forget what he saw as a snub. Soon after this he walked past my team in Army HQ without acknowledging us and after that he refused to discuss further reserves issues. Without wanting or intending to, I had made an enemy.

The Government wanted reserve recruiting to grow fast, but the media were keen to show growth was poor. Most media supported Project Fear, the plan by some senior officers to show that reserves could never provide the numbers or quality to replace regulars and so the Government should reverse the downsize plan. We knew that the reserves could provide both quality and numbers, but what we needed was a standard system to calculate progress, not something I ever achieved.

Intelligence HQ was giving numbers showing that regular recruiting was consistently achieving higher numbers, while the numbers for reserves were lower. This indicated that adequate numbers of reserves couldn't be achieved, which I was certain was not true. Was Intelligence HQ no longer neutral? I asked my team to investigate and they found out that our HQ did not want the reserves growth plan to be seen as more successful than the regular one, so they delayed uploading reserve numbers until they had finished training, but recorded regular numbers when they started training. This was blatant manipulation.

Throughout this phase I had learned a great deal. The work was physically hard, though manageable, but I was saddened by some of what I saw. Learning about institutional power games wasn't fun, I wanted to believe in fair and open systems and they often weren't there. I understand that networking your way to success is necessary in senior roles, but I wasn't ready for the level of secret and dishonest manoeuvring. Nor was I ready to find that elements of the military were willing to damage the fighting power of the Army rather than accept change. And being naturally enthusiastic and energetic, I found it hard to work alongside any factions who were apathetic and who had worked out that they would still be promoted if all they did was clear their desks and get to the gym.

I also worked under great leadership and I felt a real sense of loss when PSmith moved on. He was one of the rare senior officers who could see that it is, at times, the reserves who are the professionals, which is why the Head of the Army wanted to bring them in. Not for soldiering skills, where they should be in support, but for their professional abilities - in HR, training, budgets, project management and niche specialities. Here, it is the reserves who could lead because regulars are not trained well in these areas and most do it badly.

I learned that one or two malign individuals can disrupt a plan from the inside far more easily than from outside. Intelligence calls this 'the insider threat', but I was not expecting to have to protect our plan from my own side, including from our HQs.

I was disappointed and frustrated that the antipathy towards reserves continued to be an issue throughout this period. Given how many regulars had served alongside reserves in Iraq and Afghanistan, the ongoing negative culture was surprising. But A2020 made it worse and a hard-core group of regulars seemed to hold reserves responsible for taking their jobs. It altered the narrative and reserve change leaders, like me, were an obvious target for anger. Either side of the entrenched middle resistors, at the top and bottom, there was genuine curiosity about what motivates reserves. Why do they serve? The assumption was that it was for money, but in my experience, there are only a few true reserves who work for cash. Full-time reserves do, but the vast majority, the part-timers, serve because they believe the UK needs a strong defence and they want to give something back.

But reserves still need that professional, regular beating heart, and morale during A2020 for regulars was low, particularly as we reviewed our humiliating withdrawal from Basra, Afghanistan and then had to face the plan for heavy cuts only a few years later. There was a feeling that government and senior leadership did not value effort or understand military needs. It was draining out the top talent, leaving behind too many who were discovering that doing the minimum was no longer a bar to promotion. It was particularly worrying because Army HQ is mostly officers and if morale was low there, it was probably worse among the soldiers.

Despite all the setbacks and roadblocks put in our way, we did succeed in creating the new intelligence reserve units. By late 2014, three years after I first took on the challenge, we had three shiny new battalions up and running, to complement the London hub. And what is more, we had stayed on target, fought for our bases and held onto most of our staff – just. Naysayers had told us it couldn't be done, yet we achieved results and had fun in the process. All the team, including me, would go on to better things. I take credit for bringing a fantastic bunch of people together, but it was teamwork that made the plan a reality.

(left) Me just before Sandhurst

WRAC at Sandhurst watching the men do tactics. We weren't allowed to join in at this point.

Learning to ski at Sandhurst – I took to it straightaway

Trying on my WRAC uniform at Sandhurst

Petticoat pass-out

WOMAN SOLDIER Diane Allen from Cheltenham made military history when she was commissioned at the Royal Military Academy, Sandhurst.

Diane, whose mother, Mrs. Margaret Allen, lives in Lockhampton-road, Cheltenham, was one of the first 30 officers from the Women's Royal Army Corps to train at the previously all-male Academy.

The WRAC College recently merged with

Sandhurst, and from May female cadets will also be accommodated there.

Diane, 19, has undertaken joint training with the men. To mark the first woman being commissioned there, the parade was taken by HRH the Duchess of Kent, Controller Commandant of the WRAC.

Diane, a keen sportswoman and a karate blue belt, now becomes a Troop Commander with 16 Signal Regiment in Krefeld, Germany

The Sovereign's Parade at Sandhurst was in the newspaper at the time

Sovereign's Parade in 1984

(below) In Germany about to serve Christmas lunch to the troops in men's mess kit

(above) me with rifle, training in Germany

(left) Parachuting in Germany

Leading a WRAC team in the Nijmegen
Marches, 1985

Kayaking off Trent Bridge

Finishing my first
half marathon

Skippering a RIB for military on the south coast

Glacier training around 2005

London – me inspecting the intelligence recruits around 2007

(left) First date with Newall

A rare shot of both me
and Newall in uniform

Receiving my OBE

Chapter Ten
Setting Up the Specialist Intelligence Unit

Nothing will be attempted if all possible objections must first be overcome

Samuel Johnson

In order to earn promotion, I needed to gain higher HQ staff experience, but because of the bias I was finding on the Army appointments boards, I couldn't get one of the top-tier, career-enhancing posts – those kept going to the same middle class white males, effectively keeping them on (and me off) what is known as the 'golden escalator' to the top.

I discussed it with my career manager and we agreed that the best way to show what I could do was to be 'double-hatted' - to overlap and volunteer for extra duties, taking on roles in higher HQ alongside my formal military roles. This is how I ended up first in the Intelligence HQ at Chicksands in 2008 and then in our military intelligence brigade for A2020 from late 2011 to

2013. By the end of this spell I had significantly increased my military knowledge and skill set including covering the senior intelligence reserve post in Army HQ, from late-2012 to mid-2013. And my efforts did work. I was getting excellent reports, and on 25 March 2010 I received a letter from the career management branch at Glasgow saying that I had graded high enough for command. This meant that I could apply for a post to command a unit – a huge step in military terms which would give me a much better chance of future promotion. But I was now playing in senior officers' territory and there were many blocks, games and challenges ahead. I needed to up my game, but to do that I needed to understand the game, and that wasn't going to be easy.

Typically, the first choice for commanding a unit is in your own trade, mine being intelligence, but when I first hit the command window in 2010, intelligence didn't have any units for reserves to command. For the small corps reserves (including intelligence), this meant we had to fight to get promoted against all other cap-badges so there were only two options: either commanding a training unit or a University Officer Training Corps (UOTC).

To put it into context, 2011 was the start of a chaotic time for the army which would continue until 2015, as it underwent a period of huge change and restructuring. This began in the autumn of 2011 when General Sir Nick Carter became the architect of A2020 following our withdrawal from Iraq. We were still in

Afghanistan, budgets and manpower were really stretched and both had been unpopular wars. The military-political decision was taken to re-shape the Army and at the same time make cost-savings. The highlights were to focus on whole force concept, integrating regulars and reserves, plus to re-structure the staff at Army HQ, move the Army back from Germany, save money and hand back army bases. Chaos.

Career management for reserves had been pretty good until then. We had our own career management staff, MS6, and it worked well. But as part of A2020 it was decided there would be the same system for both regulars and reserves. Great in principle, but messy in practice and disastrous for reserves, who became second class soldiers and officers.

The biggest change took place from the end of September 2013 to December 2014, although it continued until spring 2015. And during this time anyone stuck in the critical career phases – and that was me – experienced cockups. The Glasgow careers staff were under-resourced, there was very low morale and many of the regulars were either not trained or not interested in taking on reserves' career management. Subsequently there was no clear policy for reserves, just vague advice to 'establish a relationship with the regular career manager' and cross your fingers.

It was messy, but despite that chaos, I had a good relationship with my first two intelligence career managers. Both were overworked but they did their best to help and I was advised to seek command of a South-West UOTC. Women were just starting to reach the level of applying for senior mainstream posts, but many appointments really needed a re-write to reflect the broader career paths that women had taken. Sadly, those re-writes didn't happen and many jobs still cited 'combat experience' as essential, even for non-combat-related roles. The Army also chose this time to reorganise the UOTCs into 'super-groups' and a complicit decision was taken to give preference to combat-experienced reserves. This was illegal, but I have a colleague who sat on a shadow-board who confirmed that it happened and top-scoring women were overlooked in favour of lesser-scoring but combat-experienced men.

The upshot was that women did not yet have equality, especially in senior roles. I lost out and was not sure what my next step should be. With perfect timing, PSmith sent me a text asking if I wanted to command one of the new reserve intelligence units we had set up. I said yes. I would only find out later that his wishes were not supported by intelligence HQ, although I never found out why. Perhaps simply because they had their own ideas about slowing the pace of change and wanted to keep three of the four new intelligence reserve units under regular command. They were able to influence those ever-present shadow-boards and I lost out again.

Frustrated, I rang my career manager, a regular intelligence officer who managed the careers of officers, both reserve and regular. He pointed out that there was still command of the new specialist group up for grabs. It wasn't yet a formal command, but the plan was to apply for that as the unit took shape. We will call this group the SIU, or Specialist Intelligence Unit, to be formed as an extension of TIU and that would work alongside regular intelligence to provide technical, regional and industrial expertise.

Since I had previously been chief of staff of the smaller TIU, this would be right up my street. Added to which it was the one closest to my heart. During my time with the TIU I had found I really loved working with this group of deep specialists- they had a slightly disruptive, irreverent, questioning and challenging mindset. The initial mission given by General Carter had been to set them up to 'bring the outside in' – meaning to capture technical skills and those from industry and science to help with defence. But, we needed a group that was also capable of bringing the inside (those rather sclerotic entrenched middle army thinkers) out to see what was possible in wider industry and of benefit to defence.

With appreciative thanks to my career manager (sometimes you need the obvious pointing out) I got my application in and got the job. It was still part-time, which I wanted, and I believed at the time it would get me a command 'tick' as my next big step towards promotion.

It was late 2012 when I heard and my official start was to be in February 2014, so I had about 18 months to prepare. Smiley applied for one of the roles in the new unit as his next posting and I was keen to have him on-board;

172

his ability to recruit the right people and to network and write on intelligence matters was almost unique. Well before my official start the two of us began to base ourselves half and half between the new site for the TIU, near Newbury, and Army HQ. Space was still at a premium, so we knew we needed to be on the ground to make sure we got a set of offices.

Before I began my new post, I went on a refresher course on internet security at Chicksands. A smartly dressed young Lance-Jack (a Lance Corporal, the first rank for soldiers) was sitting near me.

'Which unit are you from?' I asked.

'6MI,' he said. 'Not many people know of us, we are quite new. It's in Manchester.'

'I do know about 6MI,' I said. 'How's it going?'

'Really good, we have a reserve CO (*commanding officer*).'

'Colonel Pxxx', I said. 'Yes, I know. Does that work?'

'It does, she understands what we need.'

I smiled- part of me wanted to tell him that I had set up that unit, but I didn't. I was happy just to know that it was doing well and growing and that the commanding officer was not just a reserve, but a woman.

I started the new job full of optimism. Getting a new unit up and running, I was told, was often 'nigh impossible'. But how hard could it be? After all, as the great Muhammad Ali once said, 'Impossible is just a big word thrown around by small men who find it easier to live in the world they have been given than to explore the power they have to change it'.

I soon bumped up against my first problem; I was in charge of a concept rather than anything tangible. We had fought for and won our location, but we hadn't yet been allocated a building, offices or furniture. We didn't even have an email address. All we had was the London intelligence hub as our support until we were able to stand alone. I did have the original 13 TechINT specialists from the London hub but that felt a little like the original 13 stars of the American flag – we needed a bit more mass to have an impact. I had authority to grow the unit to over 100, but first I had to find them and to do that I needed a home ... and a budget ... and some staff. The size of the challenge began to dawn.

Even top cover was unavailable because so much was in transition. The Intelligence Brigade was being merged with the surveillance elements of the Royal Artillery and a few others under A2020 plans and the new, bigger organisation above us was yet to form. We were like teenagers about to leave home: excited, itching to leave, but not knowing what was ahead.

Take a breath and focus on the 'what?' My task was to *bring the outside in*. General Carter wanted to increase intellectual horsepower, decrease paralysis of innovation and reduce institutionalised thinking. The draining of talent, as I have mentioned, had been worst in the middle ranks, leaving a disproportionate number of plodders. There was the vision at the top, the bottom had the energy

– but the blocks were in the middle. The general didn't want specialists to replace his professional soldiers, he wanted people who could offer alternative, knowledgeable views and who were willing to think for themselves. This vision really wasn't about money. It was about diversity.

My vision was to pair these specialists and experts with reserves who were ex-regulars and intelligencers. There is a known challenge with specialists, something that was illustrated well in the TV series, *M*A*S*H*. Deep specialists are deep because they focus on one thing, in *M*A*S*H* it was army surgeons, saving lives at the front-line of the Korean War. Regulars are usually the opposite, rarely specialists but adaptable to most situations and trained to know what the commander wants and when. As the surgeons in *M*A*S*H* found, trying to do your best work in the crude disorder, fast pace and brutal chaos of war will always require compromise. The deep specialists need the regulars and vice-versa. My job was to find people with deep expertise, provide them with enough military training so they could integrate and understand the Army and then, most importantly, pair them with seasoned military operatives who understood conflict.

Would the regulars welcome this type of reserve? Or would it turn into tragicomedy, like *M*A*S*H*? I was determined to find out. What I didn't expect was the journey to last as long as the Korean War. At least it didn't last as long as the TV series.

The social background at this time was important. The optimism of the 90s was over and, 70 years after the

D-Day landings, we were forgetting how to enjoy peace and nationalism; intolerance and polarised views were returning. We were entrenched in old feuds: Syria, the wider Middle East, Israel-Palestine, India-Pakistan and more, yet at the same time we were less willing to be involved.

Softer liberal coalitions in Europe had created harder outliers: the right and left extremists were polarising and circling for opportunities, Momentum in the UK, Trump's right in America, among many others.

At the same time the great post-war collaborations (EU, UN, NATO) were weakened due to lack of common purpose, repeated financial bailouts and poor leadership. Spiralling, ageing and unhealthy populations threatened future prosperity. Single states were on the rise. Russia and China were making gains against polarised coalitions and exploiting new trade routes and collaborations through investment, particularly in the South China Sea and the Arctic.

Newer, non-state ideologies were rising – most notably ISIS with its siren call to arms, particularly for young, disenfranchised Muslims. Unbound by state legislation, they could exploit online messaging in a way governments were unable or unwilling to do. A global caliphate led by strong men was considered more appealing to some than an increasingly leaderless western society. Physical fear of terrorism was heightened and so was emotional fear, what with non-stop news online and trolls and bullies reaching into our homes, to young and old. Trust was fading while fake news, opinions over fact and censorship were tarnishing the joy of information. And despite the many channels for communication, there was a sense of growing loneliness.

Mob hysteria was easy to provoke, hard to turn off. We became incensed, shocked and outraged by minor things, yet silent on bigger things: use of drones, AI, robots and autonomous vehicles. Our online innocence was being stolen by new tools for propaganda - the whispering voice online not necessarily Eve from Croydon, but possibly Ivan from Moscow (or a trained bot).

There were increasing concerns over poor mental health as we were less able to speak of our views and, in the absence of real debate, what was left was banal online entertainment rather than engaging with the real world. None of this was making us feel good.

We were changing and so was our planet, with global warming, rising sea-levels, plastic pollution, antibiotic resistance and Ebola. Scientists were advocating a precautionary approach and action by governments to curb human effects even as the debate on human responsibility for change raged on. And meanwhile an excess of input had made us fat, anxious and disinterested in civic duties. We were becoming victims, not owners of our destinies.

Did all of this make me worried? Yes, alongside many defence thinkers. I believed we needed to be building our resilience, emotionally and physically, for these changing times, and at the same time re-establishing our responsibilities towards society and one another.

My new unit, SIU, was to be one small part of that plan. But there was a lot to do to make it a reality. On the 70th anniversary of the D day landings, June 6, 2014, I sat in Southwick Park, Hampshire, home of the D-Day maproom. I arrived early and sat alone as I had so often on Friday evenings, in a deserted military officers' mess. It was the perfect spot for reflection, with the original map still there on the wall, inspiring both awe and determination. My aim was to be visionary not only in who we brought in, but how we led them. I wanted to allow reserves to serve in a way that suited them and to find a way to reduce the experience of too many reserves - that the full-timers found them a nuisance. I wanted my permanent staff to be willing to attend weekends and to grasp every opportunity. And I wanted to bring in reserves who understood the importance of being honest with their time, turning up when they said they would. It started well - we were still a fresh concept and all the reserves in the group did turn up that weekend.

A few weeks later we were given permission to move into the new site. In the summer of 2014, I left Bedfordshire in a transit van, along with my one full-time officer, Smiley, and a few bits of furniture and office supplies. The Army way, if the system can't help, is to 'acquire' what you need. It's not stealing, as such, since it's army property and we asked the former owners, it's more a case of 'liberating' or re-homing items.

We met a representative of the local 'get you in' team at the Berkshire site and were allocated an office – a room with broken chairs, a single phone and no internet. It was like being on operations overseas. Smiley and I stood in the middle of the room staring at one another, bemused by the whole situation.

Smiley and I were both from the Werner Herzog school of thought that 'everyone should pull a boat over a mountain once in their lifetime'. We loved and were frustrated by the military in equal parts. He had pulled a few large objects over mountains in his career, while writing a PhD along the way – I hope someday that he'll write his own book about it. This time we were about to find that the large object had a sign on it saying, 'We don't want reserves on our camp'. We walked around the building, reading the structural survey. It was condemned, with broken toilets, non-existent heating and no air-conditioning. There was Legionnaire's Disease in the pipes, the ceilings leaked, and the power was intermittent. A normal army building then, we joked.

I made a quick case for a second office and the space in between so that we had somewhere for our reserves. There was already pressure to recruit - amusingly, we had been classed (alongside all other new units) as 'failing', before we got an office. This was true army Catch 22 thinking during the chaos of A2020 transition. All the cap-badges that gained new units under A2020 (Intelligence, REME, Engineers and so on) started, inevitably, with very low numbers. And we had to get into our new locations in order to recruit. Since settling into our location had been delayed by more red tape, we couldn't yet recruit. Meanwhile the Army, defensive in the face of adverse media reports, started recording all units, even the new ones, as a percentage of their final 2020 numbers. So, I started with 13 of 115. So far so good – except that any unit that was less than 60% manned was rated as failing. I had to send a quarterly report explaining why.

When we finally moved into our new home it was quiet, as few of the other new A2020 tenants had arrived. I was allocated one regular PSI (permanent staff instructor), a sergeant-trainer who was outstanding and worked hard to get us going. And we recruited an excellent pay sergeant. These two worked very well together and began to build a wider team and an ethos while Smiley and I worked to recruit and create the broader organisation.

My orders said I was commanding a unit, yet my status was not command. A number of posts in the Army are stuck in this limbo - they are what I decided to call 'near command' posts, with all of the responsibility and none of the perks. Near-command posts don't get drivers, cars, a house (with cleaner), an adjutant, a clerk and so on. And they don't get recognised as having been in command by career managers. So, wait … I start up this unit, run it, all with poor and inadequate resources, and I get less recognition? Hmmm. Also, it didn't authorise me to attend the commanding officers' course. This meant I was doubly disadvantaged as I didn't get the training to command either. I read on a forum that the advice given on the course was to 'keep your head down, just pass the unit inspections and don't cause your boss any problems' as the surest way to the top, so perhaps I wasn't missing much.

There is no obvious reason why my post wasn't full command, since there were smaller units that did get a full command tick. That lack of a command tick would turn out to be a huge setback to my hopes of progressing in my career, as the Army career path selectors could choose to ignore 'near-command' leaders, but when I took the job I didn't know any of this.

At one stage I spoke to a general about it. He said that my unit and quite a few others deserved to be commands and he would write me up as if it was command, but the Army would resist making them commands because they were unwilling to offer all the budgetary perks that came with it. My view was that you should at least get a promotion tick for this - you do the same job but without all the things that make it easier. It was a tough lesson for me to learn.

For a blissful few months we were on our own, waiting for the other reserves' unit, the Security Assistance Group (SAG), to arrive. The SAG was similar to our unit, all reserve specialists, with a small regular core – they just had different skills. But when their vanguard arrived, it seemed that things had changed. A lot. The numbers were the same, but the concept was now bigger. It was the start of one of the Army's 'big ideas'- a step towards an 'information formation' as I liked to call it. The SAG boss, a quixotic brigadier I will call Don Quixote, wanted to build it around the ethos of the Chindits, which seemed a little odd to me. The Chindits were the creation of a British Army brigadier for the Burma Campaign in the latter half of WWII. My understanding of Don Quixote's reasoning was he was looking for a strong brand and he liked the long-range penetration, targeting of enemy communications and 'special forces' mystique that the Chindits had. The fact that the Chindits weren't universally seen as a successful brand and its leader was killed would probably have steered me away from that particular choice.

Officially we weren't part of his empire- our own parent brigade was still forming, many miles away. My boss was brigade commander of a different brigade, besides which he was not yet in post and would be based near Andover. We were working to a station commander who was supposed to be neutral and treat everyone fairly. Except that our station commander was one of Don Quixote's officers and was in no way neutral, so we ended up being placed second on every priority list. For example, my brilliant regular PSI came to see me and told me that he had been told that the drivers, the vehicles, the clothing store, the feeding and training facilities were all going to be held back from us. I had never come across this attitude before on any camp- it was a truly hostile environment.

When the SAG settled in and re-branded (I will call them the Long Rangers), they ordered us to surrender posts to form a larger station support unit, claiming that if we all pooled resources, it would be cost-effective. I fought against it; we had already surrendered some posts to Blue's 2012 plan to form the basic support unit even though experience told me it wouldn't work reserve-friendly hours. But even better, when we looked for it, it didn't exist. The Long Rangers had hoovered up those posts, now wanted more and said they would now support 'anyone on camp', something that was already proving to be untrue.

We needed to grow the SIU very quickly or risk being disbanded as a failing unit. Smiley and I knew the types we wanted, and he took on the role of going out to find them. Soon, we had a steady trickle of incredible CVs coming in. At interview we were reminded of just how many people do exaggerate their talents, but there were also some excellent candidates. The ones we selected demonstrated three things: intellectual rigour, a career focused around one subject and compatibility with the military.

Historically intelligence in defence started with intellectual outsiders supporting a military centre. Now we were continuing that tradition and at the same time making our own history. I asked some of the first cohort to pick our emblem and motto. I was inundated with beautifully explained Greek and Latin symbols and mythology, some of which I have kept as mementoes. Yet, like Einstein, many of these great brains struggled to boil a kettle and were unable to stay together in convoy or find a classroom. What I needed was a small team of ex-regulars to 'herd the cats'. It proved difficult; we could get ex-regulars to join, but it was hard to get them to attend at weekends, which was when we needed them.

Despite the many hiccups, within a few months of starting, we were growing. Our Friday night gatherings became legendary for fascinating conversation. I boasted once to a potential recruit about these erudite discussions, only for the team to discuss the science of porn on the evening he visited. Our children will try us...

I travelled to our career centre in Glasgow, to explain what recruits we needed and was warmly received. Our intelligence HQ willingly provided top-cover and the small issues on site were handled by our London hub. I had planned a six-week trip over that first Christmas, island hopping through the Pacific, and I felt able to take the break. Things were running okay.

The first harbinger of deep difficulty was my brilliant permanent staff instructor promoting early and having to leave. He had been the epitome of the professional regular, sharing his knowledge and herding the SIU 'cats' as he described them – and they loved him for it. What he said at his leaving do was tough to hear. He had been told by the Long Rangers that they had been ordered to block our growth (just as at Sandhurst and again at Army HQ, groups had been ordered to impede change). It explained why the facilities were mysteriously closed at weekends when we needed them. He confirmed the obstructive plan by the station and apologised to all of the SIU as he couldn't believe that we were getting this treatment – unprecedented in his experience. His replacement was fine, although he didn't have quite the same breadth of talent.

In theory, the Government's decision was right, and it makes sense to have reserves on a regular base. Regulars use facilities from Monday to Friday, reserves use them at weekends. The original A2020 plan by General Carter had a balanced set of units at the Newbury site; the SAG was made up of mostly reserves and smaller and the SIU was to be paired with a regular intelligence hub. We would be about the same size and there was also to be a third, smaller reserve intelligence company on the site, all of which meant that there would have been parity. The site was also the right size and had the right facilities for this plan. What changed and how is not completely known to me, it was a decision by the heads of the Army of the time to offer the command of the SAG (which would probably have been a colonel's job) to a more senior brigadier. This meant that it became a Brigade and therefore much larger. The Newbury site and the allocated SAG units and numbers didn't appear to match Don Quixote's ambition, so he was constantly trying to grow it by pushing out us smaller units. Incidentally, the issue is still not resolved. The Long Rangers is now on its third commander who is still trying to get it to work because the site and the numbers are fundamentally wrong for the new task.

The Long Rangers' change in plan meant they didn't have enough of anything for their ambitions. To them it made sense to keep everything they could and drive us out, but it was institutional bullying. We were part of a strict hierarchy and weren't authorised to speak directly to their HQ. It was hard to fight back.

I spent many fruitless hours negotiating with the station commander to keep our resources, but gradually we began to lose ground. As more Long Rangers arrived, they started to push us out. When we didn't move, the station boss declared the offices we were in as an 'essential coffee-room'. Yes really, coffee was essential.

A sofa appeared. I called this phase 'sofa-wars' as he ordered his people to maintain a steady roster of individuals to sit on it throughout the day. My team were bemused. It got worse. The station boss put in writing that reserves were not to use facilities without his permission, but regulars could. The Long Rangers still had a few reserves who also found themselves relegated to tents or transit bunks when they turned up for weekend work. We were paupers looking in. One such weekend, when reserves were accommodated in a tent during a snowstorm, they held a regular selection for what was described as an 'SAS-style forward unit'. The regular candidates were accommodated in heated rooms, with beds and duvets; the reserves in cold canvas tents on cots as the station refused to allocate them any rooms.

It was time for me to raise the matter higher.

Hierarchies are really important in the military. We all have a chain we must follow from the soldier at the bottom right the way to the top. In this sense it isn't that different to any business. But where it differs from business models is in the rigidity of the rule that soldiers cannot negotiate or discuss business outside of their chain of command. It's essential in battle but a pain in peacetime. The rules meant that I couldn't talk to Quixote because he was senior and not in my chain of command; I had to approach my superior.

By this time the intelligence brigade had been absorbed into a much bigger, nineteen-unit formation (which I will call Spider19), and we were the smallest unit. My new boss was now in post. And although there were no combat units in the brigade, it was run by a combat specialist, since commanding one of these brigades is necessary for future career progression and he was one of those carefully selected to succeed. We will call him Flashheart.

Flashheart came to see my situation, amused that the station lead had put in writing that he would treat reserves worse than regulars. He took him aside and said, 'You might want to think again on this one, you don't want to be a Sun headline'.

I was hopeful, but in fact nothing changed and within weeks, the Long Rangers increased the pressure. Our own chain was able to push them back the first time but were not based on site. When it kept happening, I was told by Flashheart that he had bigger issues to resolve and I had to sort it myself.

I was on my own.

188

Chapter Eleven
Trouble Brewing

Hard pressed on my right, my centre is yielding, impossible to manoeuvre, situation excellent – I am going to attack
Ferdinand Foch at the Battle of Marne

Early in 2015 I was blue listed, which meant being put onto the shortlist for senior promotion in the next twelve months. It would mean leaving the SIU early, but I knew I still had time to get it going and meanwhile the prospect of upward change to full colonel was exciting.

I had a new career manager by this time, we'd established a good rapport and when he was visiting Chicksands we sat down together to plan my next role. The idea was to look at positions coming up in the next year, consider which I might be likely to get and see whether there were any courses that would strengthen my case.

My expected promotion made it easier with my near-command issues. One of the residual issues we had from A2020 was the rank structures. The plan had been to rank-range all specialist posts, but instead the Army allocated all the highest ranks only and that meant I had seven others the same rank as me. It only worked if all accepted my near-command authority and now that promotion was on the cards, most of them did.

There was one tricky character though, a new major posted in purely to gain promotion. He challenged my authority and while it wasn't quite mutiny on The Bounty, it was close. My senior team became split, unhappy with the slow progress and some supported his more aggressive approach. This was trouble - I needed them to back me, but one or two were now backing what was an obvious leadership bid from my colleague.

Although I had little line-management or mentoring, there was a lead reserve who was an ex-regular with a lot of experience and who I could talk to. He had a busy day job, so I wouldn't say he was keen to take the role of mentor to me, but he had the skills. I'll call him Sirius, after the brightest star in the night sky (or Harry Potter's godfather and mentor). I went to see him to discuss my problem and he diagnosed two issues: firstly, if I didn't have line-management authority over the seven at my rank, of course they would go to whoever did and secondly, although it was exactly what my mutinous colleague wanted, he advised I let him move to where he wanted to go. While I didn't want to do it, Sirius was of course right. I was desperately short-staffed but keeping a troublemaker on the team was worse. Sirius arranged for me to have career management rights over my senior team and we moved the mutineer. It was the right decision because his behaviour was unpredictable and an unnecessary distraction from what I needed to be doing. He had only been parked with me to gain promotion.

I found another ally in my boss' boss. He was an engineer and a more approachable individual than Flashheart. He could see the challenges for reserves' leaders in regular HQs and was active in making it easier. He had published guidelines for the new commanding officers. My favourite piece of advice was, 'Don't let the troops see how much it hurts'. I followed this bit of wisdom; I was upset by two colleagues who had supported the rebel, but I let it go and used the negative energy I was feeling to build my network. I emailed an intelligence colleague and luckily, she was available to join SIU part-time to lead the day to day operations. I will call her Barbara, after Barbara Lauwers, a strategist and influencer in the US Women's Army Corps.

Despite the hitches and 'two steps forward one step back' moments, things were progressing well. I had a great relationship with the Intelligence Corps and, other than Blue, who was not a true intelligencer since he'd transferred from infantry, I had found them my sort of people. Blue had now moved, on promotion, to an influential role in Spider19 and was causing me niggling difficulties, but he was only an isolated voice. Until a new intelligence lead arrived.

I will call him Major Orange. He came with a mixed reputation and I had been warned he didn't like women or reserves, so I knew I was already two strikes down. I met him for the first time in London to give him an introductory brief to the SIU. He was abrupt, offering me only 20 minutes, even though our meeting was pre-arranged. At the end, he asked no questions and said only that he didn't like my briefing style.

Alarm bells went off. As an ex-regular myself, this is not how such a meeting normally goes. I would have expected an interview with coffee (you will recall this means friendly – whereas without coffee means trouble) and an effort to build rapport. Back in my office, I sought out views from friends within intelligence. Why had he been so hostile? I couldn't understand it. I could only hope that this was just him on a bad day and things would get better.

I wanted him to be proud of the SIU and invested in its future. It was growing and gaining accolades. We were running technical weekends; blowing stuff up, showing new reserves how the Army worked and applying great lateral thinking to gnarly military problems. I was growing a great team and it was fun. All I wanted was to have the backing to carry on with that and get the unit up to full strength before my coming promotion.

Spider19 first established in September 2014 and that month the senior soldiers and the officers went to Cyprus for a week for its inauguration. The build-up was tough. The Long Rangers were being more intransigent than ever, refusing us vehicles, insisting we re-do our military driving tests and blocking access to funds. I eventually got a hire car to get to the airport, to see all the regulars arriving in their chauffeured staff cars, their adjutants handing them briefing packs.

At the start I was the only reserve and the only woman. When I arrived, I went over to sit with the intelligence regulars, most of whom I knew. This event was their first time in front of the new boss, Flashheart, and there was a distracted atmosphere in which a primordial pecking-order was being established. Although I knew them, each one in turn moved away from my table to join other regular groups and I was left with my coffee. It was awkward and I was left wondering where things were going.

Over the next few days as the jostling went on, I started to identify the high-flyers. They were the ones who were not threatened by a reserve and who welcomed me into conversations. They had grace to spare and were friendly. It was quite an eye opener. There were gaps in my military knowledge compared to most of the regular commanders and while some were keen to expose my weaknesses, others took the time to support me. It was a difficult and informing week.

One day, we did a squadded run up the Troodos Mountain. Running as a squad is challenging, as you have to adapt your pace to the pack, and this was a tough uphill run. I knew my fitness had slipped and, along with others, I dropped behind the pack. That evening, as it got dark, I decided to run it again, on my own. I was enjoying the solitude and thinking that I had to be the only mug running in the dark, when three runners went past, with a cheery, 'Hi Diane, nice night for a run.'

They went cruising past at three times my pace, still chatting easily. These three, who I recognised as a trio from special forces, had been friendly all week, as had the artillery group. It was only the main body of intelligencers who shunned me, which had come as something of a shock. It was my first realisation that senior leaders need to be thick-skinned and I wasn't. I needed to grow some armour quickly.

Flashheart was a talker, not a listener. We were briefed early that 'he doesn't like bad news'. At the Cyprus inauguration, Flashheart kept repeating how the Army was run by 'middle class, middle aged white men' and emphasising that this 'needs to change'. Looking around the room, I didn't see any evidence this was likely. It was a classic example of when words and body tone don't match: his words said the right thing, but his tone and body language said it was working just fine for him. There were only 2 women, 1 reserve and 1 person of colour out of around 60 people. The chief staffer, a floppy haired officer I will call Rupert had already set his stall by telling us that when he was unsure of a decision, he always asked himself, 'What would the Queen do?' I decided that this brigade's definition of diverse was probably 'representing all of the home counties and public schools in UK'.

One of the decisions we had to make collectively was to select the new brigade emblem. We had been sitting for an hour debating; would it be a dog, a panther or a spider? The unit leaders, we were told, were to get a free vote and Flashheart would leave the room to ensure this happened. Rupert turned back after Flashheart left, and with a wink said, 'By the way, the commander likes the spider'.

The spider it was. I voted for the panther.

The week finished on a low, with a deeply misogynist lecturer from the Army Warfare Centre. Seeing his male-dominated audience, the speaker expressed views I hadn't heard in years. He kept using the phrase, 'women in comfortable shoes' (a derogatory term for lesbians) with a wink. This time I did speak up. But by doing so, I had marked my card. It wasn't done to raise this kind of issue – to do so instantly branded you a troublemaker, we were expected to simply grit our teeth and put up with sexism and misogyny. I had tried to raise it subtly, mentioning it to Rupert when he was on his own. He responded positively, the speaker wasn't invited back, but it changed our relationship and after that I could sense his wariness towards me.

The week highlighted my status in Spider19 as 'different'. It was, and still is, the challenge for true reserves. We don't quite speak the language; we are juggling a second job with the Army job and are more likely to be out of tune. In highly competitive, male-dominated arenas, the pack can be quick to spot weakness and take down an individual. There is a subtle difference in language between the regulars and the reserves. When I was in the camp during the week and talking to regulars wearing the same uniform the conversation would be friendly – at first. But in some cases (they weren't all this prejudiced), as they noticed my use of reserve phrasing, they would become wary and treat me as an outsider.

I needed more allies, some wingmen and women to watch my back and negotiate with the Long Rangers support staff. And soon after Cyprus, I found one. A smart Rifles officer turned up in response to my open advertisement. Despite my wariness towards infantry, there was an instant rapport between us. Here was a poacher turned game-keeper type. We had almost nothing in common except our love of the military and a desire to make SIU work. He was to be the third element I needed alongside Smiley and Barbara. He was my Patrick Harper. (In the Sharpe series of novels Sergeant Patrick Harper was the belligerent rifles sergeant who became Sharpe's most trusted companion).

Within weeks, Harper started to ease the situation with the Long Rangers. He went across and sat down with them, pointing out that he knew all the tricks of the game and could not be hoodwinked. They had been running rings around us precisely because I hadn't been allocated someone with the training for this role. Harper made all the difference.

In November 2015, Newall went solo to the South pole for nearly three months (as part of the Seven Summits Grand Slam). I didn't want to be at home alone all that time, so I left Smiley in charge for six weeks and roamed alone, with just my backpack, across Chile, Easter

Island, Tahiti, Fiji and Samoa, returning back via Hawaii and Los Angeles.

It was the most beautiful time. As I roamed from island to island, Newall and I were connected by satellite tracker and could text. We didn't talk except on his birthday and the day he reached the Pole – it was too expensive – but we were probably closer in those two months as I wasn't focused on work and I had time to talk to him via text. We did remote physio consultations when he hurt his ribs and I shared his journey as he did mine. It was a surreal bond we shared as we travelled and one of my happiest shared memories with him.

I went back to work refreshed and believing that things were on the up, but I couldn't have been more wrong. There were rumours of big plans and reorganisations on camp. We had fought them off before and hoped we could again. Within weeks of me returning, we were ordered to move immediately. I challenged this, only to be shown an email which confirmed that Blue had secretly agreed this with the head of the restructure team. The second time he had booted me out.

This time I was shocked. As a commander, the higher formation should have let me know and given me time to tell my staff, but instead I found out alongside my team. I went to see Blue, whose dismissive response can be summarised as, 'Reserves are not entitled to offices, computers or phones'. He had allocated sufficient rooms in another building for my team of nine full-timers only.

I was part-time, and so was Barbara, so we weren't included, along with the other 45 or so reserves.

'It's a reserve centre as well,' I pointed out.

He shrugged. 'I have more important priorities. Make do.'

'Where am I meant to command from?' I said. 'The corridor?'

He was already leaving for another meeting and he ignored me. My relationship with Blue broke down that day. I took the evidence to his boss, Orange, who declared it, 'Untidy and unsatisfactory'. He promised to look into it, but as far as I know, he never did.

So, we made do, because that is the Army way. Harper and I thrashed through a compromise with the base to give us a few extra rooms and computers in another building in return for a quick move. What they wouldn't fix were the carpets. They had been using the building as a dog kennel. Harper and his team arranged for paint and new carpets and fixed it themselves.

I have spoken to other reserve commanders of this time and found they were experiencing the same kinds of prejudice and pressures – the result of the regular army's anger about reserves taking jobs under A2020. In meetings, regulars would express antipathy towards reserves unchallenged. Resentment of pension rights, medical care and leave allocation were the commonest complaints, but mostly there was a reluctance to support any reserves' growth activity of any kind.

Spider19 was half reserves, yet our meetings focused only on regular issues. Flashheart would talk solidly at his 19 commanders for an hour or more (which at least had the effect of bonding his unfortunate audience). Only Sirius would occasionally speak up. At one meeting, focussed on a large change that had occurred within Army HQ, Sirius interrupted to ask how it affected reserves. He was slapped down with an angry, 'Not now'. It had been clear for months that there was tension between the two of them and Flashheart did nothing to hide his contempt.

After talking to other reserve commanders, I realised I couldn't fix the anger many of the regulars felt towards us. The brigade was over-busy and had little time for reserve support. It was raised at a reserve meeting, only for Blue to turn to all of us and say, 'Get used to it, it's going to get worse not better. We have too much to do'. Ironic that he was the one who had given away so much of our manpower – now, I felt, conveniently 'forgotten'.

Was I frustrated? Yes. But my way is always to look for the path through and the best way to carry on. And to take seriously my responsibilities towards others. And I had some excellent people now with me. The reserves call the volume of paperwork needed to run an army NAB (Nugatory Administrative Bo****ks). In our HQ, Barbara was doing a great job of eating up the NAB, checking the quality of everything we produced and connecting us with other intelligencers. And Smiley was finding ways to build a network and to expedite the recruiting process. He built the external network with customers, found potential recruiting opportunities and conducted all the interviews. He was outstanding at writing think-pieces and working with technical, industry and science specialists. Recruiting is an 'extra' role for reserve units, regulars don't need to do it, they just have troops posted in. The Army recognised this and allocated short-term recruiters during A2020. Despite these positive moves, there was trouble brewing within. We had recruited a man who, it rapidly transpired, didn't fit in – I shall call him Mac.

Because he was wearing officer's rank, although actually still a soldier, only Smiley and I were available to interview him, no others in my unit were of the right rank. Our 'parent company' offered to do a phone interview and he was interviewed by the head of personnel (the RAO) and I spoke to the personnel branch chief at Chicksands who knew him and 'thought he was all right'. I also rang and spoke to two of his former employing officers who gave him good verbal references, checked his annual reports and he interviewed well, telling us how keen he was to be part of the new unit. But there were warning signs. He had a delayed annual report, which should have been a flag to me, and Smiley warned me he wasn't sure about him but couldn't put a finger on why. Despite this I hired him – I was desperate for someone to sort out the admin, which wasn't Smiley's strong suit. It was probably the biggest mistake in my career, because I found out later that there was no probationary period and no ability to remove him from post once he was appointed. To be fair, I didn't have a lot of choice since he had been given preferred candidate status by Glasgow, having been made redundant from another FTRS post in the same region. But it was my first big error; I had fallen for an old trick and recruited him too quickly.

Mac didn't settle well, and I knew within a month of him starting it wasn't going to work out.

Almost immediately it was obvious his knowledge was out of date. He wanted to work from home, even though we had no laptops or military phones so I had no idea how that might work. And he wanted to leave early, play golf and go flying. For Smiley, who was his line manager, it became an immediate issue. Smiley decided to conduct a performance review and encourage some refresher training. Except that he couldn't pin Mac down for the meeting. There was always an excuse – Mac couldn't make it, he got the date wrong, something had come up elsewhere on camp and so on.

We only found out later that Mac had been avoiding performance reviews in this way for ten years. He had become an expert in avoidance and he clearly wasn't about to accept a review now. Sadly, if he had put the same effort into producing any work, he might have been a good employee.

Further down the line, I spoke to two units that had given him good reports and they admitted they had given him the grade he had asked for rather than risk a complaint. The second unit provided a file of the actions they had been taking to address his insufficiencies. They had taken the easy way out by making his post redundant.

By early 2015, when Mac had been with us for 6 months, Barbara told me that his subordinates were reporting difficulties working for Mac. Harper added that two of our staff were threatening to leave because of his behaviour – he was refusing to work with them and claiming that they disliked him. My second error was getting involved, although even with hindsight, I had very few options with such a small team.

I decided to sit him down, formally, to agree a way forward. I hoped we could get things back onto a positive footing, but his reaction to my intervention was immediately aggressive. I have seen it before with difficult staff but what I hadn't witnessed before was how quickly the support from my bosses melted away. Mac went secretly to our HQ, claiming that both Smiley and I had bullied him from the start. He claimed that I was responsible for everything from his marriage problems to his ill-health. It was malicious and untrue, but he was at pains to tell everyone he had a relative in the complaints team at Army HQ and he was going to get me sacked. Had I known he had gone outside our team, I would have been able to manage it better, but the regulars above me hadn't let me know.

At that first meeting, I issued the documented informal warning to insist he did the review and he seemed initially to accept it. I was due to be in Bosnia for two weeks about a week later and the day before I was due to go he brought in a letter to me, making allegations against me. One of my other lieutenant-colonels was in and we read it together. As he made allegations against me, it was necessary to report it to Spider19 so I informed Mac that I was going to do that. I didn't know he had already been to see them and they hadn't told me. When I rang, Rupert wasn't available, so I emailed him the details and said I would come over as soon as I was back from Bosnia, which I did. Only then did Rupert tell me that Mac had visited 'a number of times' and they advised (ordered) me to attend mediation. I pointed out that this was about poor work performance, not personalities, but they insisted. When I asked why they hadn't told me, Rupert said it had been confidential. I had never come across this before – the normal procedure if a member of a unit goes above the chain of command, would be to inform their immediate boss.

We made them aware of Mac's former history for causing problems, yet it was me they decided to investigate, blaming the victim rather than investigating the underlying issues, which is all too common, both inside and outside the military. I was ordered not to investigate other financial, security and medical irregularities in Mac's activities and to allow him to transfer, on full pay. For troublemakers it's a standard trick to kick up a fuss and demand a change in order to avoid investigation or trouble. Bosses won't take any risks by saying no, and in any case, they want the problem person gone.

For the first time, I had to endure the dreadful, long-winded and non-transparent army complaints system which would lead to nearly 16 months of investigation. And much to my frustration, it was Flashheart who was appointed to manage the investigation, worsening an already difficult relationship.

My staff were interviewed, with very little notice, about my character. Several felt very unhappy about this, but they had no choice. And Mac was able to visit the higher HQ and make fresh allegations, without my knowledge. I did attend mediation (in October 2015), being forced to answer questions before being shown the accusations (and where the mediators assume that the accuser is telling the full truth). Mac was able to pick the location and date, and I spent an hour sitting outside the interview room after the agreed start time. It was like sitting on the naughty step without knowing why. When I went in, the questions started. I had to say, 'You really need to tell me what he is alleging first'. We were then brought face to face and not long after, Mac walked out. This was not a neutral process; the assumption was that he had been wronged and I had done it. From my experience, it seemed too easy to manipulate the complaints system and having looked at the comments online, from the Service Complaints' Ombudsman, I am not the only one who thinks that.

As was the medical system. He went to a doctor and claimed that the 'bullying' had left him with health problems, which allowed him to have an extended leave of absence. Without any independent checks, medical or otherwise, he could move away from our team to work where he chose and when. Despite clear and corroborated protestations from my team that his allegations were false, the Spider19 management team refused to investigate any irregularities and caved in to his every request. After 15 months, Mac finally admitted he had been angry, wanted to withdraw most allegations and had no witnesses or evidence but claimed that he still believed he had been wronged.

Thankfully the process finally cleared me of all his allegations anyway. But nothing was done to punish his actions and, to add to the ridicule of the whole process, he never had to do that performance appraisal. Compared to every civilian complaint system I have been involved with, the Army system was defensive, reactive and amateur. If the Army had to pick a way to investigate staff complaints, this was not it. It needed a professional HR approach.

And then it got worse.

A new boss, we will call him Bert, had started at Intelligence HQ. He came down for our Christmas party and gave an excellent 'fireside chat'. He said he was proud of all we had achieved. It was a great night. Yet during that evening, Harper (always one to enjoy a drink), told him about the investigations. It shouldn't have made a difference. Innocent unless proven guilty, right? Bert asked me if it was true and was angry Orange hadn't told him. Other than that, nothing else was said. But a week later, he sent his reserves' lead down to see us and withdrew support for sponsoring our recruits. SIU was bringing in some specialist reserves who needed intelligence cap-badge sponsorship. The Intelligence Corps had agreed to sponsor them but after this it refused, and we had to create a whole new system at very short notice instead.

There was no explanation and when I rang Bert personally, he diverted the call. I switched to the mobile and he answered. I greeted him warmly, but his tone had changed, he was cold, with a curt 'talk to my staff'. Our relationship had altered that quickly. I was never able to confirm exactly what happened. But when I most needed a support network from my own cap-badge, it was cut off. Ex-regulars had warned me that we now had a difficult cohort in the power seats; they were right.

In that same month, November 2015, I was expecting promotion. My career manager and I had thought that becoming the new head of reserves' intelligence was a shoe-in. I had the qualities and besides, I was the only candidate. I had applied for it and then taken my eye off the ball, dealing with the Mac allegations. Harper came to see me, his voice strained.

'Have you seen the results? You didn't get it'.

They had extended the previous incumbent in post, even though he had been absent for a year. Up until then, the Intelligence HQ had been backing me to take over but now they had filtered me out. Was it that Blue had just been posted to be my new career manager (the nice one had been posted early)? This had certainly worried me, and a few friends had offered condolences. Was it because the candidate who was extended was a freemason? Was it really the complaint hanging over me? What had changed?

In the final blow the same week, a friend called to wish me Happy Christmas and mentioned that the Intelligence HQ were investigating new claims from Mac. I rang the HQ and they confirmed it was true. I then rang the investigators. Their response was, 'Who told you?' None of them had called to get my side of the story and there was no apology after the allegation was found to be untrue. But Mac had promised to destroy my career and I lost a promotion that day.

His campaign was working.

Chapter Twelve
Under Attack

*What counts is not necessarily the size of the dog in the fight it is
the size of the fight in the dog.*
General Dwight D Eisenhower.

What saved my sanity during this time was the support of Smiley, Barbara and the can-do professionalism of Harper. All three of them believed in me and they simply sat down and figured out their own ways to get the work done when I was caught up in the rigmarole of the complaints system. This was a fantastic senior team I knew I could rely on.

For the duration of a complaint the Army will offer an 'assisting officer' or mentor, and thankfully I could pick my own. Initially I was offered Orange; I declined. I chose a calm, measured and highly principled RAF police officer who I will call DC. I picked a police officer because I needed someone who understood the military police system as Mac had made criminal as well as bullying allegations against me.

DC's plan was simple: he checked the criminal allegations with a specialist who confirmed there was no merit in them, so refuting them was simply a matter of stating the facts exactly as they happened. For all the other wild and angry allegations, we agreed a simple 'what happened', 'what I did' and 'why' approach and we provided a witness to each event. The advantage of only having two offices was that there had rarely been a time when I had been alone with Mac so there had been witnesses.

DC's support and sage advice got me through the allegations; he was outstanding. He was calm in the face of my anger and he worked patiently to help me refute all the claims. He was a busy man, but he made himself available at any time and put himself out to see me through a tough time. After it was over, I didn't hear from him until a year later. He had heard I received an OBE and he simply said, 'Thoroughly deserved'. The military is full of these unsung, professional heroes, but unfortunately, it is the blusterers who we hear of most.

Yet despite that simple plan and confidence that I was right, I was driving home from work one evening when I received a call from Flashheart. He informed me that 'just to be sure' army lawyers wanted to refer me to the military police. They were worried Mac would create a fuss if it wasn't criminally investigated. I tried to say I was a reserve and they were applying regular terms of service to the investigation, but he made it clear that he was doing me the courtesy of telling me directly, not of discussing the matter. With a heavy heart, I rang DC and we agreed that I now needed a lawyer.

At this stage, the events were beginning to affect me. I wasn't sleeping and was worried that I was now being set up. Despite these allegations being integral to my work for the Army, there was no legal support; I was expected to pay for a lawyer myself. I rang the HQ to find out if there were any more accusations. I spoke to one of the officers who had supported Mac. He said, 'He just keeps popping in' and. 'He seems to really hate you'. Brilliant, I thought. Very observant. Maybe you could try being objective and getting both sides of the story.

It was Harper who saved me. Mac had, by this time, cast his allegations widely, accusing all the officers in our team and Smiley was now also under investigation. Harper knew of military duty lawyers, who would at least accompany me to the police station. The speed at which this all escalated had numbed me. I had been in Bosnia in August 2015, when Mac had first gone to our HQ and within months I was now under criminal investigation.

Newall was supportive – and concerned for me too. He had noticed the change in me when it all started. He could not understand why an employer would treat me so badly or why I couldn't insist on legal support. He has since said he felt powerless during this phase as he watched me suffer and become embroiled in something so unnecessary and painful.

We decided to take mountain bikes to Cuba and spend Christmas 2015 on a freelance tour. It was the break

I needed, but I still couldn't sleep. The actions of one aggrieved individual didn't particularly scare me but the fact that my own line managers had all backed away immediately to ensure they were not involved did. I felt very alone. If it wasn't for the few who stood by me in this low point, I would probably have called it a day.

I knew I was fighting too many battles by this stage. I wanted my energy and attention to fight on behalf of the unit, and it was frustrating to have to divert so much of it for my personal battle. I felt forced into a corner, several corners, and when that happens all you can do is come out fighting or surrender – and surrender wasn't going to happen. I knew of at least one reserve who had walked away from command when it got tough, but for me this wasn't the answer. So, I fought on.

With Blue gone (posted early to a new role in the north), I hoped there was now the possibility of building a relationship with his replacement, White, who I had worked with during A2020. He wasn't a leader, more of a henchman so, unfortunately, he quickly joined the group I came to think of as the Clique. The leaders of the Clique shared the same area of intelligence specialty and were a tight-knit group. It included the Intelligence Corps lead, Bert, and his female chief of staff. There is a quote from the American newscaster David Brinkley about 'building houses from the bricks that are thrown at you'. Well I was collecting enough to build a mansion.

When I returned from Cuba, the Clique unleashed a set of calculated, persistent and personal attacks.

Suddenly Orange and White wanted job descriptions re-written, organisational numbers reviewed, the recruiting system re-authorised. All while aware that I was under-staffed and preparing for a police interview. I requested a delay, but they insisted that these requests were urgent. At the same time Intelligence HQ withdrew all support for our specialists. As I explained earlier, SIU was recruiting specialist officers and we needed a cap-badge to sponsor them. I had negotiated for the Intelligence Corps to do this, but after the Christmas function this support was withdrawn by Bert. Pretty short notice. We had people already booked for interviews and had to put all of them on hold. I went to Orange to try and resolve but instead received an order to work with White to conduct a full unit review. It felt like unnecessary intimidation. The reason I was quietly given was that the Clique wanted to slow down reserves' growth and paint a narrative that reserves couldn't lead units. I was fighting back so they hit me harder.

This is when I started to read about how nasty attacks can be against women in leadership roles. I received a private message, from a friend who would not be named, about the complaint, saying, 'Go carefully, we don't want to be embarrassed'. He confirmed that what was happening was affecting my career chances. So, despite assurances, and the policy, that investigations of a complaint are not to affect interactions, here suddenly was proof. This was quickly confirmed when I had a routine security vetting interview and it was the first thing mentioned.

I am resilient, I always have been, anyone who set out to lead must be. But to remain resilient in the face of multiple attacks and challenges you need support from allies and mentors. So, I turned to my allies. I sat down with Sirius and worked through a new method of recruiting our specialists. Sirius brokered the deal and, while the Clique was still telling us to delay all recruiting until they decided what to do, we opened the new door. Sirius also sat in when Orange and White visited to conduct a review of any irregularities in my unit. The meeting turned out to be a textbook example of how bullies melt away in the presence of a strong push back. They didn't find any irregularities because there weren't any, and in the presence of Sirius they weren't able to 'discover' any.

Yet if Sirius knew what was going on behind the scenes, he wouldn't tell me. All he said was, 'Diane, I don't what you did to p*** them off, but they are out to get you. Be careful'. What did I do to p*** them off? Succeed in setting up the unit? Rise up the ranks as a woman? It was a puzzle to me too.

I had worked for the Intelligence HQ since 2011 and the task I had been set was directly in support of the Head of the Army and intended to grow military intelligence. So, these attacks were, to put it mildly, hard to swallow. The HQ mantra at the time was 'welfare and support in tough times' but judging by my experience, it wasn't being universally applied.

I spoke to Mason, the former reserves' Head of Intelligence who said he had given up on trying to build a relationship at our HQ, because of the dislike of reserves. I asked if he knew what the change of heart was, he said he had been told that one junior reserve had failed to salute Bert and he had been very upset.

I emailed a colleague within the Intelligence HQ and asked why we weren't flavour of the month. He said we were, he just wasn't sure what flavour it was and apologised if he had contributed to our pain. He gave a general message that we should ensure we followed all protocols to the letter. I had to smile; this was the same HQ that was happy to change its rules for 24 hours to let an MP promote without the usual career courses.

Once the initial shock phase of the attacks wore off, I worked out a strategy to fight back. White was sending weekly emails to me with multiple, small complaints as well as demanding a unit review. He rang me when I started ignoring these weekly rants.

'Diane, I suspect you are writing your own job descriptions.'

'Yes, I am.'

'What? You're admitting it?'

'Yes. Sirius knows about it. It has been authorised.'

When recruiting deep specialists, it is hard to find the ones you want in the right order, so sometimes we would find an anthropologist when we were looking for an armour expert. Sirius, my reserves' boss in Spider19, got this and if I ran all CV and interview notes past him, he understood that I might need to re-write a job description to say we now needed an anthropologist. Flashheart got that too, it was just the Clique who didn't.

White backed off that day, but the emails started again the following week, asking about jobs we had done and who authorised them and informing us of courses he refused to support and numbers he refused to approve. He ignored command status reviews and kept us outside the plan for future structures planning. It was continuous harassment, unnecessary and not the normal army way. What did he want? The unit to fail. Or just for me to fail? Or both? It was impossible to be sure.

Finally, nearly 2 years late, our paired unit arrived. Under A2020, all reserve units, including the SIU, were to be partnered (or paired in army parlance) with a mutually supporting regular unit. We were paired with the regular intelligence hub. It was supposed to arrive before us, in Summer 2014, but it was delayed because its new building wasn't ready. After they arrived things on camp were immediately better. The Long Rangers still worked against us, but now we had two Spider19 units on site (plus one other small, poorly manned, reserve intelligence company) that were standing up to them. And surprise, surprise, the Long Rangers found it wanted our products. Our specialists were asked to run seminars, provide in-depth input to analyst reports or to write papers. Smiley and Barbara were in their element and swiftly built a great relationship with our new colleagues. The fusion between the very young intelligence analysts and rather older SIU was dubbed 'the old peoples' home meets the creche' but it worked. Their boss, a bright and fair-minded man I had first met in Cyprus, also held 'near command', so we had much in common. Things were on the up again.

Despite this I was beginning to feel that it was time for me to prepare for moving on and returning to a civilian job – pain is a great driver of change. I had retained a small physiotherapy practice throughout, and I was also the (unpaid) trustee of a scientific charity, but I had stopped running leadership courses. Now I was tired of the harassment and bullying and ready to do something different. I asked around and a defence contractor was hiring. Soon after, in mid-2016, I was taken on and teamed up with an excellent group of contractors, all bright, cheerful and forward thinking.

The job was two days a week and flexible, acting as sprint lead for a 'social media in defence' project. My voice was being heard again and it gave me the balance I needed.

As for the service complaint, after months of delays, I was called to the military police station where I sat in a grim waiting room, the only woman among a bunch of young soldiers up on charges. I was taken into a side room where I met my lawyer – for the first time – and the allegations against me were finally revealed. Mac had accused me of taking a military vehicle to my house. The lawyer was highly professional, and he told me that they wanted to charge me but were ready to hear my story. He asked to hear it first and I explained the background.

I explained to him that I was a national reserve, which meant I was entitled to be paid for home to duty travel. I had taken a military vehicle to my house after a duty, as have many, many other military people. Sometimes it is cheaper that way and there are trackers on the vehicles so that you can show you didn't then drive it to the pub. Even though the journey was signed off properly, Mac decided to report it as he felt I should have instead taken a taxi to the train station, got a train ticket and then got another taxi to my house. This would have involved the cost of a train plus 2 half-hour taxi rides. Instead I used the works vehicle for a journey I was entitled to be paid for, and in doing so I probably saved the Army a couple of hundred pounds.

Mac had made a second allegation: that I had used a member of SIU staff to drive me in a military vehicle to the airport for a military flight because the Long Rangers refused to give us a driver, but that one was thrown out immediately since I was entirely within my rights.

After hearing my explanation, the lawyer said immediately that the military police didn't understand reserve regulations or that Mac had a performance review hanging over his head. However, he warned that, 'the young military police officer is keen to take the scalp of a lieutenant-colonel, so stay sharp'.

I felt incredibly calm at this stage. It was, frankly, extraordinary that 'they didn't understand reserve regulations' and that they hadn't listened when we had told them, many times, that Mac was trying to avoid a performance review. But this was what had happened all along – most regulars not listening to the reserves, not respecting them or treating them fairly.

I was taken into an interview room where my lawyer sat between me, the aggressive young officer and a corporal who asked the questions. My rights were read to me and my lawyer would interrupt if he felt they were trying to lead me deliberately the wrong way. I had to sign documents and was questioned, on tape, for over an hour. I pointed out the lies, the flaws and the reserve regulations and I finished by pointing out that I had saved the Army money. If they wanted to be pedantic, the Army still owed me about £50.

I wasn't euphoric as I left. They said they needed to go and read reserve regulations and 'continue their investigations'. To be honest, even after so many months, I was still in a state of disbelief that I was being interviewed under caution for using and parking a military car at my house for an official journey. Almost all commanders I knew had done this at one stage or another. Most of the time I had been denied access to military transport and simply used my own car instead, putting thousands of miles on its clock. I had willingly dropped off military personnel without asking for expenses, yet on the one occasion I needed the military option, the regulars took the harshest option as punishment. I worked hundreds of free overtime hours, showed immense goodwill to my employer and in return, was ordered to undergo a full police investigation for the most minor administrative infringement, which had actually saved the MOD money. What the hell was going on? And where was common sense? No regular officer would have ended up at a police station over this, but one malicious accuser, an unsympathetic regular management team and unwillingness to actually read reserve regulations had caused a toxic mess.

The night after the police interview, I stayed in a five-star hotel as part of my work for the defence contractor. I was randomly selected at check-in for an upgrade and ended up in a huge suite with a pamper package, special coffees, chocolates and a movie suite. It felt like good karma. As I lay in the huge bath, I received a text from an old friend who worked for the Clique. I had been short with him and he was asking if we were still friends. I said I needed a break, I had lost trust. He and I had been friends for many years, we'd worked on A2020 together, but his loyalties were to whoever sat as the Corps Colonel and he did know and couldn't tell me why my promotion was blocked. I respected his loyalty lines, but it was hard to regain that close bond we'd had. But as I lay soaking, I understood why so few commanders deal with difficult staff in the Army; they know that if they do, they will become embroiled in time-consuming revenge attacks and a system skewed towards support of the alleged 'victim'. Mac knew that he didn't need to win, just to cause me pain and stall my career.

Army investigations move very slowly, so it was another 2 months before Flashheart called me to say the police had dropped the investigation. I was never allowed to see the formal report; a clerk in Spider19 sent a rude note to confirm in writing that I was cleared, with a terse, 'don't do it again'. It didn't feel like a victory, not only because of the sour way in which it was delivered, but because I still had the long list of non-criminal allegations Mac had made to answer.

That trailed on for another 4 months. During this time many of my staff were interviewed and while they were loyal and supportive to me, they were not allowed, at any point, to tell the full story. All they could do was to answer very carefully scripted questions. Meanwhile I had another day-long interview, followed by further months of delay while the Army lawyers re-checked all of our responses.

Finally, 16 months after the allegations were first made, I was cleared. I received a full report from Flashheart (well, probably from his legal team) which laid out in depth his findings and exonerated me. This report also went to Mac. When he didn't appeal the findings, I received a short letter in November 2016 to confirm that I was exonerated and that it was over. Newall and I felt the same way - just tired and bruised. I rang DC, who of course knew that would be the outcome.

I was due to hand over the unit less than 3 months later, in February 2017, and I still had no military job to go to. So, while I did feel relief, I also felt disillusioned and let down. How could an organisation the size of the Army let one poorly performing individual, with a history of making complaints, pull so many strings? I felt the real problem was weak leadership and a poorly designed complaints system. Even the Army personnel team told me that disgruntled soldiers were known to threaten complaints, knowing that their bosses would back off rather than go through what I had just endured.

None of my bosses was willing to risk Mac turning his anger on them by standing up for me. They allowed him to use coercive behaviours to get his way and lacked the moral courage to stand up to it. It is leadership cowardice and yet keeping quiet is the surest way currently for officers to get promoted, unless they are very well connected.

Do I think I was treated more badly because I was a woman? Because I was a reserve? Because I wasn't privately educated? Yes, I do, on all three counts.

Did I see myself as a victim? Briefly. During the nastiest phase I started to go under, but I pulled myself back, because that really wasn't what I wanted. Male pack behaviour is harder to understand as a woman and working in a regular military environment is tougher as a reserve, but if I am going to choose work as a minority in workplaces, it is me who needs to work out how not to be held back and to then hold to account those who still won't create a path for me. In Spider19, many of the female support staff left, tired of the misogyny. I couldn't do that, I had taken on a commitment, but when I went

221

to work as a defence contractor, and as a trustee in the charity sector, I was treated so differently – with respect and appreciation - and that gave me the confidence to challenge the bigotry in the brigade.

All in all, it was a very tough lesson for me to learn. It affected my civilian career, my health and my performance. And I am pretty sure it was the reason Intelligence HQ blocked my promotion. I don't blame Mac; there will always be difficult employees. But I do blame the Spider19 management team for giving me a horrendous 16 months rather than just resolving things simply and quickly.

Leadership is lonely, by definition, but here it was a different loneliness. I suspect only those who have gone through being accused of false allegations can understand. It is not that I wanted to block Mac's complaints being investigated. I really do get that many people end up too scared to complain, so any system must appear friendly and to initially at least assume they are telling the truth. But surely big organisations like the Army can interview a complainant, listen and make a fairly quick judgement on the likelihood it is vexatious? 16 months. A career held in abeyance, hours, probably weeks of interviews and bureaucracy. That was the price I paid for trying to hold an individual to account for poor performance. I've read newspaper stories about others who have been falsely accused, and all of them, after being exonerated, said exactly what I felt: that there needs to be more done to hold false accusers to account. All felt a sense of abandonment by bosses and had little or no legal support. The loneliness and isolation of fighting to clear your name, the moments of self-doubt and the nagging sense of guilt, even though you know you have done nothing wrong can be torturous. And the looks, whispers and gossip of others around you can be incredibly demoralising. I read a poignant quote from a 22-year-old who was falsely accused of rape, whose accuser was allowed to stay anonymous. He said, 'Everything you build up can be torn away. You are powerless to affect it. You realise how much you have to lose and also start losing things as the process gets longer'.

As a society, we must maintain that principle of innocent until proven guilty; a principle I don't believe the Army offered me. I really don't want to put off those who truly feel they have been wronged from being able to come forward, but please, please, these difficult cases must be handled by professionals – and quickly. For me, I would add that this experience has meant I will never trust in the same way again. It didn't break me, and I held to my values, protecting my HQ staff and the SIU reserves. But the lack of support or real leadership from above broke the military covenant for me. I hit cognitive dissonance - no longer feeling part of the Army because it had separated me from its core.

George Eliot put it well, 'What loneliness is lonelier than distrust?'

The positive out of it all was that, for the first time in decades, I re-bonded with *sisterhoods*. At home, a close-knit circle of female friends nurtured me through the worst of the attacks. Online, I found various military blogs; networks of professional military women officers-both serving and veteran. And I also re-found many of WRAC 4, those women I had met and bonded with at Sandhurst. With this group I could be authentic me, with my love of science fiction, my *Star Trek* ringtones, my love of a good glass of red wine. It was the uncritical bond I needed as my relationship with the Army got tough.

Chapter Thirteen
The Cut-Glass Ceiling

Leaders are visionaries with a poorly developed sense of fear and no concept of the odds against them
Robert Jarvik

I am proud to say that I stuck it out. Despite juggling civilian work, commanding the unit and answering the details of a complaint, SIU grew ahead of our plan. Our original 13 became 60 and continued to grow. We were now working on projects across the Army, defence and beyond. I loved spending time with the specialists. Flashheart called them the 'butterfly catchers', I called them a box of frogs, but either way, they were special individually and outstanding collectively. The A2020 vision worked.

After 3 tough years, I was tidying my desk to hand over at the end of my tour. I thought back to Southwick Park and the map-room. It was Winston Churchill who advocated KBO (Keep Buggering On) as the main tool of resilience. It was my approach too; I was determined to keep believing in my vision. And it had worked, with the help of my loyal support staff. Harper built the support team quickly and trained the staff to work professionally, while Smiley and Barbara worked on and grew the output until we were in high demand.

The deep specialists (I called them the Geek Squad and meant it as a compliment) worked well with the pragmatic 'get things done' regular staff and the intelligence fusion hub. There were different styles of course; the rifles support cohort were louder, made deals verbally and liked to push through the work, sing and then get drunk, while the Intelligencers were quiet, introverted, worked best on paper and were more sober (and they couldn't sing). But I loved all my team.

With Mac gone, the HQ thrived. Sometimes, it is necessary to stand up to bad behaviour, however painful the consequences. This is the cliff edge that I was slow to recognise: that many will allow the strongly principled to deal with complex situations and difficult people and by doing so, put ourselves in the firing line. Then when we are wounded, those who stood by put themselves forward, untainted. A learning skill for the near-senior leaders.

My successor commanding SIU was an ex-regular. The Intelligence HQ knew what buttons to push with him and so the vision of what we do has remained intact, but the way he does it is no longer the reserves-focused vision I had, it has returned to a lower-risk, don't rock the boat approach.

For me it was time to move on to a new role. With Blue now managing my career, I knew it would be hard, but I had to keep trying. After missing out on the intelligence promotion, I identified a different role that I knew I would fit and my boss' boss worked with me to ensure near-command status wouldn't be a problem. I met all the criteria and was confident that this one was mine. Then the results came out and again and I hadn't got it. I watched as it went to a male officer with less experience for the role. I was suspicious, as he worked for the reserve lead of the shadow-board, but I was persuaded to hold back from contesting the decision.

I tried one more time for the role of Head of Intelligence Reserves and missed out again. Blue denied that I was being blocked, but I could feel the clique was strong and I realised that, whatever they believed I had done, I could not beat this powerful group.

I talked to influential women mentors on what a glass ceiling actually looks like and I realised I had hit it. Some of the women I spoke to were regular army women, others were in civilian businesses. Most of these women had left at the rank I now held, and what they said was that the boards weren't fair, that the results were opaque and that the complaints system was non-existent, effectively making it very difficult to identify the bias. And because there were good opportunities outside the military, senior army women were mostly choosing flight over fight, leaving the Army and seeking other challenges.

I was alarmed – I had a lot still to give, I was arguably at the peak of my professional career and I wasn't ready to have it stalled. I knew so many men who had been promoted from my level who were no better qualified. It was wrong.

I started to build a file of evidence, all the ways in which I had been undermined and blocked. And there were many. When I had been told that the reason I couldn't have full command status was that the Army wouldn't fund all the perks my peers had (cleaners, drivers, PAs, a house and many others), I could have spent a lot of time fighting for command equality but I chose instead to give priority to building the team, on the basis that it was good people I needed to deliver the goal, not the status of command. I trusted my own bosses would have my back, but I was finding out now that they did not.

Anything new bothers people, especially in slow-changing, hierarchical organisations. And those driving the change are often painted as the threat, rather than the catalyst. The level of overt bigotry had been far more prevalent than I expected. Part-time workers are protected by legislation, but the armed forces have worked hard to avoid giving the reserves protected employment status. And since military personnel are reluctant to speak up and have no formal representatives, we learn to keep quiet and carry on. But only for so long – there comes a point where the cost-benefit no longer works, and I was reaching it.

Even in an infantry setting, most of the men are not inherently bad. I never saw Flashheart as a bad guy, just one who didn't get military women, which is a common problem with infanteers. But what bothered me most was that even though I heard him make many bigoted comments, his behaviour went unchallenged. He was not hauled in front of police for minor infringements, as I had been. He was not even confronted or questioned. I wanted to understand this old-school privilege that fuelled power, because the small favours offered to this privileged cohort to assist their progression are as damaging as the big acts of the few in holding minorities back. For the whole force concept to work it needs more reserves involved in its development and it needs the Head of the Army to stamp out this bigotry, both the covert biases against women, minorities and class and the overt ones against reserves.

Imagine if the same energy that was put into blocking the A2020 plan had been applied to making it work? What if that group who had it in their heads to show that the plan wouldn't work with reserves, believing that if they did the government would retain the regular numbers, had been on side? How different it might have been. And their plan didn't work; over the next year or two the regular numbers were reduced even further.

The covert bias against women showed itself in so many ways. One of them was language. In senior, male-dominated professions, language is often used to undermine minorities, intended to constrain and hold back. Women in the military were described as using 'hyperbole' (emotional), or not understanding the background (there, there dear). It opened my ears to the language used against national female leaders: Theresa May, Hilary Clinton, Angela Merkel and so many others were all undermined by the use of language, dismissed as housewives, brittle, unfeminine, drab and so on. And yet they refused to be undermined and most succeeded in their goals. I wanted to learn how they did it, how to armour myself for the attacks.

I had experienced many 'fear of witches' moments in my career, but my 'perfect storm' only came when I was asked to stand up SIU, bring in different types of reserves and bring change to certain working practices. It was an exciting challenge that should have been universally supported. Instead tribal fear, stoked by a group of entrenched 'old power' individuals, brought me, as the harbinger of change, into the firing line.

Once I was identified as the target, support for me dropped, but interestingly, as the tide turned, people contacted me and quietly passed evidence, although all wanted it off the record. With my file of evidence growing, I spoke to the complaint's investigator, who made it clear that he would not recommend it be treated as a malicious complaint until 'after I had left the Army'.

The constant drip drip of small allegations over months is as damaging as the occasional big ones, this is why the #MeToo movement is right to mention the small stuff as well as the big. Many women are undermined daily, each incident 'minor' but all adding up to an unacceptable whole.

The Army does still have a problem with bullying, it has finally admitted it. But there is a bigger problem right now with poor performers bullying their managers into inaction for fear of repercussions. I would think twice about challenging a difficult member of staff again, and that was the point of the complaint Mac made. He had succeeded in avoiding reviews and contributing little for years, and he knew that complaining about me would affect me detrimentally, and not him.

This pattern would be relatively easy to fix, by bringing in more professional human resources management and taking the complaints procedure out of the hands of amateur regulars. Organisations deal with complaints effectively all the time – so why can't the Army?

Just before I left, Orange rang me. 'You sound grumpy,' he said. 'Do you have post-command blues?'

'That would be difficult,' I replied, 'as I was apparently never in command'.

But I did have the blues on leaving command. After dropping all the responsibilities and walking out of the door I experienced withdrawal pains. I had coffee with one of my contractor colleagues who had previously commanded and he summarised it well. 'You know what I noticed most? Suddenly my jokes weren't so funny, people didn't listen to my ideas and my plans weren't so well received. I had to start earning my place again.'

Command is hard, but it is also an incredibly nice place to be. In command I learned to stop bringing others my problems. I found my confidence and learned to make decisions and to lead. The way I did things wasn't always perfect, it could be messy, but the job got done. And when I moved on at the end of my tour, I handed over an organisation that I had taken from a discussion in a bar, to full operating capability. In leaving, it carried on, as if I had never been there. That's exactly as it should be, but it still felt like letting my teenager go; it still had a lot to learn, but it had now outgrown me.

Smiley regularly teased me that I had promised him the light at the end of the tunnel was growing brighter, when it spent most of the 3 years of this project flickering on and off. But we did get there. As I walked out, there were no big farewells, just a series of enjoyable small ones. And the last day ended as it should, with my intelligence cohort chatting quietly with me in the corridor. I knew as I closed the door behind me that I was no longer in command and it gave me a strange but powerful sense of closure.

Leaving was tough in many ways. As I was still working with the Army careers team to find my next appointment (but not getting selected) I ended up going 'cold turkey'. There was no gradual departure; one minute I was a commander, the next I was back on civvy street. And while, thankfully, I already had a defence contractor role, I didn't have any military re-settlement time or transitional 'gardening leave' as a regular would.

I had a farewell interview a few weeks after leaving command. Flashheart had been posted, so I saw his replacement who was completely different: a measured, intelligent officer who listened. As I arrived, Orange was hanging around outside, keen to see if I was going to make a complaint about him. At this stage, I was looking to resolve my concerns informally, rather than make a formal complaint. As a reserve being appraised by regulars, I was concerned that my reports would be harsher than for other reserve colleagues. So I asked the new boss to ensure that all I had achieved be included in my appraisal. The new boss admitted that Flashheart hadn't liked me. And he agreed to take the time to review my achievements before finalising his appraisal.

Finally, I had spoken up, and I thought – hoped – it would be enough. The appraisal he produced was outstanding and it did cover all my successes. He placed me as his top reserve. Surely after that I would get a promotion? But despite that appraisal, despite being awarded an OBE for my successes on A2020 and in putting together the SIU, I was still no nearer to penetrating the bullet-proof ceiling above me.

Over the next 18 months I applied for posts. Each time my enthusiasm was fired up, I fitted the spec, I knew I could do it; surely it should be a shoo-in? I sent off my long and detailed application form and a job preference form, indicating why I felt I had the skills for the role. And then I waited.

No-one called. No-one offered feedback. Instead, I would see the results published on the MOD internal network, find my name not among them, deal with the surge of disappointment and then ask for feedback from my career managers.

It was always vague. 'We can't tell you much about what the board thought'; 'The committee was unanimous'; 'Your experience was not broad enough'; 'Sorry, pipped at the post'. By now I was deeply suspicious. I analysed the results over that 18 months and as far as I could tell, almost all those appointed to the jobs I applied for were white men, privileged, ex-public school, deputy lieutenants, members of the equestrian club, the Polo set, the yeomanry. In other words, they were 'connected'.

My frustration grew. If I couldn't get any useful feedback, I was just another Prometheus, growing a new liver each day only to have it pecked out, in his case by an eagle, in mine by the Army shadow-board system.

I spoke to those I had worked with to understand how 'connections' worked. I had helped a lot of people over the past five years, so now I hoped those among them with influence would explain to me what I was missing. Did I need more qualifications? More experience of a different kind (and how would I get that)? My written career plan said I was ready for promotion. So, what was standing in my way? How was this obscure, opaque system working? And why wasn't it working for me?

No-one could – or perhaps would – give me answers. I was fobbed off, avoided or given unhelpful platitudes. How long could this go on? I was in limbo, neither in a role nor out of the Army. No-one was going to explain what was happening.

Eventually it had to stop. I couldn't go on applying and being turned down without any explanation or guidance as to what to do next. And so, at the end of 2017, I woke up one morning and realised my military career was done. A moment of real grief. This was not of my choosing. Not what I had ever hoped for or thought possible. I had been badly let down and it hurt.

No wonder so many service leavers walk away with a bitter after-taste. I always wondered how my time in the Army would end and now it had. It was not at all how I had imagined it. And it was not what I had worked so hard for. I had done all the courses, the attachments, hit the top grade, reached the Top 10 (I was 7th in line) of those reserves eligible to promote, achieved an OBE – and all I got was a member of staff in Glasgow telling me he couldn't actually tell me why I wasn't succeeding, just that I was 'up against strong competition'. But he couldn't share what they had that I didn't or what I could do to become equally strong.

A pause for reflection. A long, dark night of the soul. Fight, or flight? Thanks for the memories, or act? So many of the colleagues I confided in had warned me not to put in a service complaint. 'It will end your career' and 'you will have to leave,' were the commonest cries. But now my career was over anyway because there is no anchor for former commanders when the military won't give you a promotion.

I decided I had to speak up. Not just for me – for those like me; women, reserves, anyone who had stuck their head above the parapet in the cause of justice, wanting to make things better, only to come under fire from their own side. So, I submitted a complaint.

After the drawn-out 16 months of misery I experienced because of Mac's complaint, I discovered there was now a 'new and improved' system, streamlining complaints. It boasted that in most cases the complaint would be resolved in twelve weeks. This sounded more hopeful.

A decent complaints system will run independently of the organisation it serves. Those in charge will listen to all parties and decide the validity of the complaint, without bias. To do that, they must talk to witnesses, read evidence and keep an open mind. And they should respond quickly, because dragging the process out just creates deep-set angst for those on either end of the complaint. A good system, run by good people, will acknowledge when it gets things wrong, including over-running and lessons learned. And it will consistently look at how to improve.

The Army complaints system is none of the above. It is a deliberately obstructive system. Why? Because its aim is not to resolve employment issues, it is to make complainants lose heart, give up and go away. Why would any system want to do this? Because it is run by serving army officers whose future careers depend on keeping the Army happy. And the army is happy if there are very few successful complaints. So, the system is set up to minimise the number of complaints upheld.

The trouble is it isn't working. Such a system might succeed in the short-term goal of registering few successful complaints. But it becomes an unhappy organisation which loses its staff. The Army's most recently available Annual Continuous Attitude Survey found that 70% of those asked were unhappy with the service. It found that career management was a major reason given by those leaving the Army. And it found that there were in the region of 14 new formal complaints a week.

The system is heavily weighted against those who complain. The Army has a large team of lawyers advising the complaints system but unavailable to those who feel wronged, so without union representation, which is illegal in the military, the only potential support offered is from fellow officers. This worked when I was the defendant, but as a complainant of senior rank, I soon discovered that there was little independent support on offer.

My case appeared straightforward. I had a clear career management plan up to 2015, with targets to hit (I hit them), experiences to gain (I gained them) and grades to achieve (I achieved them). My line managers recommended me for promotion, and I hit the blue list in a high position in 2015, had a plan with my career manager and expected to promote within 12 months- that's the norm.

Then, career managers and board membership changed, I wasn't selected for any of the posts I applied for and the career managers couldn't or wouldn't tell me why. When I eventually complained, they made statements saying that I was 'never competitive', they had lost my written career plan (but hadn't told me), that I did deserve to promote, but only in certain areas (which I applied for and didn't get) and that I was missing key experiences (which ones? Why wasn't I told?).

There was a transparent refusal to investigate and the supposed 'investigation' was no more than collation and weak open questions. Their witnesses were not challenged, my witnesses were not interviewed, and the answers provided were not analysed. When an evidence pack was put together key documents had been lost. It is hard not to conclude that truth was the casualty here.

The Army could delay the investigation as and when it chose. But I missed a deadline and much of my evidence was timed out, even on appeal. These are dark times when the head of the system appears to have already come to his conclusions before statements are received.

If this was the way a formerly committed, upstanding senior officer with an unblemished record was treated, how were, and are, the soldiers being treated?

This is the power of the privileged white male elite and the few women who find a way to join them at the top and, in doing so, usually change sides. It is not just a bullet-proof ceiling, it is that the air is different up there and it changes those who make it through. If you make it beyond the rank of lieutenant-colonel, you are part of the Patriarchy. And to stay in the club, you must keep quiet.

I reached lieutenant-colonel. I was within touching distance of the Patriarchy. I have wondered what I would have done, had I got there. Because keeping quiet and joining the club was never going to be my style. Arguably this is exactly why I and other disruptive types are blocked for promotion – once in the club we would not stay quiet. We would continue to be advocates of change, but from more powerful positions. The Army, like so many deeply conservative organisations, prefers to appoint 'yes-men'. This works reasonably well in times of peace, but it won't work in times of war because conflict scenarios need mavericks as well as rule-followers, it is a necessary part of out-thinking adversaries.

I have been faced with delays, temper tantrums, threats via lawyers and endless paperwork. And false promises too. All of these the tactics of those who wished only to delay, until I gave up and went away.

Chapter Fourteen
Divorce

The most hurtful things are not what comes from our adversaries,
but from our friends
Gloria Steinem

The complaints system and I have now been doing a merry dance for 18 months. They are only required to keep me updated every 30 days. I email in May 2018 to say they have missed yet another deadline. I am phoned, with apologies, by a senior officer in the complaints team – I will call him Major Twistleton Whitewash III. Judging by his name and his voice over the phone, he is a privileged white male. He is brusque and aims to get me to narrow my complaints. He tries to reassure me that the system is highly regulated and fair. When I say I disagree, he finishes with an irritated, 'So you want me to ask the senior reserve on the Board at Career Management if he influenced the Boards?' 'Yes,' I say, 'I do.' And a few others.

I looked Twistleton up on LinkedIn. I re-run my analysis of Board successes and see a new clique around this same corps. Of course it's possible it's all coincidence, but if heads of Boards don't declare an interest and then refuse to provide an alternative explanation, naturally we have suspicions.

I am due to apply for more posts but then I receive a new grading letter; I am still on the Blue List but have now dropped in rankings. I ask to submit this as evidence as it shows I have now missed my promotion window and am told I can't, I will need to submit a separate complaint as this is 'new evidence'.

What? I haven't even had the interview for my first complaint yet. Why can't this simply be added to it as information?

During this time, I was frequently reminded of the 1980s (but timeless) TV series *Yes, Prime Minister*, a brilliant satire on masterful institutional inactivity. Forgive me if I include a few particularly pertinent extracts which made me smile as I faced the wall of obfuscation that was the Army complaints system. Here's the civil servant, Sir Humphrey, advising Minister James Hacker's Principle Private Secretary, Bernard Woolley, on how to guide the hapless minister towards making the right decisions:

Sir Humphrey: If you want to be really sure that the Minister doesn't accept it, you must say the decision is 'courageous'.

Bernard: And that's worse than 'controversial'?

Sir Humphrey: Oh, yes! 'Controversial' only means 'this will lose you votes'. 'Courageous' means 'this will lose you the election'!

In my own case I had nothing left to lose- I could only promote by getting past this opaque, shadow-board and they wouldn't tell me how I could achieve that or what they objected to. By this time, I had a following; with social media it was easy to find others going through the same system and many shared stories of befuddlement, avoidance, delays, narrowing investigations and frustrations. None were satisfied. Each shared evidence they had found. They pointed out that the 30-day update only has to say that the complaints team are 'still working on it'. They are not obliged to report progress – or lack of it. This even though in February 2018 the MOD stated that it aimed to complete all complaints within 12 weeks.

The farcical nature of the complaints system means that although there is a service complaints ombudsman, they cannot get involved until a decision is made re the complaint. Even better, their findings are only advisory anyway. And best of all, it is not possible to complain about the complaints system. There is a specific clause the armed forces have included so that being late, not investigating or interviewing witnesses cannot be challenged. So, the Army is allowed to mark its own homework? To decide what to investigate and what to ask? And to take as long as it wants (years) to investigate, while it sets an army of lawyers against an employee? Is this possible in this day and age?

In late June I receive a letter saying the 12-week period for resolving complaints may not be achieved. Again, this delay is allowed on their side but not on mine.

A young civil servant, one of the MOD complaint investigation staff in Glasgow, is assigned to investigate and assures me she is fully independent. She flies down with a more senior civil servant and comes to my house to take a statement from me, promising to investigate thoroughly, but struggles to understand the military ranks and nuances of the case. It takes weeks to complete a draft that reads well, but even then, it is very limited.

After discussions with my mentoring team, in July I submit a second complaint with the new evidence. This includes my dropping down the priority list; I was no longer 7th of 47, so my chances of promoting had been reduced and effectively I had missed my promotion window. I also submit further evidence of the boards showing changes that Glasgow is making quietly, for example that feedback is now compulsory, filtering out pre-boards is now to be regulated and job descriptions that say 'combat experience essential' must justify it – that is, not discriminate against women. But there is still no assurance process for board results and still no women sitting on these selection boards.

I have now left my old unit and submit this quickly via an independent unit at Glasgow. In July the young civil servant's 'fully independent' report is shown to me for comment. It doesn't even spell my name correctly. It does not include my previous career plan, has conflicting statements and is laid out in a way that minimises my achievements and record. The previous 18 months of vague feedback is now replaced with comments such as,

'She never stood a chance, wasn't competitive'. Major Whitewash, in a phone call, tells me to accept that I had 'never been good enough'. I tell him that the facts do not support that statement. I consider both the report and his call to be efforts to gaslight me. As far as I can tell, Whitewash's job, in its entirety, is to reduce the number of complaints, limit investigations and try and get complainants to give up.

I called the jobsworth I had been dealing with (re: promotion) for the past 3 years, Master Whitmarsh. I discovered a wonderful old book, written by Sir Patrick Moore under the nom de plume RT Fishall, based on the premise that Britons were being harassed, bullied and driven to distraction by the 'Whitmarshes' of the world. He said that parliament doesn't rule us, but the minor officials and bureaucrats within the civil service who revel in red tape are immune from dismissal and can look forward to nice inflation proof pensions. It gave me great solace through the complaints process as I realised, I was simply facing a tried and tested civil service obstruction system.

Anyway, Master Whitmarsh told me that there isn't a Reserve Blue List. Even though I have letters referring to it and it's stated on my appraisals. I could go on but essentially what's happened is a whitewash. So, I submitted a response detailing the bias, asking why evidence has not been analysed and when they became aware that they had lost my career plan.

Mostly, I was angry that I had spent three years with a set of expectations that they have now casually said were unrealistic – and they have 'lost' the paperwork and refused to interview anyone who counters that view.

Jim Hacker: What's the difference?

Bernard: Well, 'under consideration' means 'we've lost the file'; 'under active consideration' means 'we're trying to find it'.

Clearly my case was not under 'active consideration'. I request a copy of my personnel file, which is held in Glasgow. When I get it, my full career back to when I joined at 18 is fully documented, apart from just one document; the vital career plan is missing. The file does add a couple more 1980s sexist comments to my already substantial collection.

More colleagues – men and women – send me evidence: sexual harassment surveys, a Chief of Defence Staff speech in which he says that 15% of reserves are women but only 3.6% are in top jobs, and this is not for lack of trying and achievements. I took a detailed look at the June 2018 Board results for the previous year. Only men have promoted. Nearly all infantry apart from a lieutenant-colonel for creative arts, awarded to a brigadier's wife. Part of the Army's shadow 'job creation scheme' for certain individuals.

Rather late, I understood the importance of coaching those not on the golden escalator to speak up earlier in their careers. I was offering this service for others, but why had no-one done this for me? I recall being told, when I didn't get command of an UOTC, that it was because they were changing to 'super-regions' and wanted infantry men in charge. At the time, I just accepted that and applied for command of SIU. Now that choice was biting me, yet the fact that command of UOTC units was only given to men was not considered relevant when looking at evidence of career fouling.

The young investigator's attitude had now changed. I had a short period of time in which to comment on her report, but these comments could only be added as a note to the file, which was not to be changed. She had told me she would include my positive former career plan and hadn't. When I challenged this, she said it had been lost. I asked that this comment be included in the file and she said no, only that she could mention it was missing – and she didn't even do that. All the positive supporting evidence I submitted was placed at the back of the file, while the statements from Master Whitmarsh, all very morose and downbeat, were at the front. And the one thing I had requested - that an independent review looked at my skills versus those of the individuals who were selected, for an analysis of fairness - wasn't done at all.

The investigator told me there was nothing I could do (even if the report was inaccurate) to get it changed. She had submitted her file and it had been passed on to the generals for a decision. With a breathtaking level of disdain, she refused even to correct my name.

In September 2018, I visit Glasgow for the 'exceptional career plan' I am entitled to, since my original career plan has been lost. Up until now, I have been refused a career review because I am 'not due one', but since they lost my career plan, they must fly me up to Glasgow to get one. Before I leave, I go up to my attic and find a copy of my old career plan- which I later send in as evidence only to be told I was now not allowed to include new evidence.

Blue had moved on, and I have a new careers manager, a woman intelligence lieutenant-colonel. She has spoken to Whitmarsh and read my file and she announces that I would effectively have to repeat the last 5 years to show my skills again – but of course with no guarantees. It is a complete Catch 22 situation. She insists I needed to go back and find a command, but first I would have to go and get a bog-standard lieutenant-colonel role and build my profile again in order to apply for one. And yet the reason I wasn't considered for a command in 2015, 16 and 17 was that I had already gone past that stage and was ready for promotion. The whole thing is mind-numbing, and I sit there, stunned. How can I do better than the A1 report I achieved, and in any case, would the Army give me the posts I am now being told I need to fill in order to gain the 'right' experience?

I then meet the three – Major Twistleton Whitewash lll, the new career manager and Whitmarsh – the gatekeeper to the shadow-board in a conference room at Glasgow. We are short of time, yet they stall by showing me a completely unnecessary presentation on how it all works. When they do get to the point the message is, 'You were never competitive'. They won't answer why. I have never been told this or why it is different to my 2013 career advice. Or even why it matters. I am also told that, 'Reserves don't really have a career after lieutenant-colonel'. Of course, some do, they know that as well as I do, but it's just the privileged few.

There are something like 20 people chasing every post (since I was 7th on the list I still should have got one) and if you are turned down you just go to the back of the queue. For regulars it would be different.

I am reminded that civilian work experience counts, although it seems that mine didn't, and I am assured that there has been no interference from senior Intelligence figures (the Clique), even though I have statements which say otherwise from people who are reluctant to be called unless it goes to courts.

Whitewash has already refused to interview some of my witnesses, he even refused to interview my career manager, Blue. He is ignoring the fact that my career plan has changed significantly and won't answer questions on this. I recently read that a judge had commented in The Times on a case involving racial bias in the Army, saying that it shouldn't be possible for the Army to decide what questions to answer (and yet they do). At this stage, I have three serving officers who have told me, off the record, that men were favoured for those UOTC commands and two others who told me that intelligence blocked my promotion. Do I reveal all this? I don't know how to play it and I realised that, for the second time, I need legal advice. But that is so expensive…

I don't trust these three, they are not neutral. It is clear their agenda is not to resolve this complaint, just to kill it. Whitewash is becoming more aggressive. 'It's for you to prove', he says, when I tell him I was 7th on a list of 47. He keeps homing in on any weaknesses in my case while refusing to answer any of my questions.

Just to show that karma doesn't always play nicely, I race back to catch my plane, only to find that it has been cancelled, so we are bussed to Edinburgh. In the air, we are then diverted to Manchester because of a runway emergency. I get on a coach which gets lost, then delayed behind motorway upgrade traffic on its way back to Birmingham, where my car is. I have prearranged to go to Chicksands to discuss the outcome of the careers meeting, so once I got my car, I drive through to Bedford where I manage four hours sleep before my next meeting.

My plan for that day was a farewell look at our intelligence home as well as a review of the Glasgow meeting. That would have to wait for another day.

In October I get a letter. My first complaint, the one about being overlooked for promotion, has been waiting for a decision. The letter is from the general's representative at Army HQ. The general has decided that he has a conflict of interest and has deferred the decision to another. Meanwhile my next 30-day update tells me that the 'very busy' generals will be too busy to look at the complaint before December. By that time, it will be almost a year since I first made the complaint. I challenge the delay and receive a short 'I will inform them you are dissatisfied' in response.

As for the new complaint? Major Whitewash is determined to limit the scope. I send him a list of my questions, he ignores them and substitutes more weak, open questions, supporting his foregone conclusion. He is only intending to interview the same two witnesses and won't interview my witnesses or answer any of my questions. And having been forced by Major Whitewash to submit two separate complaints, Army HQ now informs me there will be a delay to the decision on the first complaint as they want to combine the two, as they are essentially the same complaint. Yes, they are. That was my point.

The letter I receive telling me the composition of the Decision Board lists several serving army generals and a civilian female I don't know. I ring the Army HQ complaint's team to ask about her background. She is the independent member on discrimination cases I am told, and she is apparently of enough seniority to stand up to the generals and encourage impartiality. Time will tell.

So, where do we go from here?

The Army uses an innovation ideas system, the Defence and Security Accelerator (DASA) and in 2018, it put out a call to ask for innovative ways to stop the loss of talent and to recruit and retain the best. The veterans' diaspora, many now in high ranking business roles, were unanimous in stating that this doesn't need innovation. All the army needs is to get a decent HR system and treat your people with a little respect and fairness and then – guess what – more of your talent will stay. It isn't rocket science.

Now those who speak up are out, we are treated as the enemy. But I, and so many others like me, are not the enemy. We love the Army, have given it so much and wanted to give more. We are Black Box thinkers, showing you what went wrong and asking to be part of the solution.

The solution is, in fact, so simple, but it will need to be forced onto the Patriarchy. The privileged few do not want a meritocracy, but that is what we need. Our promotion boards, our career management and our freedom to speak up when lessons need to be learned all need to be in the hands of independent professionals, rather than army officers with no HR skills, whose careers rely on limiting the number of complaints upheld and refusing to investigate anything that would support change.

Army bosses are encouraged to ensure that when people leave, they don't tick the box on their resignation forms that says, 'Because of discrimination or harassment'. I know of those who were told that if they didn't remove the tick before leaving, they would not be allowed to leave until there had been a full investigation. In other words, if they wanted a quick discharge, they had to remove the tick. All of us knew that if we made a serious complaint, our career was finished. So, I did not enter this arena lightly.

There are so many questions which still go unanswered. Why do so many posts still insist on combat experience as a way of excluding women? How do you address the narrower career options for women if there is only one route to the top? How come my 'lost' career plan said I had no weaknesses, but the replacement one said I had so many I couldn't be promoted? And how have we developed a 'whole force' career management system which still has completely different rules for reserves and regulars?

As I made my arduous way through the seemingly farcical complaints system, colleagues started sending me statistics from the yearly army survey; 70% of respondents were dissatisfied with the complaints system. And commanding officers are getting bogged down dealing with these complaints, so poor quality staff use it as a threat to avoid sanctions.

I don't believe Mac wanted to go through the full complaints process, he wanted to threaten me with it, knowing that all his previous bosses had backed off at the threat. He picked the wrong person in me because I didn't know, and I would have continued even if I had known what was about to happen to me. Mac knew what he was doing when he said he would destroy me, but it was the Army chain of command that allowed him to.

I now understood why the advice of so many serving, is to leave rather than complain- because the process is 'gaslighting' in extremis. A pretence of a fair and independent system, looking objectively at the facts, interviewing witnesses, promising anonymity or witnesses. But my witnesses did not want to be named because they knew they would be career damaged. And I needed a lawyer, but the costs are huge- I spent a lot on basic advice and then was lucky to find a barrister within the Sisterhood- and I am now linked to many going through the system and have been a witness for the Defence Select Committee.

It's hard to believe that in 2019 an employer can effectively stall an investigation, decide what to investigate (and what not to) and lose vital evidence but make no comment on this.

Hacker: Will you answer a direct question?

Sir Humphrey: I strongly advise you not to ask a direct question.

Hacker: Why?

Sir Humphrey: It might provoke a direct answer.

Hacker: It never has yet.

The Army complaints system is an intentionally obstructive process to discourage complaints. And while this may work in the short term, it's a disaster for morale and for retaining those talented people who are not on the golden staircase to the top.

The ombudsman is toothless and under-resourced. My appeal in July 2019 has been accepted, with a timeline to START looking at it in 15 months due to lack of resource. So, a complaint made in February 2018 can be obstructed completely for 3 years before the ombudsman will even look at it. No wonder Glasgow were confident in refusing to investigate.

The Army's latest acknowledgement is that the system to complain doesn't work and they need to set up a Defence Authority to manage it, which may or may not make a difference. It would be a bold move towards retention, which is a bigger current challenge for the military than recruitment. But most service people can already tell you the answer. Bring in a time limited process (12 weeks), after which it is either resolved, goes to an employment tribunal or is passed to a professional human resources organisation. Throw out the current toothless, under-resourced ombudsman who cannot get involved until all the steps have been taken, who has no resources to reform and who currently has an 18-month waiting list for appeals. And remove the bloody clause that prevents complaining about the complaints system because there is no incentive to do a good or neutral job with this clause in place.

I realise that it's way too late to fix my career now; the Patriarchy has beaten me and that is a source of great sadness to me. The Army and I are now in the process of a messy divorce, but the alternative was to keep quiet about my experiences and I decided that was no longer part of my values. I can still speak out in order to help the next generation of women; that has become my next mission.

My last day in command of SIU, in January 2017, would not be my last day in uniform. That would happen at Buckingham Palace, in November 2018, when I received my OBE. I didn't get it courtesy of the intelligence HQ, who never thanked me for doing what they had asked me to do. My achievements were recognised by the willingness of one of my mentors, Sirius (along with a few supporters), to stand up and speak for me. And despite my great sadness at the way I had been treated, receiving it from Her Majesty, Queen Elizabeth II was a proud moment.

There are many who work as hard as I have and who deserve awards but are not recognised, simply because they don't have a champion. There are others who get their awards along with their privileged appointments, undeserved and without any additional work. But the biggest lesson I have learned is that I am not here to put the whole world to rights, just to hold true to my values and give it my all. The warrior spirit is still strong within me – I just need to pick the battles I can and will fight and to champion my beliefs. I still believe that I have a role within Defence in the UK - I just no longer believe I can achieve that role within the armed forces. I am no longer a woman at war with myself – I am only at war with those who are selecting for personal power and privilege and who are willing to damage the UK's defensive abilities, disrupt the armed forces ability to recruit and destroy its ability to retain the best. All for the goal of retaining personal power.

Part Two: Reflections

Chapter Fifteen
Tea and Medals

Never doubt that a group of thoughtful committed citizens can change the world—indeed it is the only thing that ever has
Margaret Mead

I needed to take a little pause after I finished command. Withdrawal and replenishment are fine military principles. I withdrew, to contemplate which battles were worth fighting and to figure out what had just happened. Newall and I took time out to spend a month cycling across the Mongolian Gobi Desert. We travelled with just two local guides and it gave us a sense of the culture and the enduring legacy of Genghis Khan. In the West, we remember his brutality, but he was famed in his homeland for his promotion by meritocracy, religious tolerance and service leadership skills so it was an important lesson in perspective.

It was a truly amazing landscape. Dry and pockmarked by the occasional well or village, it was a mixture of stony, sedimentary rocks with occasional pockets of deep sand and dunes, dry riverbeds and, in the west, the Altai Mountains.

Among the nomads, camels and angora goats, we were a novelty on our bright orange touring bikes. The wildlife was extraordinary; snow leopards in the mountains, rare ibex and the soaring steppe eagles circling above. We wild-camped in a different location each evening, avoiding the scorpions and cooking on camel dung stoves.

As I rode my bike for mile after mile along the dusty desert roads, I realised that I needed to write my story, for clarity, insight and catharsis. Although I hadn't realised how hard that would be - almost a year spent collecting my thoughts, re-reading diaries and reports and talking to colleagues. Another six months writing, reviewing and settling on a final draft. An introvert by nature, introverting myself further to look backwards and inwards was tough; I needed the support of all my friends and family in order to retain my perspective and sanity. But eventually I had over thirty years of military and civilian life experiences distilled into a few chapters.

It was good to be reminded of how much I had enjoyed and achieved. The benefits of military training were many, both in my army life and in my civilian one. And there was so much I owed to the Army and to army people – good people whom I valued as friends and colleagues.

But there were also some seriously bad bits. And while in some ways I felt the Army owed me for a few of the shitty moments, more importantly I actually felt I owed it to the Army to do something constructive and point out a few of its flaws.

When I left SIU, my hope was to do what regulars do after a successful command - be promoted and take my experience to a new military role. But I found that without patronage, I wasn't going to get through. It was a shock and it hurt.

Was it just me? Were the lessons I learned just personal or were they common to most women, reserves, intelligencers and the non-elite? In other words, all my sub-groups.

Was the Army culture just fun and quirky or was there an aspect that was more sinister?

I had put my head above the proverbial parapet and found a handful of bigoted 'nasties' out there keen to see me fail, if it furthered their cause. I had repeatedly witnessed overt bigotry against reserves, women and change leaders. I had encountered an entrenched, resistant middle cohort who preferred to coast along rather than to do anything or get involved. And I had watched too many talented soldiers and officers leave.

I had also seen cowardly lack of support, for me and for others, from senior leaders. I had seen change in the attitudes of the majority and in legislation, but no discipline or consequences for senior leaders who didn't change their values. When had genuine service leadership, the very mainstay of the British Army, vanished?

Why do individuals whose leadership is poor and selfish continue to thrive? Why does the institution fail to deal with these failed leaders? What is the risk to the efficiency of the Army, its ability to meet new threats and to demonstrate its relevance to politicians and to the public? Reflecting on all these questions I felt I was getting there. It wasn't about me; it was about re-igniting and nurturing the warrior spirit across the ranks. Talented, open-minded people need to be promoted for the Army as a whole to change.

I felt ready to let go of the personal stuff, but only if I could take a good hard look at the structural and institutional failings, why they happen and how much harm they are doing to 'being the best'.

And that meant speaking up – about what happened to me, and about the big issues where the Army is getting it so wrong. I had come across all of them over the years, but in many ways the handling of the vexatious service complaint against me summarised all that is bad and apathetic and misjudged in the Army's leadership and approach; a lack of diversity, back-stabbing, fear of women and diversity and change, protection of the privileged over efficiency and unwillingness to acknowledge it when we don't know what to do and need to ask for help.

When I left the Army, I had to re-integrate into civilian life. I had to set up a routine, an income stream and friendship groups. And I wanted to let the pain I felt settle. I broadened my leadership experience, becoming a trustee for a scientific exploration society and working as a defence contractor. And I reached out to others, in and out of the Army, and heard stories from many women, reserves and intelligencers about why they too were disillusioned. What bothered me most was the high percentage that left military service angry, bitter or just 'lost'. Where are the great alumni of positivity enjoyed by most universities and schools? That undoubted force for good, a veterans' network supporting its former employer? We don't have it. And all too often it's tough for ex-military people, which is why too many fail when they leave and re-enter the civilian world. How do we stop that?

Many veterans do stay in touch with regimental associations and attend reunions. But what we need is a more joined up foundation to support and mentor those currently serving and to include those who have left, to retain their sense of belonging, of being invested.

I can't fix the woeful under-resourcing, the gaps now in the critical middle ranks or the dreadful decisions already made in procurement, housing and equipment. I can comment on but not influence the foolishly counter-productive in-fighting between the Royal Navy, RAF and Army. Those are not within my gift. But what I can do is to speak out on behalf of others, focussing on the 'people' part of resources. This is what I understand best and where I have the most knowledge, specifically around women and reserves. And I know that one of the easiest ways to judge an organisation is by looking at how it treats its minorities.

I don't think the Army is getting the best out of many of its regulars, but I really think there is wholesale ignorance of how to adapt to get the best out of its reserves. Being able to adapt is a key military skill, so why is the Army now so rigid?

Getting the best out of reserves would benefit the Army enormously. If reserves could play a key role, then the whole force concept could really work. This is something I have lived from both sides – I know what it is to be a regular and a reserve and how, at their best and strongest, they can support each other.

I am an idealist, not in any way naive. I have been there, done it and have the ripped and bloodied t-shirt to prove it. So, I know it will be difficult. Those in power now will not willingly give it up or share it, even for the greater good of better military morale and efficiency. The weight of evidence has been building- the announcement in July 2019, summarised in the Daily Telegraph by Dominic Nicholls was 'The Armed Forces (still) has unacceptable levels of sexism, racism and bullying, because it is led by a pack of middle-aged white men'. There are 'unacceptable levels of inappropriate behaviour' and the Army has announced a new Defence Authority to tackle it. I want to believe this will make the difference. It will of course depend if they mean business- from my experience of the deliberately obstructive and delaying complaints system, I have my doubts, but I intend now to be part of the group that holds their feet to the flames to deliver it.

Change is a journey, not a destination. But where to start? From my experiences, I think I would be well qualified to have a view.

The Army has a beautiful phrase: 'Home for tea and medals'. It is a way of saying our task is done; it's time to go home and pat ourselves on the back for a job well done. Tea (the opportunity to sit down and talk through the shared experience) and medals (the recognition of those who have put in that 'extra bit', to get the task done) are important. They summarise the fundamental human need for motivation, aspiration and appreciation. And they sum up why people stay in the Army. It isn't for the money – pay is low for all but the top tier – and those on full time reserve service contracts coasting along on middle management pay while doing non-management roles.

The rewards that make all the pain of service worthwhile are the comradeship, being listened to and being appreciated – in public uniformed service, honours, awards and promotion is part of saying thank you. They are the only bonus system we have.

At the moment, the Army is struggling to recruit and, more importantly, to retain the right people. Why is such a high percentage of the top talent leaving early? Why are so few joining up? Well, one reason is the Army is not delivering tea and medals in the way that it needs to. To answer the why, I need to explain 'tea and medals' and particularly, the discrepancies between the Army's approach to part-time and full-time workers.

Mates in the Army are the best. Sharing a beer or a 'brew' (NATO standard tea – milk and two sugars) is a way of sitting down and talking things through. Many problems are resolved this way. And every ex-soldier misses these conversations, the camaraderie with others who understand what has been experienced. Okay, some of the 'old and bold' do swing a long story here and there (it is said that 'old soldiers never die; young soldiers wish they would'), but at this level – drinking tea – the Army is one family and it's an art. We can talk serious stuff or nonsense and what we say is usually tolerated, counselled or laughed at in equal measure. I miss it already. It is the commonest reason why regulars, who swear they will never, ever join the reserves, find they start to consider it after about 18 months out of uniform. That's how it was for me.

So, at an individual level, listening skills are pretty good. At the organisational and senior officer level though, not so good. There are a few bosses who actively listen, but, it has become a forgotten art, confused, perhaps deliberately, with negative assumptions. Soldiers have learned not to raise issues, even ones that need fixing, for fear of being categorised as whingers. Solving your own problems (often a good thing) is seen as showing backbone, but it can mean that where soldiers can't fix their own problems, they end up desperate before they ask for help, even for mental health issues. The Intelligence

Corps hit a huge retention problem a few years ago with its Captains and Sergeants leaving in high volume. With some reluctance, HQs eventually agreed to meet with this cohort, but came away with a view that they were 'just whingeing'. The outflow continued.

At a recent senior reserve command course, senior reserves attempted to 'have tea' with regular commanders and discuss some of the disparities between regulars and reserves. The reaction? The guest speaker, a very senior, regular military officer had not realised reserves were in attendance and then alluded to them as whingeing and made further disparaging anti-reserve remarks. Once he realised he had a mixed audience, he tried to retract by saying 'it was all banter'. This was not an isolated example. Far from it. So how can we open doors if we don't call this stuff out?

Tea is meant to be a safety valve, the ability to discuss issues, both good and bad informally. To celebrate successes, commiserate with failures and a chance for any decent commander to get a sense of what his troops are thinking.

Soldiers know that amongst our peers, propped up in staff rooms or at the bar, military colleagues still offer the best pair of ears for your troubles that you could possibly want. (Just don't expect a subtle answer.) For reserves 'tea' matters just as much – perhaps even more, because they are on the outside and need to regularly connect with peers and bosses, both reserve and regular. But these genuine listening get-togethers are not happening. Why? Because fundamentally most regulars don't trust reserves – from the top down. At one stage I sat with the head of military intelligence and he said he had never met a reserve who hadn't let him down. I was silenced by hearing this from a senior leader. Nearly 50% of the troops under his control were reserves. This was Orwellian-level bigotry: 'Four legs good; two legs bad'.

How do we change that?

Plenty of good reserves will travel down at two am on a Saturday morning or midnight on a Friday, work a full weekend and then go home and do the household chores, before returning to work the next day. Why don't we salute that? The US mostly does.

The Army has improved at providing feedback and listening forums – there are 'lessons identified' sessions after conflicts, women's forums, young officer forums and continuous attitude surveys, reviewed annually. The problem is not the opportunities for giving feedback, it is getting things changed without being labelled a whinger. In other words, getting any kind of constructive response to the feedback. The Army is still not good at separating genuine grievance from unnecessary grumblings or getting the important lessons identified to army chiefs. Not least because bad news tends to be buried by the Red Lighters.

Alongside the forums, there used to be a system where all ranks could submit their ideas for improvement and even make a few quid doing so. It was popular - I am not sure why it was stopped - but it was another way the troops felt they were being heard.

Clearly, societies and their defence forces need resilience, or we become 'snowflakes'; that lovely insult for those who we anticipate will melt at the first sign of heat. But resilience shouldn't mean putting up with everything. To feel enabled, empowered and to buy into our organisations, we need to feel we have a voice and to know that our voice can be heard. Closing down these channels, especially the listening skills of senior officials, is very dangerous. Without a voice, what happens is the best leave knowing their energies will be wasted.

An organisation that has stopped listening tends to lose the next war. That is why drinking tea together has never been more important. It makes us sit down, it creates a safe forum; all ranks together to share ideas and thoughts. And of course, beer – as an alternative to tea – does have some advantages; when inhibitions are lowered, soldiers will tell you honestly why they think you are great or just a w*n**r. My rifles crew did this to me many times, and sometimes it gave me worthwhile feedback.

Active listening takes time and means taking responsibility for meeting other people's needs. I ensured our HQ was open to reserves at any time. It wasn't always convenient, but it ensured that there was always a cup of tea and the opportunity for a chat. I also attended at weekends and encouraged all my permanent staff to do the same, leaving the door open for anyone to drop in. It's a lot to expect reserve unit permanent staff, who need to be there during the week, to be there at weekends too. But getting together is so essential to preventing the 'them' and 'us' attitude developing and to understand what I used to call 'gripes and gratitude'.

Most of all, spending time together takes away the mystery of difference and makes us hear wider views. Reserves can share the knowledge of the 'outside world', regulars their wisdom on military matters. We can all ask questions of culture and values. Of course, we should practice the art of drinking tea together. It teaches us, informally and without rules, how to appreciate each other's strengths and knowledge. It is one of the greatest skills the Army possesses.

Nowhere has 'them and us' been more evident than between reserves and regulars. In the past the two were kept apart, other than for training and military operations. With a shrinking Army, the need for quality reserves is recognised from Industry, Government, even the big, defence Think Tanks. Yet there remains a blind spot for regulars. There has been much talk of merging systems to the mutual benefit of all serving personnel. As far as I could work out, it was translated as reserves coming into line with regular systems. The result was regulars doubling their workload without being trained, reserves following systems not really designed with their needs in mind and both regulars and reserves getting a poor deal and feeling resentful.

Career management is a prime example. All regulars physically move every two to three years and reserves move posts on the same timeline. This cycle has to be adjusted for changing conflicts, rotating through operational posts, military exercises, training, promotion and trade courses. For officers, there is also the need to rotate through staff posts, the 'how the Army runs' roles.

The army mantra is that it will try to give you your first choice of posting, but the final decision will be in the interest of the service. The reality is significant numbers of compulsory, short notice moves, which for full-timers means moving home, moving schools for the children and so on, and is the reason they get higher pay.

Career management for reserves used to be separate since it's quite different. As reserves live in their own homes and communities (which is why the reserves used to be called the territorials), there is rarely a need for housing, most are content to stay in their local unit, except when called up to support conflicts. About half of reserves actively seek a career, others are happy to do their minimum bit and see where it takes them. As part of the whole force approach, senior reserves are now managed by the same Glasgow personnel centre that manages the regulars and this is not the best method for most reserves.

Some of the desk officers in Glasgow are permanent staff (but it seems to attract those Whitmarsh types- the obstructive jobsworths), but most are soldiers posted in and completing what is an HR role as part of their standard service. They have little experience, compared to their civilian peers, and most have no experience of the reserves they are now expected to manage as well. I have never served in Glasgow, although I once applied – not because I wanted to work in HR, but because I wanted to know how the system worked. From the outside, it appeared to be a dark art. A series of boards, run by often unknown panel members, usually regulars, known as grading boards, placed us all in a pecking order by rank. If we were graded above a quality line, we were eligible for promotion. For a regular, this means they would be promoted over the next 12 months; for reserves there was an extra step as you had to apply and be successful on an appointment board as well. I call this extra step for reserves 'double-jeopardy' - it can take years, if it happens at all, whereas regulars are guaranteed promotion if they are above the quality line.

Having a regular manage my career during a critical promotion window was seriously detrimental – peers of mine who were being managed by reserves did better. I simply wasn't important to those regular managers and I suffered from that institutional neglect as much as from the rarer and deliberate vicious moments.

Perhaps surprisingly, despite the whole force approach, it is still possible to complete reserve service with almost no exposure to regular forces, other than a few regulars in the units or when called up to war or training. However, in some specialist reserve units and for all senior reserves, there is a real need to be exposed to the wider world of the regular army more often. These niche groups really need to create opportunities to sit down and talk. My experience was that this wasn't encouraged; there was little sense in regular HQ or units that reserves were entitled to a voice. Nor was there transparency in decision making that might have advanced the whole force concept. All the 'leaning in' (contributing and taking up opportunities) came from the reserves' side, with many taking time off day jobs to pick up kit or attend meetings during the week.

I did hear of one brigade in which some officers started to stay late one evening a week to enable conversations with the reserves and I applauded their openness and foresight. But why only one? My intelligence brigade boss, PSmith, made reserves' growth the 'main effort' for over 6 months. It wasn't seen as a popular decision, but leadership isn't always about popularity, it was the right decision to support the whole force concept. I haven't seen this approach since he moved on – the new boss returned the priority to regular troops.

There is so much to be said for spending some time together. It allows us to hear other people's views and ideas, it dissolves prejudices and fears and it enables us to see what we share and have in common, rather than what divides us.

I took great pleasure in managing the reserves under my command. I wanted to see my team, my family, do well. If I was guilty of an error in command, it was drinking tea with my troops more than I drank tea with my boss. Both are important; look after the people and they will look after the job in hand but look after your boss and he or she will do the same for you. Being fairly senior, I had multiple bosses, and most were regular, which meant they worked during the week and I worked mostly at weekends. Opportunities for tea were scarce and while the responsibility was not all mine, with hindsight I could have found ways to prioritise it more. Those shared conversations would have built trust and trust would have given my bosses confidence that I would not embarrass them and that my actions would support their careers as well as my own. As it was, I struggled to build the necessary bond with those senior regulars because we spent very little time together, because we were all struggling with the whole force approach and because I was the outsider.

Trust is instinctive, and therefore subjective. But its mysteries can be diminished through spending time together, whether in the office, on an adventure training course or in the tea-room. And drinking tea together reduces the effects of the blocks above us because once we meet and talk and exchange ideas we are people to one another, rather than 'person unknown'.

When I saw promotions, honours and awards go to those in the image of the boss, I was hurt and disappointed, but I knew that one of my weaknesses was finding it difficult to big myself up to bosses. It was uncomfortable, it always felt like altering my approach to just ticking boxes, which has never been my style. As a reserve, I am not as institutionalised as regulars and so am less inclined towards tribal thinking and peer pressure to conform. But what I didn't fully get back then was that offering less risk and more success to my senior officers was important to *them*.

The Army has always struggled to integrate outsiders: women, ethnic minorities and reserves in particular. It's easy to see why. Getting to know fellow Etonians, or masonic brethren (and I am told that a possible 50 percent of army officers are masons) feels easier, there is more work in bringing in outsiders and listening to their views. But not doing so has dangers too, because outsiders bring skills, ideas and energy to the table and the Army needs all of these.

The reactions I experienced (and those that many others have experienced in the military as well) approached the scale of a witch-hunt at times. What was harder to isolate was why I was classed as an outsider. Was it because I was a woman, a reserve or because I came from an insignificant cap-badge/grammar school/tribal background? With hindsight, some of the witch-hunts that dogged me during my command could have been avoided, but I doubt I could have avoided the widespread hostility, given the low percentage of women, reserves and non-public school power bases at the top.

It is when Institutions become 'closed tribes' that resistance builds, and they become hostile to perceived 'outsiders'. For the Army, sense of isolation is exacerbated by living in barracks, being away from family, the regimental systems (designed to enhance the warrior spirit), and finally the unwillingness of our tribal chiefs to allow independent review.

When I was wrong-footed by HQ Intelligence in late 2015, it was because I wasn't prepared for the hostility towards the growth of reserves. It wasn't something I had done wrong. I was simply the instigator of change, and change was not seen as something good.

Hostile resistance to change is fixable. But our leaders cannot just talk about being behind the principles of change. They need to lead with actions and bold moves to show us that they welcome change – and outsiders.

When Flashheart visited SIU a few months before I left and stood in front of a fully reserve audience, one of my team – someone who was not enthralled by military hierarchy – asked him why regulars seemed so bitter towards reserves, why reserves were treated as second-class and why A2020 seemed to have exacerbated the bitterness. Flashheart, always an honest speaker, looked him in the eye and said, 'Because we got the narrative wrong'.

Reserves have a huge amount to offer the regular army. They are the Army's link with the civilian world and the many skills and fresh ideas that those who still work in the civilian world can bring to the military. I want to do more than just hope a day will come, not too far into the future, when regulars and reserves will work together with mutual appreciation, goodwill and respect. The next steps I decided to take after that period of reflection, cycling across the Gobi Desert, were part of my plan to do more.

Chapter Sixteen
Who You Know and Who You Are
(or The Tyranny of the B Grade)

*Praise and recognition, based on performance, are the oxygen of the
human spirit*
John Adair

One of the biggest headaches the Army faces is
that troops are leaving in significant numbers, often far
short of the time they signed up for. Reasons I've heard
include under-manning, being promoted too early,
spending less time on operations, too much paperwork
and not enough adventure. And then there are litigation
worries; the combined effect of shady lawyers and those
willing to take a punt at blaming a soldier, plus the lack of
support from army leaders when the prosecutors are
circling.

Several recent cases illustrate this only too well. In
2018, the decision was taken to prosecute one ex-soldier
over Bloody Sunday, an event that happened 47 years ago.
It was an awful event, one that caused immense heartache

and regret on all sides, and mistakes were made, but is it right, at this late stage, to prosecute one or two elderly men for activities conducted when under military orders? If soldiers become too scared to engage in a fight, for fear of long-term litigation, we are already halfway to failure. I learned much of my fighting spirit from my time in the full-time army and I wouldn't like to see that resilience lost for short-term political aims.

Who wants to see elderly people tried for an act that happened many years ago and that has already been subject to judicial review, in the case of Bloody Sunday, multiple times? Why are lawyers allowed to keep coming back, hoping that the Army will settle financially rather than go through yet another review? We need judges with a better understanding of army service and conflict. Of course, there will be one or two rotten eggs, but the overwhelming majority of troops are serving with the intention of doing good. Please stand in their shoes before supporting these actions, or there will be very few willing to take the job on.

I believe it is important to any soldier to know that if they have followed the military rules of engagement of the time, they will not face individual prosecution, even if they have made a genuine mistake (and before you judge an individual's action, take a look at the footage still available of what those paratroopers faced on that day – the ugly violence of the crowd, the knowledge that fellow paratroopers had been murdered recently by paramilitaries). If there is to be a political reckoning, then it is service chiefs who should answer for the military decision that was taken to engage, not someone who was a junior soldier at that time. The individual needs to know that they will be supported by the military leaders, even while they face the consequences of any mistake. They need to know that only if they break the rules will they be expelled from the military family. This way, soldiers can join, serve and leave the Army knowing that they will not have to face looking over their shoulders for decades to come, for political-level choices. To offer any less is to reach the situation we now have, with soldiers leaving and potential soldiers choosing not to join for fear of prosecution, sometimes many years later, for events over which they have no control.

Aside from the threat of prosecution, there are many other reasons why soldiers leave early. While pay up to junior captain or senior sergeant is comparable to civvie street wages, by around the age of 28 the good ones will easily find better conditions in the outside world. Throw in poor accommodation and reduced opportunities for unique experiences such as going overseas to train and fight and no wonder so many of the brightest and best leave. I particularly liked a comment on one young officers' forum asking for 'more of a Harry Potter staircase of a career ladder, rather than a narrow, one-route escalator' (which only favours the select few who have patronage). I imagined the senior officers reading that request and harrumphing, 'A Harry *who* staircase? And they want a meritocracy, promotion on quality, not time served or who they know?' Double harrumph. Feedback is being provided through all these forums, but very little change is happening. So inevitably those contributing to the forums, for lack of any genuine 'tea' situations, are going to feel that what they say is not heard and that speaking out is pointless.

If tea drinking is the art, then fair application of rewards needs to be a science; objective, system-based and well-regulated. I have not met many who think the Army does career management well. It isn't easy.

The rewards that the Army offers in order to motivate, encourage and appreciate soldiers for their efforts and achievements come in the form of gradings, promotions and medals. The system should be based on merit, but all too often it isn't. It is skewed, so that in many cases promotions go to those who don't deserve them while those who do are overlooked. And at the same time genuine feedback is often discouraged.

The grading system insists that all serving military get an annual report and a mid-term appraisal report - the MPAR, which is like the system in most workplaces. The report system requires an A to D grade, alongside promotion prospects and recommendations for the type of job the candidate should go for. Other than the arcane, unnecessary complexity of the system and the time it takes, the system design is all right; the problem is in the enactment of the system.

In 2011, I had to re-enter the world of writing reports for those under my command. And right at the start I had a difficult one to write; multiple line managers were concerned about the performance of a particular officer. The system had changed since I last wrote a report, so I checked on what the new gradings meant. There was a guidebook on the gradings A to D, which were all explained, as was the plus and minus that could be used to 'shade it'.

Having done my homework I looked at my notes on this officer; his line manager's report was poor, his work output low, he hadn't responded to a chat with his line manager so I decided that this must be a C. I completed it and showed a draft to one of the desk officers who said, 'You can't do this, he must be a B'.

'What?' I consulted the guide again. 'But that's not what the guide shows.'

A shrug from desk-officer. 'If you give him a C, he will put in a complaint, because you will disadvantage him compared to others. No-one gets a C.'

'So, I can only give an A or a B? That's it?'

Nod from desk officer.

'Why would the poor performers be motivated to do better if they can all get a B?' I asked. My response was a look of pity on the desk officer's face.

This is a huge problem. Line managers either give over-inflated grades, to ensure their best individuals get above the quality line, which simply escalates all good people into an A, while everyone else – the average and the poor – are lumped into the B group. On my report I decided to give the chap a C and, sure enough, he put in a complaint and I was ordered to change it.

We are not following the guidebook or using common sense. So, what was happening? I could see that without professional HR advice, soldiers and officers were being bullied by the threat of a brutal complaints system that would tie them all in months of paperwork if they didn't offer a B. I discussed it with my mentor. 'Aah,' he said. 'This problem is known, so don't worry about the grade, focus on the Performance and Potential section'. Except the grade does matter. It is difficult to motivate a low performer if they can have a B, whatever they do. An inability to give a C, let alone a D, alongside the threat of complaints makes some poorly performing individuals virtually un-touchable.

I remember one officer who announced he was leaving, so would be going to play squash every afternoon, rather than work. I asked him when he was leaving, assuming it was in the next few weeks. 'In three years' time,' he said. He wasn't mine to report on, but in the time, I worked in the same HQ, he did play squash most afternoons and let his warrant officer cover the work. I heard that he got a B+ on his report. He knew he was untouchable. And he wasn't alone, he is one of many I have witnessed who are serial under-performers.

When the Army decides not to include lower grades in its appraisals, it strips individuals of their will to perform. An appraisal system that won't give C grades (let alone Ds), has a problem. Because keeping your head down and putting in a low performance gets you the same grade as the 'good but not brilliant' cohort. Only the truly excellent (or privileged) beat you. I remember listening to a conversation about a full-timer's report. The (middle class white male) individual had been coming in late and leaving early every day for about 12 months because his wife had taken a new job. He had taken responsibility for collecting the children so arrived around 9.30 and left at 3 while still being paid full-time. His output, even when he was there, was low. The draft report writer was on the phone, recommending a C.

'He's not been doing well, his work output has been poor, but he needs to promote this year, it's his last chance,' he explained.

'Just give him a B and a good write up,' came the answer.

So, nothing to do with performance. It was his 'turn', so that meant he could coast for a full tour and still promote. He was untouchable. Newton's third law states that for every action there is an equal and opposite reaction and in practice this means that apathetic B grades produce apathetic performances, and this lowers productivity. This is why morale in public bodies is often low (church, NHS, police, fire-service, education and military, as examples), but the B-graders still stay, because although pay is generally lower than in the private sector, they are guaranteed annual increases and promotions, jobs for life and above average pensions - all without requiring excellence (or even adequacy) of performance.

But what exacerbates the problem for the Army is the lack of any professional HR. There is no-one to talk to independently about poor people management. The reporting system leads everything; the collection of grades and appointments – collectively known as your 'book' in army parlance – is the only career tool. This rigidity of career management is why the Army has a current inability to *be the best*. What does this look like? It means indifference to how public money is spent. It means that that the privileged classes are attracted to public roles because of the higher power, lower accountability model prevalent in the public sector. It allows a handful of privileged committees to control their own remuneration and rewards. It discourages high quality outputs that would be seen in private companies who are accountable to shareholders.

Aside from higher grading for the privileged as reward, there are the medals. One of the great things about the Army is seeing someone's career and achievements displayed through their medals. There are two broad types of honours: operational medals (for heroism on operations) and those for achievements away from the front-line. Add in medals for long service and good conduct, reserve service; formerly the Territorial Decoration (TD) but now a post-nominal of Voluntary Reserve (VR), Jubilee medals and different campaign medals, for example for service in Iraq, and you can end up with quite a rack.

There are also internal commendations and national honours: MBE, OBE, and the rare CBE, which I have only seen awarded to senior officers. For reserves there is an additional one called the Queen's Voluntary Reserve Medal (QVRM). We don't have as many as, for instance, the USA, but it is possible to acquire around a dozen through a full career.

The awarding of medals should be a glowing testament to the fairness and honour of the Army. Except that this is not quite true. While you can't nominate yourself and the award of a medal is supposed to come as a surprise non-operational medals are skewed to certain ranks and cap-badges. Before I was awarded my OBE I received calls telling me that I was in the running but that Intelligence HQ was trying to block me as they didn't want a reserve to get an award that might be 'used better' for a regular. Operational medals are also skewed, but for more understandable reasons – you are more likely to earn one if you are a bomb-disposal expert or a front-line medic than if you are in a support role. I asked a bomb-disposal expert who worked for me why he had a QGM (Queen's Gallantry Medal) while a fellow bomb-disposal expert in the team had an MBE. He smiled and said, 'The MBE was earned for getting a group of infantry out of trouble. My medal was for getting myself out of the trouble I got myself into in the first place.' He did tell me his story later and it was well worth a listen. The QGM is an operational medal awarded for outstanding acts of physical bravery, while the MBE is for an outstanding performance on a broader basis.

The nomination system for honours was – and still is – organised through another secretive military panel. As far as I could tell, it ran on a barter system, with each cap-badge agreeing who would take their turn and when. I heard lines like, 'It's not the reserves' turn', 'We don't have any more for our cap-badge this year' and, 'It's a guaranteed award that goes with the post'. I couldn't find out who sat on the selection panel or how meritocracy was retained, but I could see that there was an abundance of middle-class white males on the list. It is another example of a system in which minorities have to be outstanding to achieve success, whereas the favoured few can rely on it as part of their privileged ride up the to the top.

The promotion system is another that needs an overhaul. Not only are there unwritten discriminations, prejudices and favouritisms, but the system means that reserves have a harder time getting promoted. They don't just pass a promotion board, they have to face a selection board too – I called this double jeopardy – and only after both have been passed, can the promotion be awarded.

The day that was to be my lowest career point, worse even than the police investigation, was late in 2015 when I was waiting to hear the promotion board results. I had applied for a job I believed I was perfectly qualified for and I was sure it was mine. It was my birthday and I was excited about being promoted. I was under investigation over Mac's complaint at the time, but I had been assured that malicious allegations by a difficult member of staff who was throwing as much mud as he could to avoid being held accountable was not going to hold my career back.

As I stood in the bar, making small talk to my reserves' boss, he looked awkward. He had seen the results. 'You didn't get it', he said. An hour or so later I had to give a speech congratulating others in my unit on their promotion success, in front of the man who retained the post I had hoped to get. It made no sense to me at all, and this was the day I vowed to start investigating the system.

What I found is that promises are made, as they were to me, to get someone to take on a tough job or role, and then conveniently forgotten. The Army no longer rewards service leadership, looking after your people, it rewards selfish leadership, looking after yourself. I was willing to make that mad journey into Uxbridge to train, and I did get a good career report as a result. But a few years later the career team told me, 'That type of training role doesn't count'. Over and over this is the story good people tell, that doing a good job isn't the key to military promotion – it's who you know and who you are. In other words, class and connections – I call it the Cult of the Individual, because teamwork, performance and results are of little value compared to patronage. To put it bluntly, it is a protectionist racket.

And as a result, this biased career management is driving the most talented to leave. A fellow top third reserve intelligence officer who had received a lower grade from a regular, dropping from a consistent A position to a B, confronted his line manager, telling him, 'The only difference in my performance between last year and this year is you'. And in the end, he left, because he was never going to be supported or promoted.

A fellow colleague from the WRAC, the group I trained with at Sandhurst, stayed on as a regular and seemed to have a strong career path – until she left suddenly. I asked her why and she said she knew she wouldn't be allowed to progress any further in the current system. She also told me that she had been on Glasgow boards where results had been 'amended' to reflect a preferred outcome for a board – in other words, the boards were fixed.

Another senior woman officer, one of the highest flyers of her generation, also left suddenly to join a specialist branch of the police. I asked one of her mentors and he told me she had been struggling to get past the regular boarding system and knew she had better opportunities elsewhere.

There are a number of women on these military blogs who reported being told they would not be given the same level of career support 'as they were going to leave and have babies' so the (male) boss didn't want to waste his time. And there are many other reserve commanding officers stuck, like me, on the unposted list unable to get promoted. What we see, and what I have raised to Glasgow, is that having skills and experience isn't getting us through these boards, only privilege and connections do that.

If the Army was recruiting strongly and retaining best quality people perhaps incidents like these wouldn't stand out so vividly. However, the Army is struggling to recruit and is retaining the wrong balance of talent (and way, way too many expensive senior officers for the size of the Army). I think we must find the will to re-set the 'fairness bar'. We must hold a mirror up to the senior leaders, even if we cannot ensure they take time to see if there is a taint in the reflection, or to own the responsibility for bringing a more diverse cohort on behind them.

A 'quick win' would be to professionalise Human Resources in the Army. Because a tweak, given the level of bias, won't fix it; shifting entrenched low performers will need a professional and consistent approach. But it would be worth it; top talent will stay if they are valued, trusted, mentored, challenged, included in decision making and above all, appreciated. It isn't rocket science, but it is a science.

Apart from anything else there is a significant benefit to be achieved in bringing in a proper HR service to handle the huge backlog of complaints and dissatisfaction with the complaints system. I am among the 70% of those who are not happy with the way a complaint has been handled. It's a startlingly high number. And it's not about sour grapes. Fifteen months to get the Army to respond to a complaint? And their lawyers decide what can and cannot be investigated? A further 15 months for an appeal even to be looked at? That isn't a system, it is a blocker.

Being overlooked is incredibly painful, particularly when there is no explanation, and initially it felt easier to blame my own failings rather than a skewed system. But I have suffered many setbacks on my way to the top, from growing too tall to be a ballerina all the way to the Army throttling of the promotion system and I mostly know how to separate a genuine 'no'. What happened to me didn't feel right and the research showed it wasn't right, which is why I decided to keep fighting. Each step takes another small piece of ground, even if I did sit it out for a round or two while I tended my bruises. I care too deeply about the Army of the future, those who will sign up who deserve a fair and transparently just system, to give up.

So much of career management is done behind closed doors, with little feedback. I have been sent commiseration emails with 'Glasgow moves in mysterious ways', as an explanation. I began to analyse board results. Writer Caitlin Moran calls it a 'testicle premium.' I would go further, it's a golden testicle premium, for the middle-class white male; a platinum testicle premium if you are also *connected* (a mason, an MP, or know the chair of the board, for example).

I found two main areas of challenge. The first I saw was an army own goal; damage done by using untrained regulars to do what should be professional HR roles. Most are well-meaning amateurs, but they create inconsistency in results, then move on after three years. And there is huge added risk of them promoting friends and disadvantaging enemies.

The second challenge is the standard power curve. If you study the demographics of the Army and cut a slice through each senior rank, you get a quick sense of how the pyramid at the top is skewed towards public school, white males and to the cap-badges where upper middle-class white males reside. Does only this group aspire to head up the Army? No, it is about 'like selecting like'. It is the bias that feeds 'biased promotion systems'. The Army term for it is as I have explained is the 'golden escalator'; if you are on it, you tend to be selected for the plum jobs, gain promotion at the first look and get nominated for awards. It is not that these golden children never deserve their success, more that proportionally they get the rewards earlier and in greater volume and sometimes they are undeserved.

Newton's third law applies to army rewarding and retention. Treat people badly and the good ones, who have options, leave. The military struggles to value its people and to understand the benefits of diversity. It has been complacent and allowed the weeds to grow across its garden. It needs to do some judicious and urgent weeding.

Most army people are resilient and tolerant of an average amount of what we call fuckwittery: being uprooted, moved at short notice and so on. The moves that are genuinely in the interests of the service are usually accepted; it is those that lack transparency, that smell of favouritism or its opposite, the random, un-explained moves that hurt. When this happens, it seems that the rewards system - the postings, promotions and/or medals that are highlights of any career, are awarded as more of an art, when it must be a science.

While the Army is struggling to hang onto those it should value, it is also being hampered by a hopelessly bogged down recruiting system. When the Army brought in Capita, in 2012, to handle its recruiting, there were many voices of concern, and mine was one of them. The recommended idea was to continue running the old system concurrently until the new system could be seen to be working. But that didn't happen. Instead, the old system was dropped, and Capita recruiting was expected to work from day one. It didn't, not least because the Army retained an incompatible computer system as a cost-saving exercise. That wasn't the only reason though; there were all kinds of teething problems. A year later several very senior officers wrote a summary of these recruiting delays which was ignored. As a result, simple problems are still blocking recruiting and it takes 18 months to three years to bring a recruit into service. No civilian company could tolerate that kind of delay. Potential soldiers drop out simply because there are too many of those pesky hoops to jump through and each hoop is placed months apart. They are not made to feel wanted or valued, so they choose other options.

The Army needs to learn the lessons of the appalling recruiting system, get professionals to set up the tender and don't just pick the cheapest without looking at the contract; it has to be about cost-benefit and value, not just the headline figure.

The Army rotation system means that there is always someone new dealing with recruiting and HR. Since staff are moved on every 3 years, too many staff officers sign and forget and then move on, which means that in the future they hold no responsibility for their past decisions. Whoever moves into the role next has to deal with any repercussions. But they know that in 3 years they too will move on, so *delaying tactics* become very tempting.

This can lead to enormous blunders. One of the classics was, and is, the current housing situation. A team of staff offices signed away the management of many service houses to a private company. In return the Army leases them back at a reduced rate, but only for several years. When this time is up all the rents will go up, so it wasn't a bargain at all.

Then there is the well-advertised maintenance contract for soldiers' housing and for other building on military sites, negotiated by an amateur army officer who was soon posted on, and so not around to see the consequences. It was so bad that when the power to our building was accidentally switched off and needed the trip re-setting, the terms of the contract stated that the military were forbidden from touching it. Even a simple flick of a switch required maintenance call out and a fee. And even better, the maintenance company had a 3-day window in which to do it.

Do I sound angry in this chapter? Well, I am, because this is the root of current military toxicity. We ARE getting the Army we deserve - under-recruited, unfit and unable to retain the best. An employer that cannot value its people, that runs a career and reward system that favours only a handful of privileged white men for top leadership and retains by preference those who won't rock the boat in the middle ranks, is not setting itself up as a battle-winning force, it is setting itself up as a cult to pay homage to the 'Old Boys' Network'.

Army life remains an attractive offer in the early years of a career – but it does attract the mischievous, lazy, bigoted or just downright evil to join as well at the great and good. However good the recruitment process (and as I have explained, the Army's is not good), this can still be managed if an organisation is able to weed out the worst people quickly. The tyranny of the B grade prevents this; and the lack of a professional and fair complaints process drives good military people to apathy or early departure, while those who are past their best linger on.

The unique nature of the military offer: access to an adventurous, professional military environment, a steady job, camaraderie, care of family and welfare, boarding school allowances for the kids, a sense of vocation and structure throughout service and priority of care and benefits on retirement, still attracts some great people.

But if the reality becomes merely 'a steady job, with decent pension' plus sub-standard housing, inconsistent opportunities for promotion, all while watching the Chosen Few leap ahead and claim the medals, is it a surprise that recruiting and retention are tough? Add in the inevitable fuckwittery and the chance to look over your shoulder for lawyers for the rest of your life, well, no wonder The Best is failing.

The military can do better in all these areas, if it has the will to change; most changes won't involve extra cost, just a new way of doing things. But to bring about the changes that are needed, it is going to have to take a long, hard and very honest look at itself.

Chapter Seventeen
The Women's Story
(or Dry Your Eyes, Princess)

I'm a feminist - I've been a female a long time now- it'd be stupid not to be on my own side. Maya Angelou

When I hear men I know to be open-minded and fair say, 'What are women going on about - surely they now have equality?' I am irritated. Because, no, we don't have equality. So, this chapter is about why we don't. It's about the small stuff and the large stuff that holds women back and keeps us outsiders and under-achievers when it comes to promotions, praise and pay. And it's about the individual and collective effects of the pockets of misogyny that I, and the women alongside and around me, experienced in the military.

The case for equality for women has been made legally but putting it into practice has stalled because the underlying values of the Army, and the attitudes towards women in some areas of the military, have still not changed. Until they do, women cannot and will not achieve genuine equality and the Army will not get the best from its women.

Change is rarely instigated by the people in power. If all the generals are men, if all the selection panels are men and these men are doing well out of holding the power, there is no incentive to instigate change from the top down. Which means it needs to come from the rank and file. And it has to be demanded because asking politely is not working.

Hearing talk about women as inferior, hearing that we are 'less', seeing women treated differently before we can show what we can do, individually and together, is damaging to the soul. I want all of us to have equal opportunities, no matter who we are or what our strengths and qualities are. I like that everyone is different. I know I am not as good at some things as at others and want to be selected for the roles in which I excel. I believe the Army as an organisation wants that too; it's just certain people within the Army who block opportunities for women.

It's frustrating that progress towards equal opportunity for women is so slow, but when any group is not the majority in positions of power within an organisation (or society) power change is slow. And in the Army, it is painfully slow. The view of most military women I have spoken to is that the Army, far from doing away with the glass-ceiling, is re-glazing it. The bias is simply more subtle because it has moved undercover. It surfaces after alcohol, on the military forums (where cries for the rape, murder and compulsory subordination of women are surprisingly common) or in misogynist 'safe spaces', like some of the infantry units. Until presented recently with overwhelming evidence, our generals have been insisting that bigotry in the military was a thing of the past. I knew they were lying - when I was serving, I often heard bigoted voices in open plan offices, when I was sitting out of sight, and I still regularly read these extreme views on military forums. Only recently, at a meeting in the corridors of the military one man said to another, who was having a bit of a meltdown, 'Dry your eyes, Princess'. All the women in the room rolled their eyes at this tired old association between women and histrionics.

So, the generals are wrong, and every woman in the Army knows it.

Some of the comments I have heard are extreme enough to count as 'gender fundamentalism', by which I mean that they are made by those who are willing to break the law to achieve their way (and keep women down or hold them back). Mostly though, what happens is gaslighting; women are manipulated psychologically into doubting themselves and their confidence is destroyed. When I was told that I imagined the bias of the promotion boards, it was classic gaslighting.

I think back to Sandhurst, and how the men were told not to talk to us, the instructors 'didn't know how to share their knowledge' with women and there was no uniform to fit us. All these actions slow women's development and lower performance, sometimes by design but more often through what I think of as masterly inactivity.

What I am suggesting is that we define what a role requires and then let battle commence fairly to see who the best person is to fill that role. A transparent process based on merit. We would see a much more balanced gender mix if that came about.

The prevalence of gaslighting makes it harder to identify friend from foe; the ones I expected to support equality, who said they did, were not always the ones who actually did (including some senior women as well as those Sandhurst academics) but over time the effects become obvious; not only are we being held back, we start to hold ourselves back. Women are seen as – and feel – second class.

It's not just the Army – we are gaslighting girls throughout society. When my niece started school, I watched her language and her confidence change, just as mine had. Society is still treating women as weak, unstable, unreliable and 'emotional', and perpetrating ridiculous myths like the one that says women are unable to read maps (with all the accompanying technical and logistical implications of that). And we deny women positions of power, so there are not the role-models that girls growing up need.

All around the world, there are fantastic females strutting their stuff. Not because they are tomboys, butch or battle-axes but because they love life and are living it their way. That's why calling out the small stuff, the everyday gaslighting, as well as the big stuff, the criminal level of sexual harassment, matters so much. Free our souls and watch us thrive.

Women have trained alongside male officers since I joined in the mid-80s. Some of those same men who started with me are now the generals, leading the modern army. If they are good leaders, they have adjusted their thinking with the times. But our deepest learning comes when we are young and our generation, Generation X, was exposed to quite different male-female relationship norms. I am aware, deep in my heart, of that voice from my youth that told me women are inferior. I no longer believe it, but I have had to re-set and fight that inequality of opportunity. And that is why I know, when I look into many senior army men's eyes, that they are not authentic when they say they believe in equal opportunities for women. And when they are back in all-male environments, like the promotion panels and some infantry settings, they revert more openly to that 1980s attitude.

Unless we open up all of the processes and show why a man has been picked over a woman, rather than endorse the all-male decision panel by saying meaningless things like, 'We just knew we had the right man for the job', we cannot know the truth or work out what is happening. It may suit the chosen few, but it betrays the values of the Army. Selecting a man over a woman without comparing their route to that point is like one football team being given all the training facilities, coaching, equipment and resources and feeling proud if they then beat an unsupported team.

In 2017, I read a stream of stories from army women, mostly officers, which appeared in an online forum. When I weaken or start to believe the promotion board feedback that I am less or inferior or imagining things, I go back and read those comments. Some of the women who contributed to that forum have achieved outstanding things, yet they were subjected to the same casual bias that said, loud and clear: 'You are nothing'.

Here's one of the comments (all are reproduced with their consent), from a woman who is a captain and a highly successful mountaineer: 'When I arrived at the unit I was told that it was my job to take the minutes at all the meetings, since the men had more important things to do. I spoke to the CO and he told me not to make a fuss'.

Here's another from a woman who is a private: 'Where I was posted, women were classified by the corporals as sluts or frigid, what was known as the 'bike or dyke' classification, and there was little difference between the two.'

And from a female Royal Engineers officer: 'There was a sign up as I entered the bar. It said 'Officers Only' so I went in and the conversations stopped. The president of the mess committee came over immediately and guided me out. He apologised, 'I know you are serving, but this room is just for real officers, I'm sure you understand'.

Enemy attacks are an acceptable risk; a knife between the shoulder blades from a colleague is not. It doesn't matter if the bigotry is minor, if it happens all the time, it is a pebble in the shoe – it hobbles you. Forgetting to let you speak in a meeting, not being invited out for drinks when all the men are, being denied an office because 'you are just a reserve', these and a thousand other slights are the death of a thousand cuts.

To bring about change, we need to take action. The 2017 #MeToo campaign was a talking point, but was it a turning point? Will anything change because of it? It gave women the confidence to speak up and achieved awareness, but it also scared good men from engaging. It won't give us our power back. To do that we need to be prepared to do some work, to ask for what we need to be fixed, to not be reliant on others to change. The suffragettes, when they stood up and demanded it, brought about change. Women who quietly took on male jobs in two world wars, and did them well, brought about change. As do women claiming firsts on mountains or reaching the poles or running governments and companies. Even with fewer resources and less training, women are finding a way to succeed. So, imagine what women could do with a level playing field.

To create that we need women on the side of other women. When I failed to get yet another promotion, I went to see a senior female officer who was reluctant to speak out on my behalf. She thought I should have got the promotion but didn't seem willing to risk her career by saying so. It made me look at the career paths of women at the top. Many were married to senior military, or to the privileged classes. All were very careful as they reached senior posts to fall in line with broader army culture. The all-male boards appeared to be picking women not likely to rock the privileged boat.

But some women are rocking the boat and fighting back. An army lawyer, Rabia Siddique, was involved in the rescue of two captured special forces soldiers in Iraq in 2005. A male colleague involved in the same incident received a hero's welcome home and a Military Cross while her role in the incident was not acknowledged and was left off official reports. In 2007 Rabia sued the Ministry of Defence for racial and sexual discrimination. In 2008 before the hearing, the MoD paid her damages and gave her a letter of apology and of praise for the role she played in the incident. Rabia left the Army – why would she stay? She had made her point and proven her case and every time a woman does this, she encourages others to follow her example. It's a shame, not least because the Army would have benefitted by keeping her, but of course with the system as it is she would have been vilified and punished had she stayed on. This is exactly why so many of us can only speak up when we leave, but speak up we must, if we are to bring about change.

Skills fall along a spectrum; life experience shows us that some traits are more common in one tribal group than another – the concept behind the film *White Men Can't Jump*. Most men are physically stronger than most women; most women are better empathisers than most men.

I have no issue with genuine exemptions, which are sometimes necessary in the military. For example, a liaison role to a country where there is no equal opportunity for women may need to go to a man. But my research of the promotion system showed it was used not simply for necessary exemptions but to block women applicants. Some job adverts would list combat experience as essential as a way of excluding women. I was not the only one to point this out and the personnel branch has quietly asked that this behaviour stops. But the sentiment behind it has not changed.

Do women have equal pay for equal work in the Army? Yes, by rank, role and length of time served, there is equal pay. That's the law. However, I dug a little deeper and found the benefits added on as extras throughout an army career still favour men: trade pay, awards and honours, pace along the career path and success on promotion boards are all skewed against women. Desire for time off is not, and should not be, a gender issue, but an issue of choice; there are both men and women who want time out - to parent, pursue hobbies, studies, climb mountains – basically a better and flexible work-life balance. When will it be recognised that people who have spent time parenting, or on other pursuits, like adventurous challenges, have added life experience which can enhance their ability to take on a job? This is exactly why army reserves are so valuable. While many regulars have only known the military, reserves have a breadth of experience they can bring, and the two groups working together can be truly effective.

What the Army needs is clear job descriptions. What does an infanteer need to have in the way of skills and experience – not just physical, but psychological too? Some women will meet these standards. Some men won't. The media published statistics on serving soldiers in 2018; over 20% were obese and another 15-20% were overweight. In addition, the age average was creeping up and the failure rates in combat fitness tests were high. The Army has more than a problem with whether women are fit enough for combat roles; it doesn't have enough of either gender who are.

I heard a female sergeant from the Royal Horse Artillery on the radio a while ago talking about their approach. A key skill for her troop is to be able to vault from the ground onto horse-back. They practice and they test this skill regularly and if anyone can't do it, they are transferred. That's equality.

As a physiotherapist I understand the closer someone gets to their physiological limits, the higher their injury rate. So, taking individuals who keep falling below a fitness line and then just scrape above it is riskier. The cause of falling fitness is variable - injury, laziness, age, but it shouldn't matter why, just whether it is temporary or permanent. If the Army sets clear standards and tests that its personnel can meet these regularly, as the RHA do, then we would have troops, both men and women, fit for role. At the moment, with 20% obese, we don't. In the future, physical fitness may become so rare that we must pay a bonus to those who can achieve it.

This isn't a gender issue. There was, for example, a case of a female police officer who lost her job because she kept failing the physical tests. She went to court saying she was thrown out for being a woman, but the judge rightly said she was thrown out for repeatedly failing to meet the fitness standards set for active policing duties. If we applied that across the military right now, we would lose about 20% of an already under-recruited army.

The first question for the Army is not whether there are still an entrenched few who see females as lesser beings, it is how to get the hierarchy to accept that something needs to be done. So how do we do this in the military, where complaining is seen as 'whingeing' and career-limiting?

I have some suggestions:

1.   Select the person who can do the job. In 2018 we saw women polar warriors trekking across Antarctica, a woman general, mixed platoons at Sandhurst and talk of the same for soldier basic training. These are all great, but they're individual cases; we need the organisation to go mainstream with accurate job descriptions and a system that can actually select based on the skills and experience required - in other words, on merit. An honest system doesn't fear transparency.

2.   The Army leadership needs to fix the many systemic inequalities by calling out the small stuff; the day to day gaslighting, the assumptions that all officers are 'Sir', automatically generated career letters that read 'Mr', dress codes which state the male dress code and add 'or equivalent'. There are many more, and most are easy to fix.

3.   We must put independent scrutineers in place and give them the power to challenge outcomes. I can't emphasise the need for this strongly enough. Only external scrutiny can counter the tendency of majorities in the Army (men, regulars, white, upper middle class) to feel that they are automatically in the right.

4.   Bust the myths about women. I lost count of the number of times men attempted to put me down. The commonest put-down women get is that they're 'over emotional' and of course the one thing which heightens the emotions is being accused of it. Besides which, the evidence shows that good leaders need an emotional range.

5.   Some, genuine and constructive, criticism is helpful to our growth. So how do we separate myths from helpful mentoring? I use a formula called SEALED: Statement, Evidence, Analysis, Link (to other cases), Extrapolate and then Decision (does the system need to change?)

Here's an example:

Statement: Women get more injuries in training and therefore shouldn't be allowed in the military.

Evidence: A higher percentage of women do seem to be getting injuries in basic training.

Analysis: Injuries in basic training are generally increasing for men and for women, since recruits are less fit on joining than they were previously. Some types of injuries are more common in women – and on analysing the training schedule it appears that the tests and courses are designed for the male physiology. We need more information on whether the tests reflect accurately the skills and experience required.

Link: The Israeli Army had the same problem and resolved it by changing their rucksack design for women.

Extrapolation: If we add a more gradual curve to fitness for men and women and change the rucksack design for women, we should see a reduction in injuries.

Decision: The British Army adapts.

6.   Have a scale for raising issues. The Army used to have a system in which military personnel could make suggestions when we saw poor value or something that needed to improve. Now, the only way to 'complain' is to make a formal complaint (that can take years and huge effort to resolve – as in my own case). We need to introduce a scale of raising issues: a 'good ideas' list, informal solution forums

and guided negotiations, all in addition to the formal complaints system. Having military lawyers as the first response to raising issues of bias is not proportionate. Nor is ignoring the issue and brushing it under the carpet or gaslighting women who raise sexual harassment or bias issues. It sends the message that women are at fault for raising concerns.

It's not just the Army that needs to make changes, training to spot bias needs to change too. Sometimes for women the hardest part is working out that we are a victim. I was in denial for a long time about the effect that male behaviour was having on my career. The first solution is to have mandatory, clear and constructive feedback. The armed forces are not obliged to give appointment board feedback, but when pushed into a corner, it remains masterfully vague:

Whitmarsh: 'You were not selected as the other candidate had better skills.'

Me: 'Okay, which skills did he have that got him the role?'

Whitmarsh: 'It was unanimous.'

Me: 'Okay, but what skills specifically gained that unanimous vote?'

Whitmarsh: 'You were too narrow.'

Me: 'Right, so what were the broad skills that I needed for this role?'

This was followed by a month of silence.

By the time I was aware of the effects male behaviour had had on my career it was probably too late to undo the damage. There is a solution: bespoke training for women on how to deal with the Whitmarshes of the civil service. And we need forums and networks of our own – I like the female equivalent of brethren – I want to be part of the sistren.

We also need to teach girls and women that the voice inside, the one that tells us we aren't good enough, is the voice of our nurture, our schools and our workplaces. We need to teach them that history is not a true friend of their future. And we need to make sure that women, and men too, are aware of everyday sexism.

Get rid of the putdowns and save the honest feedback. If women become suspicious of putdowns, we may miss useful feedback as well. Writer Caitlin Moran calls this the 'how many f**ks should I give' approach. We can teach women to respect comments only from trusted colleagues and put on their armour for the rest. And we can teach men to be specific and non-sexist in their feedback.

My partner is a white male. He listened in on a phone call I received after I had raised an issue with Flashheart. He overheard phrases like, 'You don't understand' and, 'It's more complex than you get'. After the call my partner told me that the words the line manager used were aimed at putting me in my place and were not those that would have been used by a man speaking to another man.

There are plenty of men who would never, ever speak to a woman (or anyone) like this. Men who actively support equality and stand up for it. Take David Beckham tweeting congratulations to the Commonwealth gold winning netball team in 2018, or Andy Murray correcting journalists who omitted the successes of the Williams' sisters when asking him questions in 2017 or Lieutenant-General Tim Radford, the official army women's advocate (not a gender-tied role, which is perhaps a good thing), turning up at the Army women's 100 event in 2017 showing energy, warmth and enthusiasm. All good and popular men are supporting equal opportunities. I think women have to start with being positive when good men reach out, and guard against alienating the reasonable men in our frustration at being held back for so long. It is why I question on social media any comment that looks a bit like 'all men are bastards' and risk the ire of my female peers. Most men I have spoken to are confused by #MeToo, so there is training needed here for men as well.

I have heard from many military men say that #MeToo is trying to feminise men, to make them more empathetic, less competitive and with lower physical standards. I don't think that's what it's saying at all, I hope it's saying what I feel – which is that we should all be our best and, when it comes to the military (and perhaps elsewhere too), men shouldn't feel the need to cheat to beat women, by rigging boards, selecting in their own image or providing equipment and training that only suits them. The Army skill sets mean that it will always be patriarchal, with women in the minority, but I am arguing that it can lead as an example to wider society by changing the narrative, so that being the best means being transparent and open to anyone as long as they can fulfil the role.

There are a group of us, men and women, who feel the call to arms as warriors. Some will want to be elite infantry; there will be more men, but some women who can meet those standards. But there are also far wider roles in defence than just elite infantry – it takes nine soldiers to provide the back-up needed for one infanteer – and many of those jobs can be done equally well by either gender.

So, where do we go from here? Ginger Rogers said, 'Women have to do the same as men but backwards and in heels' and all too often that's still true. For some time yet, women, particularly non-privileged women, are going to have to work harder to get to the same place as men. But there is hope; plenty of good men aren't threatened by competition, all they need is to hear the new rules and they will adapt. We must aim our battles at misogyny, not at men.

How will we know when we have won this fight? When women no longer have to prove themselves anew each time we are posted. When the Army is willing to open its promotion system to external scrutiny and women start promoting at the same pace as men. And when women speak out. In the last 12 months I have stood up for myself more than in the last 12 years, and while it's been tough, it has felt good. I want to be part of seeing misogyny go the same way as Flat Earth believers - a quaint but laughable and obscure ultra-minority view.

To get there means setting standards and enforcing them, so that gender is not the deciding factor in any situation. If I am held hostage in some foreign field, I want someone to come and rescue me who can run faster, think quicker and is highly trained. I don't care if that person is male or female, I just don't want it to be the individual who failed their basic fitness test for the last 3 years and doesn't have the discipline to fix it.

There are easier paths to success for women, and non-privileged men, than the military. It is why so many good people leave. If the Army wants the good ones to stay, it must reduce the personal attacks, gender-related insults and career fouls. We should follow the Caitlin Moran test for bias and ask: 'Are the men doing it?' If they are, then we should take our turn, but if they are not then we should 'gripe about groping', 'bitch about bias' and shout our heads off about career fouls. We can keep the humour (I can think of at least one benefit for women in the military – the queue for the loo is longer for the men) but let's ditch the assumption that 'men are competent until proven otherwise and women are incompetent until they prove otherwise'.

Let us tell stories of great women as well as men. We need a meritocracy; it really shouldn't be about gender. You can identify as anything you like in my experience as long as it is ' warrior' and you understand the enemy is going to kill you if you aren't at your best and better than the enemy.

For women, I believe that there is a wind of change coming. Army generals and Air Force equivalents, once they are unconstrained by military law, having left their posts, state, 'We need more women at the top'. General Sir Peter Wall said recently, 'I want every woman in the country to know the service is open to them and we need to make sure we get that message across. Women need to see they have equal opportunities right throughout the organisation.' Lieutenant General Robin Brims and Air Chief Marshal Sir Stuart Peach have publicly said the same thing.

I think, and hope, that women are ready to speak up because if we don't get what we need, we must demand it. I now understand what feminism is and it is not about having power over men but having power over ourselves.

Chapter Eighteen
The Warrior Spirit

The price of freedom is eternal vigilance
Thomas Jefferson

The UK has enjoyed the longest period of peace for generations, but I think it may have forgotten the importance of appreciating warrior culture. I call this the 'Tinkerbell Problem'. Peter Pan said that Tinkerbell was at risk of fading and dying because the public no longer believed in fairies. Similarly, if the British public, and government ministers, no longer believe in our army, the warrior spirit could die. Britain, now, is reluctant to go ahead with the kind of overseas engagement tasks and practical training with equipment, at home and with allies, that is necessary to keep the Army on its toes and ready. But if you don't use it in conflicts and don't want to fund tasks and training, there is high risk we are heading for failure. The challenge for the UK is that it isn't going to notice if its military is failing until it is needed. And then it will be too late.

Nobody knows how close we are to the Failure Line right now. But the level of disquiet is high. I am not a lone voice, though my voice is focused on the people and the systems we use to prepare them for role. Others are painting an equally alarming picture of our equipment and training. And everyone is raising alarms about the budgets, although I believe we could spend our budget better, if we really looked at where the money is going.

The Army has a long history of stealing success from the jaws of defeat, but past success and optimism don't guarantee results tomorrow. The British Tommy is still a professional and resilient warrior, but Britain isn't giving much support.

Here's a quote, posted anonymously on Twitter:

'Let me tell you about war. War doesn't give a f**k about the colour of your skin, your race, religion or sexuality. It doesn't care if you identify as male, female or a plant pot. It certainly doesn't care if you need a lie down in your safe place because the horrible man said some nasty words. The only thing war cares about is whether you are up for the job, because if you are not, you are dead. Worse than that, the people around die because of you.'

Those of us who join the Army are willing to be on the front line, out there, doing our jobs so that others can stay safe. But to do that, we need support from our chiefs, from our government and from our fellow citizens.

Military culture is bound by our fighting spirit, which itself is bound by our morale and sense of belonging. The warrior ethos, the fighting spirit I believe is vital, and that we need to nurture, is based on mission first, common purpose, shared beliefs, values and practices and commitment to sacrifice and service. It is powerful, worthwhile and the basis of a good army. The warrior spirit embodies mission first, family second, team ahead of individual needs, sense of duty and regimental honour ahead of personal glory. It is more than just ensuring we leave no-one behind on the battlefield (or alone when returned to civvy street); it is how we train, live and fight.

And that warrior spirit is in danger of being extinguished. We are currently getting the Army we deserve, and it isn't the Best. Talent is leaving at a far faster pace than the Army can recruit. Bias, bullying and weak leadership seem to be internal causes; poor resourcing from the government, lack of buy-in from the public and threats of litigation the external causes.

There are many things the Army can celebrate and keep, but others it needs to kill off if it wants to truly 'Be the Best'. The Army needs young, resilient people. It needs the many to join for short careers, the steady to stay on in the middle third and the talented few to rise up and set strategy. It doesn't need that many generals. And while many of us will need to move on and out, good organisations see their people leave happy, join a reserve or perhaps an alumni and become a supporting force for good.

Most of army culture is healthy; strong traditions merge our individual warrior ethos into coherent fighting spirit on the battlefield. But all traditions, like old trainers, need to be smelled and assessed occasionally - then retired if they have run out of mileage. The trick of course is to keep the good and retire only those aspects which are no longer optimising our fighting power, rather than to follow every whim or trend of broader society. Very few in the media, the judiciary and government have served. Before judging any individual soldier, they should try standing against an angry, armed mob in Northern Ireland who have already killed your colleagues or patrolling a village in Afghanistan where your best mate lost a limb the previous day. Our politicians need to be honest; if they are seeking a political settlement, then hold those in charge of an organisation responsible, don't hang an individual out to dry for a command decision.

Army culture is a powerful thing. It is the outward expression of values and how we operate, but also the inward reflection of our sense of belonging. It allows us to always know who is in charge (if you kill the boss, the next in line picks up the lead until the last warrior is standing) and it means we will always keep fighting. Military culture is designed for conflict zones. It must reflect wider society, where citizens are recruited, but train us to cope with the culture of armed conflict.

And once soldiers have experienced war, it is hard to lose that sense of separateness, so it can be a challenge to re-integrate into the differing rhythm of civilian space.

The culture is still strong. It produces those who are resilient, pragmatic, humorous and level-headed in crises, problem solvers who are capable of game changing energy or incredible patience. Most veterans make great civilian employees because of this culture. Our warrior hearts know that human behaviour dictates we will sometimes have to fight for what we have and believe in; not everything can be resolved through talking. But we also know that talking, mutual respect and understanding is the best way to resolve any conflict.

For military roles, hierarchical systems are not inherently bad. Arguably they are necessary in war. But, during long periods of peace, they need regularly weeding out. Not by their own leaders, letting them mark their own homework has led to the 'near-fail' position we are in now. To weed out the military flower bed, we need to bring the outside in.

A2020 was a big change for the Army - it caused emotional grief for the regulars who were seeing the Army reduce to a size below what they believed was an effective fighting force. And it caused physical workload grief because the level of staff work it generated in Army HQ was huge; each change in basing, role, every new unit required huge bureaucratic effort. Many staff officers just didn't have the skills or time to deal with it; budget and project management skills were particularly scarce.

People like me, coming in and embracing the change and quite happy with living in times of uncertainty, were not always popular. Around this period of grief, a lot of good army people left, accelerating the downsizing of the regulars and leaving two distinct groups: the toxic leadership who began to look out for themselves and a cohort of entrenched and resistant middle-ranking soldiers and officers who were often overloaded or simply closed down under the excessive workload. It was not that there weren't good people still in the Army – there were many – it was just that they were not being rewarded for effort and army pay and conditions were eroding fast, which meant that many were leaving.

The Army can't fix all these at once, but it can, and must, fix them. I have learned a few lessons in my 30 years of service. So, these are my thoughts on what we must, should or could do, to get the Army back on track. I believe that if we put a handful of 'muscle moves' in place, we can slay the worst of our demons very quickly. They're all achievable, but we shouldn't expect our senior leaders to initiate them, that will take outside forces:

Cut adrift the entrenched middle

Not all of them, but the lowest 10%. Every year. Don't then move the worst of the regulars across to take full-time reserve posts. Because the military kindly guarantees you stay on the same pay levels, even if not the same grade, adding in a bonus that you won't be sacked for low productivity unless you get lower than a B grade (no chance of that) it's a job for life. Cutting out some dead wood may make the Army smaller in the short term, but we won't be less productive, I guarantee it. All those pensions and salaries saved will mean more money for other stuff. And while we are culling the hangers on, let's include those drawing specialists pay, for example Special Forces pay, when individuals haven't worked in that community for years.

Create an independent HR unit

We need independent professionals to really look at what job skills are needed and then to select based on skills plus effort, not pedigree and connections. As I have said before, we are not served at all by the current system of using untrained soldiers and officers to manage our people. They are following orders, not fair process. Outsource all the tough, long-term stuff; HR, complaints and awards and leave military personnel with input but not control. The current system of brutally quelling all dissent by throwing a pack of threatening lawyers at anyone who dares to speak out and insisting that even senior officers and soldiers leave if they dare to challenge, is arcane. It may maintain the autocratic narrow power base in the short term, but the Army will continue to lose its best.

Get a decent recruiting system

A system that loses approximately 80% of its applicants through poor administration, long delays, an incoherent medical strategy and the inability to match applicants' skills to roles is not a service. After five years of this, I am not judging whether it is the fault of the current private company, the military interface, the IT system or the CEO's cat – it doesn't work, and it isn't able to change. We need to move on.

Drop 10% of the senior regular posts

For the size of the Army today, we just don't need as many senior posts as we have. Include in the ones we dump all those who fail to live up to the stated army values. Make a further 10% of senior posts job-shares, open to reserves. It will broaden our thinking and reduce bias. Asking senior leaders to cull their own numbers is pointless - this will have to be done by an independent panel.

Refuse promotion to selfish leaders

I'd like to see feedback gathered from a wider range of peers, asking the soldiers if their leader 'served them'. Appraisals should include the views of more than just the immediate boss (and his boss above). And ditto with awards, no more honours simply for turning up to work. Here are my starter questions:

What measures is the Army taking to rate its leaders?

What does leadership success look like?

Why do our line managers get the only voice on our leadership skills?

What support are individuals getting for 'doing the right thing'?

Why is there not a 'great leadership' award?

How do we rate units on their application of the Leadership Code?

I would like to see tales of great military leadership highlighted; the small successes of peacetime as well as the tales of daring-do on operations. No-one can call themselves a military leader unless they find genuine joy in the success of all those under them.

The toxic apathy of our current army leadership is a vital issue. Whenever I look at an organisation that is saying it wishes to change but still failing to move, it is the senior leaders with whom I want to sit down.

Being a leader is not about getting it right all the time, it is about the vision and grit to keep pursuing that aspiration, despite setbacks.

Max De Pree said, 'The first responsibility of a leader is to define reality - the last is to say thank you. In between, the leader is a servant.' The Army knows the importance of service leadership - the motto at Sandhurst is *Serve to Lead*. Officers are issued a book on leadership. I picked it up again recently; cringing at how it only refers to men (I hadn't noticed that bias in the 1980s). But while my book needs updating, it still has some great messages about the sacrifice and passion needed to be a great leader. Yet now, selfish leadership is dominant. Why? Perhaps this is now addressed through an updated book for the 21st century? I haven't seen the most recent one – I would like to.

This brings me to the next tier of action we need to take; what I think of as 'bite the bullet' stuff. These are the changes we may not like in the short-term, but we know will be good for us in the long-term.

Value your people

It isn't about men, women, caste, class, sexuality or bloody hair colour. It's about valuing talent. When it was announced recently that Defence was running a competition to come up with novel ways of improving recruitment and retention, the veteran community (and probably a few anonymous, but still serving people too) roared with laughter. The thrust of the response? 'The Army doesn't need 'novel' it just needs to value its people.

Reward them fairly and stand up for them, even if they make a mistake (don't hang them out to dry every time a lawyer comes sniffing). It is not about subverting the justice or any other system, it is about showing the soldiers they are one big family.

Listen to trusted people

Trusted doesn't mean privileged by birth or saying things the generals want to hear. Trusted means trusted to speak truths, pleasant or unpleasant, in a respectful way. But for that to happen in the military, leaders need to give permission for others to speak out. Good people who aren't heard leave or blow whistles. So, let's hear the music of our people, of all ranks, through genuinely open forums. Create healthy debating platforms not governed by rank, but by ideas. Do not punish thinking. And stop giving an ear to those who shout loudest. There is a small group of low performers bullying upwards now and threatening to destroy the careers of any who challenge their personal powerbase.

Stop throwing away all our information

The Army has the same problem as everyone else; we are deluged with data, struggling with storage capacity and cannot file or retrieve the information we need. The Army exacerbates this by deleting all kinds of information when people are posted – and so effectively re-doing the work over and over. One young officer spoke up on this last year, suggesting we label our important information differently. We would retain this valuable information, archive other stuff by different labelling and delete all the rest as 'fluff'.

Improve our productivity

It's time to look at the hours the Army works – do we get value for money? How many days are 'undertime' versus overtime? And how many hours are just spent on repetition? The head of the Army spoke passionately recently about 'using or losing' young troops, so let's not bore them into leaving. And let's be honest and look at the annual military cycle both creatively and objectively. Posting too many people at once in the summer means loss of knowledge, projects being re-started and loss of momentum. Henry Ford said, 'The best people get ahead during the time that others waste'. I agree.

Re-condition the wolf-pack

Healthy wolf-packs are diverse. They lead from the front, develop their young to take over, mix male and female traits and run together. And I do mean run together. The Army must get serious about its lack of physical fitness. 20% obese? Even more overweight and not fit for role? In industry, if you have a skill that is hard to recruit, it becomes more valuable. So, increasing pay for physically arduous roles may be a way forward. Asking nicely isn't going to change this.

Youth needs to roam free, to have fun and learn about risk. When I think of the adventures I have had on my travels - SCUBA diving wrecks solo at night, rescuing groups from lions, climbing mountains and biking across deserts – this is how I learned my limits. My later success was not based on avoiding risk, on fearing failure, it was based on learning the consequences and deciding if the risk was worth taking. We must guarantee young army leaders the chance to heed the call to arms, to adventure and take risks and to see it as career-enhancing. I'm pretty sure boredom kills more people than lions or deserts.

Let appraisals reflect broader talent

There are industries that have cracked the appraisal process. Let us trawl our HR reserves first for the skills and if we don't find them, approach industry direct. We need a system that both recruits the right talents (which means almost certainly a flexible offer, based on the type of skills required) and then retains only those who remain fit for role (which means a broader range of grades than just A or B). This really is a 'bite the bullet' moment - it won't be cheap to come up with a better system, but it is going to be more expensive if we don't, because the top talent is leaving at the moment, knowing they cannot 'beat the bias' of the current appraisal system.

Outsource the army brand

If we want to show the people of Britain what we do, we need to do more than the traditional parades and air-shows. Sending our best out to schools and universities to sell the benefits of army life would be a good start. But I think we can take it further. There are commercial companies selling 'military fitness' and many veterans doing army-type roles in industry. We could bring in revenue to the military through outsourcing our best skills directly. Sending people to train others in junior leadership, resilience and discipline would be a start. We already rent out real estate so why not also rent out people? It will teach soldiers the skills they will need when they move back to civvy street. What a great transitional role for the right military person to set up. And if you run competitions and competitive training events, you can tap the ones you want on the shoulder as well.

Set up the right 'how are we doing' groups

Leaders don't need to have all the good ideas, but they do need to create the conditions in which good ideas thrive. And that means forums in which all ranks can speak up and know that they will be heard. At the moment we do have some innovation forums, but they tend to tell the boss what he or she wants to hear. Of course, innovation takes time and sometimes fails, although I like the way Edison put it when he said, 'I haven't failed – just found 10,000 ways that won't work'.

The military is woefully bad at listening to its own ideas, so this is another area where we must bring the outside in. And these are the kinds of groups we need if we are to allow fresh ideas and input:

External Initiative Groups

Let's chair a pool of our best officers, soldiers, regulars, reserves and civil servants. Let's get a little competition back in there, but without the current senior leadership as the sole judging panel.

External Continuity Groups

An external group with the power to monitor outcomes of projects after regulars have been posted and to hold them to account for their successes and failures. To run the 'lessons identified' sessions and keep the best parts of the military at the forefront of our thinking. If our current military project managers knew they couldn't just walk away at the end of a tour, but were accountable, many of the current poor project decisions would not be made.

External 'Black Box' Review Groups

The air industry drastically reduced its accidents and errors through being open to its mistakes. Black Boxes were placed inside all planes and the outcomes after disasters were shared. But the military (like other public bodies) gets very defensive and prefers to obfuscate and deny its errors. This is not going to change if we let the military mark their own homework. We need an external panel looking at military accidents, complaints and mistakes and we need to admit to our faults. This is not weakness, and it is a move away from blaming the individual soldier caught up in the incident before an investigation has been completed.

Pretending we don't have problems with, for example, bullying, equipment and fitness isn't making the problems go away. In my own experience the complaints team simply denied any wrongdoing; they didn't look at the evidence, just asked me to trust the system. Outside of the rigid military command, people don't trust the military to tell the truth. So, we need an external review group. An OFSTED for the Army. As the original American self-improvement expert Dale Carnegie once said, 'My business exploded when I started truth-sharing because people are starving for the truth'.

Influence and Outreach Groups
The Army needs to do more about shouting out its achievements. There is much it does well. If we can admit when we get it wrong, let's also have a group shouting when we get it right. A healthy ego is about

climbing up and climbing down when necessary. Most readers love to hear tales of people taking the knocks and getting back up.

Equality and Diversity Groups

We need a more innovative way of showing why equality and diversity matters. There is an important rule of war, known to all soldiers: no plan survives first contact. Meaning that just giving soldiers orders may not work, they are likely to need initiative and to outsmart the opposition. If you think like everyone else on the battlefield, it's hard to come up with a game-changer. Our head of reserves at Spider19, Sirius, was a great thinker who struggled to get on with Flashheart who just wouldn't listen to wider thinking. The police were recently lambasted for slowness and delay in sexual harassment investigations. Well the Army has the same issue, just more privately. And they're doing the same thing – ignoring the problem, hoping it will go away.

Realistic Red-Teamer Groups

These are the devil's advocates. The ones willing to say no when the government expects the military to fight on multiple fronts with scarce resources. We don't have to be negative about it, we just need a simple, clear statement of what we can do for the resource level. There are a lot of under-worked soldiers and officers in UK. So, there is more we can do. And we don't need to pay huge fees to contractors for this role, there are plenty of quality reserves, if the Army can get over its hubris about regulars versus reserves. Many regular troops are also knowledgeable when they're allowed to speak up.

All six of these groups need to mix industry plus officers, soldiers, regulars, reserves, civil servants, men, women and so on. What they must have in common is the willingness to speak up and on behalf of defence thinking differently. Newton said he could 'see further by standing on the shoulders of giants'. There should be no shame involved if our institutionalised military minds ask for help.

There's one more thing. An army, by its very nature, must be prepared for war. We don't want war, but wars happen and those of us in the armed forces are prepared to go out there and fight to win when we have to. But at the moment the Army is not making the case that sometimes you are going to need fighting power. Warriors. Those who enjoy competition and want to win. Not all our troops need to be infantry, but all must understand the nature of war and defence. So, we need to make the case to the public, explain why we need an army and what it needs to be able to deliver a credible defence. Social media can help here. Because just standing up an army when the Russians are coming over the top doesn't work. We need a full-time, combat-ready armed force that can be augmented with reserves when needed.

The types of people attracted to military service are broad. So, what the military environment must do is unleash their potential. There are more roles than bayoneting the enemy on the front-line; potentially the infantry role may be taken by automated robots in the near future, needing new technical teams to support these robo-infanteers on the front line. You might be a cyber geek, engineer, intelligence or signals expert – we need them all, and many more. But whatever area you choose, sometimes you will go to war and find yourself making split second life and death decisions in life-threatening, confusing battle zones, where it is hard to tell friend from foe, you haven't slept properly for days and you still need to function. War is horrible at times. So, we also need to make sure that our warriors know that when they do leave, there is a great network of support and alumni opportunities. The troops don't have to make a lifetime commitment to service – armies need to be, mostly, young – but the Army needs to make that lifetime commitment to the troops.

Many will only serve 5 to 7 years. This means we have a large pool of veterans. And far too many of them leave feeling bitter, with no desire to help the military further. We can change that; we can do so much more to make sure those veterans are proud of their service and willing to extend military recruitment and capability beyond active duty. But only if the Army's commitment to them is for life. I remain humbled by the way the US honours former service people. We can do far more for soldiers through simple respect. Let us remember them, alive or dead, with pride.

Most of the class of '84, the band of sisters who graduated with me, had their wings clipped and left the Army within a few years. I was one of the last still serving. Most of those who left have done brilliantly; they, along with the wider army sisterhood, have become leaders of industry, heads of charities and scored successes in multiple fields. Imagine if all that energy and ability had stayed in the Army, even for a little longer, and had been valued, appreciated and used intelligently.

The Army didn't get the best of me. It doesn't get the best out of most women, or reserves, and intelligence, particularly the way it is run, is not as good as some of its people think. But with a little energy, initiated from the outside, we can do better. If we continue to do what we have always done, then we will continue to have what we have now. We will carry on paying out on claims, letting our veterans leave disillusioned and losing our defence edge. It is not a good battle-winning strategy.

I have moved on now. I would still recommend a short tour in the military for most citizens with warrior hearts, but I could not recommend longer service, particularly for minorities and especially not for women. The level of bias is still damaging, and the narrowness of the culture will damage your soul. Time, resilience and humour lessen the impact, but I remain saddened that I could not find my way through to the highest and most influential posts while in uniform.

I still believe in the Army and the need to defend the realm. I have seen it when it works and there are many good people still serving, we just need to give them the headroom to grow. But what my journey hopefully shows is that it is past time for an honest look at how the Army fights. Because it can reduce the conspiracies - by becoming more transparent with its own people. It can mitigate the level of cockups - through being prepared to explore failure. And it really, really can eliminate most of the misogyny if it puts its mind to it, by re-setting the leadership style to a merit-based career system – back to service leadership. Then all the current and future warriors will be freed, to focus on fighting power, standing ready to win the occasional battles that we will always need to fight. While avoiding un-necessary skirmishes with those we should instead be calling friends.

As my army journey ends, I am aware that the military will always be part of my soul and I was honoured to serve. But like many veterans, I do not believe my service has been honoured – by the army hierarchy. And unfortunately, for most women serving, I don't believe theirs will be either. Through sharing my story and hearing the stories of others who served along that path, I hope to have opened your eyes to the pleasures and pain of service life. I am more at peace now I have left the Army, but I haven't left the warrior tribe. Because that tribe taught me to be part of something bigger than myself and above all to 'cope' in extreme environments – to thrive and prevail.

I am going to continue to speak up, to share my thoughts on how the Army can find its way back to be the Best. Until it does, I intend to remain a woman at war.

9 781912 964376

BV - #0057 - 010722 - C0 - 197/132/19 - PB - 9781912964376 - Matt Lamination